DISPATCHES FROM THE VANGUARD

D1557271

DISPATCHES FROM THE VANGUARD:

THE GLOBAL I AAM VERSUS DONALD J. TRUMP

Edited by Patrick A. Howell

Afterword by Marvin L. Mills II

Special Editor, Tori Reid

Published by Repeater Books

An imprint of Watkins Media Ltd

Unit 11 Shepperton House

89-93 Shepperton Road

London

N1 3DF

United Kingdom

www.repeaterbooks.com

A Repeater Books paperback original 2020

1

Distributed in the United States by Random House, Inc., New York.

Copyright © Repeater Books 2020

ISBN: 9781912248667

Ebook ISBN: 9781912248940

All rights reserved. No part of this publication may be reproduced, stored in a retrieval system, or transmitted, in any form or by any means, electronic, mechanical, photocopying, recording or otherwise, without the prior permission of the publishers.

This book is sold subject to the condition that it shall not, by way of trade or otherwise, be lent, re-sold, hired out or otherwise circulated without the publisher's prior consent in any form of binding or cover other than that in which it is published and without a similar condition including this condition being imposed on the subsequent purchaser.

Printed and bound in the United Kingdom by TJ International Ltd

MIX
Paper from
responsible sources
FSC® C013056

Cosmic Spirit Force, My God

To Daddy, Dr. Bing P. Howell, the brilliant Trinidadian, former Consumnes River College, Stanford and Roger Williams University professor, co-founder of the Alternative to Western Civilization Program and author of 1999's *The Ideology of Racism* (Simon and Schuster), who often said to me as a little boy, "Our people are some of the most brilliant, most creative, most creatively-endowed people in the world — bar none!"

I know you receive this missive Spirit.

CONTENTS

DISPATCHES FROM THE VANGUARD IS PROUD OF, MADE POSSIBLE BY, INSPIRED BY AND SUPPORTS THE LITERARY ARTS.

Proceeds from *Dispatches from the Vanguard* are made in donation to:
  100 Black Men of America
  PBS SoCal

Many of the essays and interviews were originally published in:
  Denene Millner's My Brown Baby
  Los Angeles Review of Books
  The Nasiona
  The Tishman Review
  Into the Void
  Huffington Post
  PoetryFoundation.org
  The Good Men Project

THE GLOBAL INTERNATIONAL AFRICAN ARTS MOVEMENT (GLOBAL I AAM, OR I AAM GLOBAL)

The Next Movement in Our Artistic Expression

There has been a virtual saints and soul revival processional in the canon of Black arts globally since 2014 — Amiri Baraka, Maya Angelou, Ruby Dee and Walter Dean Myers, and before that Chinua Achebe. Our griots — the repository of our culture(s) and original technologies — are moving to the other side of our cosmic reality where creativity and audacity color the demarcations between day and night. Most recently, there have been the literary giants and our laureates of the twentieth century: Toni Morrison and Derek Walcott. We would include Gabriel García Márquez, Carlos Fuentes and Julio Cortázar in that tribe for their engineering of the Latin American Boom which set the global stage for a new school of thinkers outside the conventions of Faulkner and Hemmingway. Mission accomplished: New Age dawned.

Amiri Baraka, our firebrand and godfather of the Black Arts Movement (BAM), was one of the first to jump in line and light the celestial fire, so others could see it was time to ascend. His movement, our Black Arts Movement, was born from Malcolm X's assassination in 1965. In fact, in the poem "Black Art" penned by Amiri for BAM trumpets, he writes:

> We want live
> Words of the hip world live flesh &
> Coursing blood.

Or as Harvard's Werner Sollors observed, Amiri saw the need to commit the violence required to "establish a Black World."

BAM helped to usher in the boom of hip-hop, born in the 1970s when block parties became increasingly popular in New York City. Popcorn raps, freestyle battles and sheer rhymes over beats went "viral" in communities all over the USA before that term even existed (events not unlike 2014's 16th annual Harlem Book Fair). From Afrika Bambaataa to Lauryn Hill, from A Tribe Called Quest to J Dilla, hip-hop packages together liberation, creativity and social commentary, and it is a global gift that the youth, marginalized and voiceless patrons embrace and cherish. Hip-hop stands on the shoulders of BAM. Lady Griot Poet Magistrate of the Black Arts Movement, Sonia Sanchez, certainly acknowledges the direct legacy:

Because when the bebop people started to play nobody could keep up with them. It was so fast you couldn't even hear. I would always say to my kids when I first heard hip-hop, "I can't hear it/I can't understand"... It came at a fast pace and if you turned your head, you missed it. It was gone. The bebop, the bam, and the hip-hop.

Now, if we turn our heads to the future, we can see that a current movement seems to have been seeded, certainly in part, by President Barack Obama's literary ambition and accomplishment, with *Dreams of My Father* and *The Audacity of Hope*, seeding a transcendent moment for America and the peoples of the world, where hope and change were homogenized and momentarily materialized in 2008 as a north star.

Perhaps, this could just as soon be dubbed "The Age of Obama," but it is not. It is something much more.

As Obama has noted, "I stand here... on the shoulders of giants." Indeed, a generation of writers, artists, intellectuals, creatives, entrepreneurs, seers, visionaries, healers, mystics, clairvoyants, knowers, followers and more are awoken and activated. Names like Zadie Smith, Chimamanda Ngozi Adichie, Jason Reynolds, Ta-Nehisi Coates, Kwame Alexander, Denene Millner, Colson Whitehead and Paul Beatty become standard bearers of powerful voices going back to antiquity, with the *invention of* culture, language and story.

The Global International African Arts Movement (or the Global I Aam) has grown organically from the Harlem Book Fair, beginning as a way to round out the global self-perception the diaspora holds of itself through mass media. For a quarter-century, the *Quarterly Black Book Review*'s (*QBR* also runs the Harlem Book Fair) mantra has been, "Our words, our lives, our stories." As such, it publishes reviews of books and provides literary content for, by, and about writers of the African Diaspora: this includes American, African, Caribbean, Latino, British, and other writers of African descent. It is fitting that the Harlem Book Fair holds space from the Harlem Renaissance, bridging the nineteenth to the twentieth century for a movement which will bridge the twentieth to the twenty-first.

In the twenty-first century we look to increase that consciousness and build upon this twentieth-century platform. Max Rodriguez's Harlem Book Fair and *Quarterly Black Book Review* occupy the same space as the independent book movements in New York City and Chicago in the 1960s and 1970s. We hold firm to director Shekhar Kapur's observation that: "We are the stories we tell ourselves. A story is the relationship that you develop between who you are, or who you potentially are, and the infinite world."

QBR has been called "The African American book review of record" by Martin Arnold, cultural critic of the *New York*

Times. Along with the traditions of Troy Johnson's African American Literature Book Club, *Mosaic Literary Magazine*, Cave Canem, *Aaduna Literary Magazine*, Black Bird Press, African Voices, *Kweli Journal*, *Black Orpheus*, Jalada, *Callaloo*, *Killens Review of Arts & Letters*, *Chimurenga*, *Black Renaissance Noire*, Third World Press, *Xavier Literary Review*, *Home Slice* and other online periodicals we see an effort made to precisely define ourselves. We can also note *QBR* and the Harlem Book Fair, the Leimert Park Village Book Fair, Ujamaa Book Festival, Virgin Islands Literary Festival and Book, Anguilla Literary Festival, African American Children's Book Fair, Schomburg Literary Book Fair, the Sacramento Black Book Fair and dozens of others are a continuing record of the global African expression.

In short, the Global International African Arts Movement (I Aam Global) is about moving our people forward through artistic and intellectual expression into spiritual expression. We recognize that triumph and tribulation have brought us to our current place as the world's single greatest ongoing creative force. We are a celebration of our culture and an exaltation of people who have mastered the art form of spiritual rebirth and pure inspiration. Afro-form.

We proverbially, literarily and perhaps one day literally, march, for enlightenment, higher consciousness, and just human BEING. We celebrate our being members of a single human race. As BAM's and Harlem Book Fair's Sonia Sanchez has spoken:

> The first writings I did were to my grandmother, this woman who loved me unconditionally. She would say to the Aunts, "Just let the girl be. She be alright. She going to stumble on gentleness one of these days." I am not sure that I have stumbled on gentleness. But what I did know is I stumbled on people who were like me. People who decided they had

to change the world. People who decided they would change the world.

The Global I Aam is this. We are now from different shores, with different stories, languages, but we are one. *We are one.* Through the Global I Aam, we can discover our collective uniqueness and common thread, curated in a way that only the Global I Aam can.

We cherish the moments when we, folks of African ancestry, connect and find each other in space and time. We find each other in history. We find each other through our differences, like the beautiful accents we infuse into and the manner in which we transform the English language, and of course, the diversity, yet oneness, of our artistic expression. Yes, we be alright. We be more than alright. Yes, We Be. Our sacred moments have dawned.

The Global I Aam, the spirit of togetherness, the divine inspiration that emanates from our ideas, voices and bodies.

The Global I Aam has already been moving, germinated in the first part of the twenty-first century. We simply aim to chart its course, giving form to the spiritual.

Patrick A. Howell & Marvin L. Mills, co-founders of the Global International African Arts Movement, 2005, 2012 & revised in 2019

INTRODUCTION: THE VANGUARD

The poet or the revolutionary is there to articulate the necessity, but until the people themselves apprehend it, nothing can happen... Perhaps it can't be done without the poet, but it certainly can't be done without the people. The poet and the people get on generally very badly, and yet they need each other. The poet knows it sooner than the people do. The people usually know it after the poet is dead; but that's all right. The point is to get your work done, and your work is to change the world.
— James Baldwin, 1924-1987

The vanguard of American and world culture is held in the metaphysical and very real hands of two American mythic figures. The first literally underwrites American society, a society that really only exists in the imagination, and is responsible for governing the lives of 320 million citizens drawn from around the world in a heretofore successful social, cultural and political experiment called "The United States of America." This construction consists of any number of tools, including but not limited to executive enforcement, bully pulpit (elements of leadership, charisma and influence), judicial jurisprudence and legislative law making. This powerful figure is the President of the United States of America. His (or her) job is literally to have their hands on the controls of what can and cannot happen in American society (or at the very least be a central focal point). The ones who are heralded as heroes expand the expanse of what can and cannot happen with their presidency, campaign, or both. Think Barack Obama,

John F. Kennedy or Franklin D. Roosevelt — expanding medical insurance for all, going to the moon or equality under law. If you want to think about control, contraction or the reigning in of that intangible circumference of power, think of the campaigns and presidencies of Ronald Reagan, Richard Nixon and Donald J. Trump — the reversal of civil liberties, Machiavellian pursuits, racist and criminal (so-called capitalist) agendas. In each case, expanse and contraction, each of the aforenoted presidencies are just an iterance of one another. Their governance is supported by a body of presidential cabinet officers, law makers, congressmen and senators, judges, law enforcers, and executive enforcers, policemen and military — *the system*, if you will.

The counter-power to this powerful figure in American life and the second set of hands on this mantle of power is not a governor with a set of laws, rules and their enforcement, but is instead something which has more of a *sway* over the hearts and minds of people. They are inspirational or *charismatic* figures. They are *leaders* in American and global culture. These figures are represented by those outside approval ratings, appellate court and Supreme Court appointments, decisions handed down and legislation passed. Sometimes they are represented by gross ticket sales, total social media clicks or thumbs up — the actual movement of cultural assets as commercial revenue — albums, books, movie ticket sales, t-shirts and hats. They exist within the collective imagination, moving souls higher or lower based upon the frequency of their creation. For every so-called president, there is a griot. Or, a storyteller of unimaginable power, skill and talent to carry the hearts and minds of citizens, capture and define the times with as much virtuoso as a president wields the power of his or her office. Their structure is supported by an army of DJs, business managers, agents, financiers, publishers, authors, intellectuals, poets, musicians, sculptors, painters, athletes, movie directors who underwrite the expressions of the soul with images, words, sounds, feelings. For every Ronald Reagan, there is a Michael Jackson, Walter Mosley or Prince, right? For every William Jefferson Clinton, there is a Maya Angelou or Michael Jordan. For every Richard Milhous Nixon, there is an Aretha Franklin or James Baldwin, right? Sometimes, whole movements serve as the countermeasure or even buttress to presidential power. From Calvin Coolidge to John F. Kennedy, it was the Harlem Renaissance. For Barack Obama, hip-hop. No less with Donald J. Trump, where there is a vanguard of poets, authors, artists, athletes who push out the expanse of their artistic expression under the banner of "the Resistance". As his so-called "power" constricts, restrains, toxifies, numbs and confuses, they free, inspire, liberate and clarify. They are the Vanguard. Their dispatches come from the fifth dimension — worlds at the axis of spiritual, emotion, cosmic and metaphysical realities. And, in reality, they are the fifth and most influential estate in American society and world culture. Godmothers Nikki Giovanni and Jaki Shelton Green represent those tentpoles for humanity, poetry and the arts, with nearly six decades as pre-eminent forces in American global culture, and are now the most dominant of those voices, particularly as their sister Toni Morrison has passed.

America's most powerful export has always been its culture — an amalgamation of the world's culture homogenized into a single society and exported to the far reaches of the planet. It's why Hollywood is a multi-*trillion*-dollar industry. Since Franklin D. Roosevelt and America's emergence as a world leader and its transformation from an agricultural into an industrial power, the world has migrated to the United States because of the promise of hope, self-definition and freedom. America's culture (e.g. music, film, books, ideas, academia, iconic figures) are the assets that move the hearts, minds and spirits of the people. The Fifth Estate is a counter-balance to the other four. It represents the spirit, the will, the vision and the hearts of the people. The Fifth Estate dials in and channels the fifth dimension in its work and deed. Along with co-founder Marvin L. Mills, I call this the Global I Aam, or Global International African Arts Movement.

This is precisely the time when artists go to work. There is no time for despair, no place for self-pity, no need for silence, no room for fear. We speak, we write, we do language. That is how civilizations heal. I know the world is bruised and bleeding, and though it is important not to ignore its pain, it is also critical to refuse to succumb to its malevolence. Like failure, chaos contains information that can lead to knowledge — even wisdom. Like art.
— Toni Morrison, 1931-2019

In the art of American politics, the virtue of checks and balances is extolled. The press is widely panned as the "Fourth Estate" after the judicial, executive and legislative branches of government. But, the most powerful estate is that of arts and culture, or art as the means by which culture is exported. The arts are the pathway to the fifth dimension. It is the work of free spirits to pull from alternative realities and merge into the blandness of man's governing body. Arts and culture are how the gifts of the spirits are merged into the mendacity of everyday life. Artists are the timeless gatekeepers of humanity. Maya Angelou. Amiri Baraka. Mark Twain. Tupac Amaru Shakur. Allen Ginsberg. Joni Mitchell. Revolutionaries, renaissance artists or political leaders? *The Matrix. V for Vendetta.* Toni Morrison's *Beloved*? Langston Hughes'

The Ways of White Folks. Prince's *Sign o' the Times*? NWA's "Fuck tha Police." Artwork, manifestos or political treatises?

In authoritarian regimes and totalitarian and fascist states, expression of the human soul will spill outside the lines of control and onto and into pages, canvasses, video screens, social media, graphic design, music. When politics lacks total art and is in fact solely a means of state control, well... then DJs, painters, entrepreneurs, creatives, sculptors, academics and intellectuals become leaders of social, the spiritual and the marginalized. Creative faculty is the spirit by which resistance to authoritarian control manifests. Publishers and producers become de facto gatekeepers of culture. In fact, their largess is expanded metaphysically within spiritual, emotional and real worlds.

Since approximately 2015, and the campaigns for this current epoch in American life (the tenure, campaign and election of America's 44th and 45th presidents), I have interviewed dozens of these storytellers of varying powers, influences, talents and visions. Some are household names over the decades. Others are not as well known or celebrated, but are the power and inspiration behind whole movements of American and global culture. These interviews and reflections are published in this volume. Each interview is titled with a name and title for the piece (e.g. Abiodun Oyewole — Harlem's Last Poet, or Nikki Giovanni — In Her Revolutionary Dream). Two essays, including this one, and a manifesto, have been included at the beginning and end of the book. The essays and interviews have been organized according to sections titled The Prophets, The Evangelists, The Seers and The Manifestors.

The list includes Pulitzer Prize winners, *New York Times* Best Selling authors, award-winning painters, professors, a poet laureate, mayoral candidates, HBO script writer, Hollywood designer, iconic poets, award-winning novelists, thought leaders, TED speakers, leaders of movements — movers and shakers who have used their platforms to make the voices of the unheard heard.

Many of the interviews included have been featured on platforms such as the *Huffington Post*, Toronto's award-winning *Into the Void*, the *Los Angeles Review of Books*, the *Tishman Review*, and the *Nasiona*, whilst some of them were conducted exclusively for this book.

Lots of the choices listed could seem unconventional. They are not all African American. Or even African. But I think about something that godmother Nikki Giovanni said to me when I asked whether the women's movement needed 50% parity to achieve its aims. Her answer as a renowned and celebrated feminist, activist and civil rights figure was not only instructive but powerful and *right*:

> Well, you know I have trouble with people who are saying it ought to be a 50 percent situation because some women are not nice or smart. And we know that some men are not nice or smart. And what we are looking for are nice, smart people... So, I think that what we want are more outstanding people.

On writing my initial introduction to this volume, my editor (who is English and considered "white," even though I consider him someone who is half Turkic (Uighur specifically) and Arab) also had some keen editorial comments about his and Dr Tom Lutz's participation:

> Also it is flattering that I and Tom should be included but do you think we should be as neither of us are Black, or can trace our midterm lineage back to Africa? I think you should

either remove us, or excuse us (explain why you have made an exception in our cases), or extend your criteria of who you have included and why...

I absolutely *love* that he noted "midterm lineage," as *all* seven billion of mankind are African. We Africans are the originals. My response was informed by my life experiences but also probably by Godmother Nikki Giovanni's sage counsel:

> As it regards yours and Tom's involvement, there are several other choices such as Richard Krawiec (white guy from Boston), Angela Narciso Torres (Filipino-American), Dr Chloe Martinez (Latino-American), William Allegrezza (Italian-American), Ingrid Baars (Dutch) or Rajni Perera (East Indian-Canadian (Toronto), that could be considered "unconventional" or non-African. But look at the quality of their work! The subjects they cover, the aesthetic they employ, the universal themes that transcend petty considerations of race. Are supreme court justice Clarence Thomas or Ward Connerly really carriers of peace and the advancement of people? Kareem Abdul Jabbar said the tricky thing about race is "it is a pretend thing masquerading as a real thing" — or as Dr. Martin Luther King famously alluded to the "content of character" versus skin pigment.

In fact, the words you're reading right now were edited by Tariq Goddard and his band of established anti-establishment merrymaking editors, designers and publicists including Josh Turner, Rhian E. Jones, Jonathan Maunder, Michael Watson and Francesca Corsini — many if not all of whom are white. The "technology" of racism insists upon dividing humanity from a shared history and creates societal caste systems based upon differences. Ytasha Womack, author of *Afrofuturism,* noted:

> Race or the notion of being Black or white specifically was created to justify the trans-Atlantic slave trade. The caste system that resulted was encoded through law and violence. People in our society have fought very vigilantly to change the system and recognize our shared humanity but the idea of separation continues to exist.

Then, there was one of my trusted readers, Tori "LA" Reid — an African American producer whose roots go back three generations in the USA before coming from the Akan and Yoruba tribes of the ancient Ghanaian empire. She said, "I can see what he is talking about. Matter of fact, I can see where both y'all are coming from. He's saying what pre-Mecca Malcolm X and the Black Panthers said — basically, 'You white people can help but this is our struggle'."

Quiet as it is told, civil rights and those struggles in addition to human rights are always fostered and brought about by a cadre of outstanding people of multitudinous backgrounds. So, just like Ghanaian, Liberian and Nigerian delegations of diplomats have been travelling to Caribbean islands like Trinidad, Jamaica and Barbados to apologize for their roles in the transatlantic slave trade and foster business and cultural ties, American Congress, which consists predominantly of white male descendants of slaveholders, would also be wise to do so. Just as 2019 is the Year of Returning Home for the entire African diaspora, it is also the entirety of the human expression that will ensure our progress. My life experiences affirm that it is outstanding people, brilliant spirits, who have moved the needle from tyranny to the light of hope, change and love.

We are the people. We are spirit. *And I Aam Global.*

The Prophets

But these things I plan won't happen right away. Slowly, steadily, surely, the time approaches when the vision will be fulfilled. If it seems slow, do not despair, for these things will surely come to pass. Just be patient! They will not be overdue a single day!
— Habakkuk 2:3

A prophet is a *griot* who sees the future and writes it into being. A prophet is an individual who has lived fearlessly, puncturing the cosmetic veil of a reality thick with superficiality, without concern for his or her own well-being. Of the prophets who are currently living there is Wole Soyinka, Ta-Nehisi Coates and Colin Kaepernick, to name only a few. Prophets bathe their spirits with justice, hope and faith. They emerge as instruments of a Love Spirit. Prophets exude an uncommonly high degree of humanity or love for their fellow human. "Prophet" is a cousin to "martyr" and "living legend." All define a person with the willingness to speak, live, and be the truth no matter the potential consequences. *Prophets can speak a future into being.* Prophets foresee, foretell and, at times, summon, a glorious future. Like their ancestors Emperor Haile Selassie, Kwame Nkrumah, Sojourner Truth or Chinua Achebe, they speak the truth into existence and, with the passage of time, come to embody that truth.

The Evangelists

All authority in heaven and on earth has been given to me. Therefore go and make disciples of all nations, baptizing them in the name of the Father and of the Son and of the Holy Spirit, and teaching them to obey everything I have commanded you. And surely I am with you always, to the very end of the age.
— Matthew 28:18-20

Evangelists speak, write or produce the truth in its raw unvarnished form, employing spirits, ancestors, magical expressions and emotional levers. Evangelists differ from prophets insofar as they speak the truth *as it is*. Prophets effortlessly travel the time spectrum (sometimes called "the imagination") into a glorious past and a bright future, bringing those spirits to shine in the here and now. The role of the evangelist is explained by the title. "Evangelist" means literally "proclaimer of Good News." Some of the most widely accepted evangelists are found in the Holy Bible, Talmud, Bhagavad Gita and Holy Koran. One might consider Barack Obama and his "Hope and Change" campaign slogan to be "good news," and he would be an evangelist. Or Oprah's Super Soul Sunday another layman's "good news." An evangelist may become a prophet. Sometimes when that truth or reality is dehumanizing or hurtful to the human spirit, they will curse it from the bottom of his or her soul — think of gangster rappers or the revolutionary expressions of Angela Davis or Eldridge Cleaver. Creative faculty is the *spirit* by which resistance to authoritarian control manifests. Evangelists lift limits of expression and spirit — *for which there are no limits*.

The Seers

God and Nature first made us what we are, and then out of our own created genius we make ourselves what we want to be. Follow always that great law. Let the sky and God be our limit and Eternity our measurement.
— Marcus Garvey, 1887-1940

Seers are visionaries who engage the spirit visually. Seers work with *perception* over the six other senses and the messages these images communicate to the spirit about our *entire* reality and all of the different dimensions and modalities that affect our interpretation. Or, as it is commonly stated, "perception is reality". Octavia Butler, Stan Lee and Sophia Stewart are some current and former seers with widespread followings. Just as ancient Kemet civilizations communicated our first alphabets by hieroglyphics, the seers channel future and past kingdoms by a common medium, translating metaphysical and extra-sensory realities by film, acrylic, watercolors, chalks, clay, bronze, pencils and, sometimes, even Bic pens. Like the sun that rises in the morning sky giving light and hope to a brand new day, the Seers see reality outside of time and space in all of its glory and reflect it plainly for all to see.

The Manifestors

A person who sees a problem is a human being; a person who finds a solution is visionary; and the person who goes out and does something about it is an entrepreneur.
— Naveen Jain, billionaire founder of InfoSpace

Manifestors make. They *underwrite*. They create. They create the accoutrements (read: magical things) of the new-age reality in a fashion that is absolute, loving and magical. What they create moves, inspires, lifts the spirit higher. Madame C.J. Walker, Elon Musk and Dr George Washington Carver are examples of current and past manifestors. Manifestors make books, jewelry, shows, musical acts, comic books and stores that seek to enliven, pick up and inspire the human spirit. Manifestors are also financiers like Mellody Hobson, Christopher Williams, Aliko Dangote, Robert Smith and Suzanne Shank. Some even create new ages with their good works. The items are taken from a glorious past and a powerful future and implemented in the here and now. Manifestors manifest the new age with their fresh good works.

THE PROPHETS

WHO WILL BE THE MESSENGER OF THIS LAND

BY JAKI SHELTON GREEN

who will be the messenger of this land
count its veins
speak through the veins
translate the language of water
navigate the heels of lineage
who will carry this land in parcels
paper, linen, burlap
who will weep when it bleeds
and hardens
forgets to birth itself

who will be the messenger of this land
wrapping its stories carefully
in patois of creole, irish,
gullah, twe, tuscarora
stripping its trees for tea
and pleasure
who will help this land to
remember its birthdays, baptisms
weddings, funerals, its rituals
denials, disappointments,
and sacrifices

who will be the messengers
of this land
harvesting its truths
bearing unleavened bread

burying mutilated crops beneath
its breasts

who will remember
to unbury the unborn seeds
that arrived
in captivity
shackled, folded,
bent, layered in its
bowels

we are their messengers
with singing hoes
and dancing plows
with fingers that snap
beans, arms that
raise corn, feet that
cover the dew falling from
okra, beans, tomatoes

we are these messengers
whose ears alone choose
which spices
whose eyes alone name
basil, nutmeg, fennel, ginger,
cardamom, sassafras
whose tongues alone carry
hemlock, blood root, valerian,
damiana, st. john's wort
these roots that contain
its pleasures its languages its secrets

we are the messengers
new messengers
arriving as mutations of ourselves

we are these messengers
blue breath
red hands
singing a tree into dance

IN HER REVOLUTIONARY DREAM

NIKKI GIOVANNI, ACTIVIST AND POET

Nikki Giovanni by painter Malik Seneferu

Sometimes, when folks get older, they age gently. The lions, once regal and fierce, become lions of winter. Think of the freedom gladiators like Nelson Mandela or Muhammad Ali in their later years. Where there was once judgment and the spirit of a fighter, there is now understanding and calmness, coupled with patience and perspective. Where there was once a spirit of revolution, there is now forgiveness, diplomacy, and statesmanship. Where there were once sharp, hard lines, there are now soft pastels, curves, and shades. But sometimes, just sometimes, people grow fiercer.

That was my impression, after a conversation with griot Nikki Giovanni — a "queen mother of movements" — whose positions on the issues are just as potent now as they were over half a century ago. Giovanni's first book, *Black Feeling, Black Talk* (1968), sold over ten thousand copies in its first year. Ten thousand books of poetry. *Her first book.* She has been dubbed the "Poet of the Black Revolution," and is one of the foremost authors of the Black Arts Movement, influenced by the Civil Rights Movement and Black Power Movement. Since then, she has completed twenty books of poetry, about a dozen children's books (from 1971's *Spin a Soft Black Song* to 2018's *I Am Loved*), and recorded seven albums. She has received dozens of awards — honorary doctorates and the keys to cities — and recognition for her social impact on women and African American communities.

When I spoke with her recently, she was in mourning over the loss of a friend, Charles. But the clarity and intensity with which she spoke about leadership (or lack thereof) in our nation, the lack of compassion in our times, and the senselessness of gun violence, was not tempered and refined but enhanced, underscored, and made bold-faced by age.

Patrick A. Howell: It is widely reported that your Tennessee grandmother, Louvenia Watson, played a huge role in forming your consciousness for justice, love, and righteousness for your people. Even in these morally compromised times in America, can you say that you have found these qualities throughout your life's work?

Nikki Giovanni: I think that the grandmothers were incredibly organized. If you think about the Civil Rights Movement, you really are looking at grandmothers. I know we all look to King and some of the other people standing on stage, but if you look at who organized, it was the grandmothers. If you look at Montgomery and Ms. Parks, it was the grandmothers that were leading people because people didn't have jobs. They were the ones making the food and taking it to them. They were the ones who were the cab drivers to make up the difference in their money. Some of them would have their clubs where they played cards, but mostly they organized so they knew each other and they knew what each other needed — what they could get done.

I was born in Knoxville, Tennessee. It was the grandmothers who were saying, "We are not going to go to Miller's Department Store." They were the ones. I think we miss them, frankly speaking.

P.H.: Are you a grandmother?

N.G.: I am, but my granddaughter is only twelve, and it is a different world now. Coming up in the age of segregation, I don't think we could have come through it without the grandmothers. Even if you look at Martin [Luther King], you look at his mother. She was a grandmother, right? Ultimately, she was going to be murdered in church. Somebody must have known: "The grandmothers are important, and if I don't get rid of Mrs. King, it'll all start over again."

P.H.: As we move into this twenty-first century, it is impossible to ignore the historical patterns that have emerged both challenging and promising the American dream. In Donald J. Trump, we have Richard M. Nixon's wildest dream. The Black Arts Movement continues in a series of streams flowing through the grassroots of Black Lives Matter and the high-culture expressions of Ryan Coogler's *Black Panther* and hip-hop. What is your American dream for the next generations?

N.G.: First of all, I would disagree that Donald Trump is Richard Nixon. I think you have to compare Donald Trump to Adolf Hitler. I think that Trump is evil, and I think that he is a murderer. We continue to see him encouraging war as we continue to see his greed. So, as bad as I thought Richard Nixon was, and I was glad he resigned under threat of impeachment, and that was led by representative Barbara Jordan, I think you have to look at Trump for what he is — he is evil.

My hope for the future — *I am a big, big fan of Black Lives Matter.* I think that the kids, the young people, have done a wonderful job. I wish that I could sit around some of the tables at dinner time and hear the grandmothers talk to their granddaughters. I bet you there were granddaughters who said, "I am not going to let my grandmother die seeing her grandson shot down." I think all of that had to do with Black Lives Matter. And, of course, the prisons are just incredibly stupid. They are bad. We know that the prisons are the new Klansmen. They no longer lynch Black men and women — and you have to remember that Black women were lynched. America has more people in prison than anybody else [in the world].

P.H.: I just think that is something that is central to what America is. Black lives murdered, Black lives incarcerated is elemental to American life. It's the way it was in the very beginning and nearly four hundred years later that is how it is today. It is like the oxygen that we breathe — that is just how America is.

N.G.: First of all, America is changing colors. The white man is already scared. America is turning brown and yellow. You can see that every place. I think as we are changing colors, we are changing our responsibility to planet Earth.

I teach at Virginia Tech, and one of the things that I teach is creative writing. I am always reminding them that it's probably time we started to teach the young children that read our books, that when somebody asks them, "Who are you?" they say, "I am an earthling." It's time that we moved into, "We are earthlings." It doesn't really matter if you are from America, North or South, Russia, or China. What matters is that you are from Earth, and we need to start teaching that to our youngsters so that they can begin to see themselves as a part of a bigger situation.

P.H.: Are you preaching love?

N.G.: You have to be careful how you use love because love can do different things. But I think that love is important — yeah.

P.H.: The new generation has taken a strong stand with the gun lobby. I thought you might have something to say about that as it relates to your own activism and your own experiences with Virginia Tech in 2007 — and as you emerged as a national voice during the assassinations of Kennedy, Evers, Malcolm, and Martin.

N.G.: First of all, I think the NRA obviously has too much power. You don't need the guns the way that they are now. How many people have AR-15s? That's ridiculous.

Now, we hear people talking about how they want their guns so they can hunt. Hunting is when other things have a chance. You don't go hunting, and the deer doesn't have a chance.

I eat the meat that I shoot. But most people don't. They shoot it because they want to show it is a trophy. "Look at what I can do." If you took that back fifty years, they put a picture of a Black man hanging from a tree. "Look at what I can do." And if you took it just a few years more, you can see the most horrible thing — that Black woman that they lynched and split open and her baby fell out. And somebody has a picture of that. So, hunting for somebody to say, "Look at what I did." That's insane. That's like husbands beating up their wives. Their wives come out with a black eye and the husbands say, "See, look at what I do. My old lady listens to me." All of that has to stop. The only way that is going to stop — and it is going to be slow — is one at a time.

P.H.: What are you now working on? Your last work was *Chasing Utopia: A Hybrid* in 2013. What comes after *Utopia*? *A Good Cry*?

N.G.: I was going to say, you are a little bit behind. I've been pleased with the fact that I have been working so much. *A Good Cry* just came out, and I have been working with Ashley Bryan, who I love so much. He is a great illustrator. Ashley and I did a book called *I Am Loved* — it's a children's book, and I am pleased with that. I am getting ready to do what I hope will be a podcast. I'm seventy-four years old and a little behind on some things but, in talking to my students, they say, "You should do a podcast, because you talk all the time." So, in the next couple of months I am working on a podcast so I can, again, reach people. People need to be talked to. People are lonely. I travel a lot.

And what you see is a lot of people have earplugs and they are listening to something. Usually, what they are listening to is podcasts. They are listening to somebody talk to them, and I am thinking, I talk. And maybe it's time that we who like people started to talk to people and not just let the haters do it.

P.H.: What was your hardest time as a writer, and how did you get through it?

N.G.: I don't know if I can really answer that. Writers are always questioning what we say and how we want to say it. I think the hard time with any writer is when you are sad. And you are calling me at a very sad time. My dear friend Charles Steger died. I was debating whether we should wait for this conversation. I really loved Charles. How do I get through it? The way you get through it is you write through it. You cry through it, too. I had to laugh at myself and say it is funny that Charles dies right after *A Good Cry* because it made me want to have a good cry. We are going to miss Charles a lot. He was a good man. There are probably a lot of good men, but not a whole lot. [Laughs.] You miss people with his vision and who cared the way that he did. So, it's been a sad week. What made me happiest about Charles is I never let him down. I never said something I did not do. If you can just say that about anyone that you love — well, that's the best that you can do.

P.H.: Who are your inspirations?

N.G.: We started this conversation with Louvenia Watson. Grandmother just meant a lot to me. I had to laugh about it. I never think of myself as going to heaven. There are just people who I dislike, like Donald Trump. I hope he goes to hell. So, I'm not going to heaven.

P.H.: I think you will.

N.G.: Well, thank you. But there are day-passes. Because there are day-passes for everything. So, I say when I go to hell, I'm going to be a good girl and get a day-pass and get a chance to go up to my grandmother, so I can ask her, "Why did you put up with me?" I can sit down with her as an old lady and say, "Were you proud of me? Did I do a good job?" Because I know that she went there. I know that. I'm sure that you are not supposed to smoke there, but I am sure that Louvenia is there smoking. I bet you she sneaks over and has a cigarette.

P.H.: Did you read poetry to your grandmother? I think you would be doing poetry while she is smoking and listening to you.

N.G.: And some red wine. I know my mother is in heaven. If Mommy is there sitting with us, I know that she is having a beer. So you can see what the group is going to look like. I would probably take a really good bottle of wine for my mother — and grandmother loved Winstons. We'll just be sitting there saying, "Well, how did this happen? How did that happen?"

P.H.: In 1972, you interviewed Muhammad Ali, the Greatest of All Time. Do you see his greatness in our new generation — in our Colin Kaepernick, in our Serena Williams?

N.G.: That young football player and him kneeling down — I see Ali's set on him. I think that is wonderful. But when Ali did what Ali did, nobody had done what he had done. And so, there isn't anybody like Muhammad Ali. Because, as you know, he had to give up his belt, and, of course you know, his life was being threatened a lot. He just decided,

I am not afraid. I'm a man, and I am going to stand up for what I believe. So, he did. I am lucky because when they took his belt, he didn't have a job and he wrote poetry.

P.H.: Really?

N.G.: [Laughs.] Yes, it was awful. We had a mutual friend: Victoria Lucas. She called me. She worked with one of his people, and she said, "Would you like to do some poetry with Ali?" I said, "Are you kidding, I would love to." So, we traveled around for a while. So, I was just very lucky to get to know him. So, I'm happy for Serena, and I go whenever I get to watch her. I'm happy for Colin. I'm happy for all of them. You have to look at who did what when. And when Ali did what he did, he was all alone. Jackie Robinson was a Republican, and I'm not against him. When Ali stood up, he really stood alone. And he said, this is what is important to me. You have to recognize that he opened the door. Now there are other athletes, other people going through that door.

P.H.: It is my personal conviction that the aims of the women's power movement ultimately fall short of the mark if women do not occupy 50 percent of the power structure positions in government and the executive suites of the United States. The challenge is that of simple arithmetic. What would Nikki consider success and equality in women's suffrage?

N.G.: Well, you know I have trouble with people who are saying it ought to be a 50 percent situation because some women are not nice or smart. And we know that some men are not nice or smart. And what we are looking for are nice, smart people. We've seen some Black female judges who have just been terrible, and some, incredible.

I am a member of Delta Sigma Theta, and we have looked at incredible women like Barbara Jordan. So, I think that what we want are more outstanding people.

I just don't want to get caught in that trap — they all have to be men, they all have to be women. I'm a Christian — oh, they all have to be Christian, they all have to be Israeli. What you want is good people. We don't have enough good people. Somebody needs to open a grocery store selling backbones. When you look at the Congress, they don't have their backbones. I don't know what they are doing, but I know that they don't have them. Americans have been bought and sold. It is amazing to have Americans that don't care if someone has committed treason in the White House just because they are getting enriched by it.

It's no one thing now. I said the other day to a group — "Fortunately, God doesn't call me." But if God called me and said, "Hey Nikki, it's God, do you have a minute?" And, of course, you know, you would have a minute for God. If he said, "I am thinking about closing down planet Earth. I'm thinking about getting rid of human beings, what are your thoughts?" I think we'd all be in trouble because you can't lie to God. I'd have to say, "Well, you know, it hasn't worked. It's been several thousand years and it hasn't worked, so maybe we need to shut this all down and start all over again."

P.H.: Woooooooow. Okay.

N.G.: Could you say that you think this has been a good idea?

P.H.: I just want to project love and positivity. It's part of my MO. Those are the choices and the decisions I have made. That it is more powerful to make a way for hope. To make a way for love. It's not as easy, and a lot of times it may not seem like it makes any sense in terms of what you are seeing. A lot of times I feel exactly as you do.

N.G.: That's not what I asked you. I said if God called you and said, "How do you think we are doing?" what would you say?

P.H.: I would say that I think we are working through it. I am going to read you a poem of yours:

> i used to dream militant
> dreams of taking
> over america to show
> these white folks how it should be
> done
> i used to dream radical dreams
> of blowing everyone away with my perceptive powers
> of correct analysis
> i even used to think i'd be the one
> to stop the riot and negotiate the peace
> then i awoke and dug
> that if i dreamed natural
> dreams of being a natural
> woman doing what a woman
> does when she's natural
> i would have a revolution

N.G.: Yes, I love that poem. It's also prophetic, isn't it? I'm going to be a natural woman. I'm not going to let [anyone] take my womanhood away from me.

1/10/2019

AMERICAN BARD

JEFFERY RENARD ALLEN, AWARD-WINNING AUTHOR, POET AND PROFESSOR OF CREATIVE WRITING

So much about our lives as Black people in this country involves this form of creation, the proverbial making of something out of nothing, of finding a way out of no way, and surviving (and hopefully thriving) off remnants, remains, and leftovers.
— Jeffery Renard Allen, "Urgently Visible: Why Black Lives Matter," *Evergreen Review*

Let's suppose, for the purposes of this article, that American history is nothing more than a series of structural patterns spawned from an original sin and high idea. Or, as Mark Twain has widely been credited with saying, "History doesn't repeat itself, but it often rhymes." And let's also suppose that those patterns have slight deviations that allow altogether different possibilities, both negative and positive. So where there was the Civil Rights Movement, there is now Black Lives Matter. Where there were once mass hippie protests, there is now the Resistance. Where there was Richard Nixon, there is now Donald J. Trump. Where there was Dr. Martin Luther King Jr., there is now a realization of Barack Hussein Obama.

Now, if you consider racism a plague, you might recognize these patterns as *no es bueno*. You might even be a little bored of the spiritual pestilence, rot, and disease. *Si si, muy malo*. You may be sickened by a system predicated upon incarcerated Black bodies and young American men murdered. Who wouldn't be, right? This requires grit and grind. We remember where we have been. If you have considered slavery and its fascinating twin babies of discrimination and institutional racism to be cancer agents of a toxic and malignant characteristic, you might consider Mr Jeffery Renard Allen, a Reiki doctor, gripping a satchel of diagnosis and cure in a tightly clenched fist. We know where we are. He is, in fact, a master mystic creating the work of a generation previously unknown. Now, forward to where we have yet to go.

Throughout the nascent twenty-first century, Allen has made work of traveling, learning, educating, reflecting, and creating. In 2006, he traveled to Nairobi, Kenya, working with Chimamanda Ngozi Adichie soon after *Half of a Yellow Sun* came out. He taught at the Kwani Litfest. In 2008, he traveled to Accra, Ghana, organizing a writers' conference at the Kokrobitey Institute and working with fellow author Arthur Flowers. In 2012, he again worked with Chimamanda's Farafina Trust Creative Writing Workshop in Lagos, Nigeria. That same year in Zanzibar, he served as program director of literature at the Jahazi Literary and Jazz Festival.

As we prepare for this interview, Allen seems most proud of his recent work appearing in the premiere online version of the celebrated journal, *Evergreen Review*. His answers to my questions were equally insightful, deliberate and thoughtful; both hands of the American Bard, prepared to do their work.

Patrick A. Howell: Jeff, you've been globetrotting in recent months, completing a residency in Bellagio, Italy, at the Rockefeller Center. You worked on completing your book of short stories, *Fat Time*. Also, you have traveled to Dublin, Ireland, to do a reading at the James Joyce Center and lecture students at University College Dublin. Did you enjoy your time away from our grand American experiment... I mean, experience? Away from the Black American experience? How have your recent travels informed your work? How do they inform your identity as an American?

Jeffery Renard Allen: I arrived at Bellagio last November only a few days after the election. I truly felt as if I were escaping my country at a time when it was necessary to do so. The good thing is I was able to spend a month there, spend a month on one of the most beautiful places on Earth, and simply focus on my writing. Of course, I was also trying to get my head around the election, so I watched things from afar as it were.

I have always had an itch for travel, and my life has been such that I have had the good fortune to travel quite extensively abroad. As a Black person in this country, we often don't feel welcome, but when you go overseas and see another American, you have a strange feeling of kinship. Traveling overseas can't help but change your understanding of what it means to be an American. You notice, for example, that nowhere on the planet do you see scores of people who are obese. You only see obesity in America. What does that tell us about who we are as a country?

Let's be frank about it. Americans are the most naive people on the planet, which also makes us the most dangerous people on the planet given our nuclear arsenal and that we have the strongest military in the history of the world. More than sixty million Americans voted for Donald Trump. It doesn't matter why you voted for him. I traveled to Dublin back in January and arrived there before Trump's inauguration. I was talking to a taxi driver who had been to America numerous times and to many different parts of the country. He clearly finds much to like about our country because there is much to like, and our country is like no other. So he said to me with great concern, "I hope Donald Trump doesn't ruin the country." My question, how is it that a foreigner can recognize Trump for what he is, but tens of millions of Americans could not?

You can travel throughout our country and find monuments that celebrate the conquest of Native Americans, and few stage protests to have these monuments removed. This means one of two things: on the one hand, either most Americans are so ignorant about our history that they are incapable of recognizing why these monuments are an affront, or, on the other, they are perfectly comfortable with celebrating certain forms of conquest and genocide. Thinking about such questions, one thinks about the overall question of the American psyche. Travel, conversation, reading, and observation have led me to understand that we have a type of optimism that exists nowhere else in the world.

We believe that we are entitled to happiness. In fact, that very wording is in our Constitution, the "pursuit of happiness." In contrast, the rest of the world has a firm and realistic Old World view where they expect nothing, and where they know that they have little chance of improving their lives. They may long for improvement, but the reality is that for most people in the world, life has afforded them few opportunities of improvement. This is not to say that life has not improved for millions of people around the world over, say, the last century. I'm talking about mindset, attitude. Americans are the only people in the world who feel entitled to happiness, a feeling that often comes with other kinds of expectations, as in an expectation to make money and acquire wealth.

How true is that expectation? Statistics from the last census show that the median income in this country is quite low, one where most families are led by a couple, with each person working a job where the annual income is just above the poverty level. And that's the kind of job most people work in this country, one that keeps them a few thousand dollars above the poverty line as our federal government defines poverty. That is the economic reality.

Couple that with certain forms of historical, political, and emotional denial — this country that has never come to terms with the strange legacies of genocide, slavery, and segregation, to say nothing of our colonial experiment that took half of what used to be Mexico. This country where the majority of white people don't think that people of color suffer racial discrimination. This country where sixty million people voted for Trump, including the majority of white women. This country where tens of millions time and again vote for a Republican and thereby vote against their own economic interests. Why would they do that? The answer is simple: because they embrace their whiteness, their feelings of privilege and superiority. They embrace white superiority. There's no other way to explain it.

To be honest, the recent election has caused me to become completely disillusioned with this country, notwithstanding the fact that the Trump presidency is starting to look like the best thing in American politics given that it has given rise to a grassroots movement that we haven't seen in decades. The election brings home once again the reality that this is a country that can never come to terms with what it is. The resistance to reality is such that it leads to a violent resentment of anyone who speaks the truth about certain forms of systematic injustices and the like, as was made evident in the rise of the fanatical Tea Party and also in the violence that erupted at Trump rallies time and again last year. This is a fanaticism, a hatred, that is steeped in the most blatant forms of ignorance.

Scientific illiteracy is such in our country that millions of people don't understand why we need environmental protections and certain regulations, and it leads millions of people to deny such factual phenomena as evolution and climate change. Given our refusal to come to terms with who we are, these troubling realities are not surprising. One might simply say that it is all a failure of education. If our government were truly interested in serving its citizens, every American would receive the best possible education, to say nothing of a livable wage, healthcare, childcare, and other essential life necessities.

P.H.: It is interesting that with the current unrest, with our civil rights moment in Black Lives Matter, with an authoritarian, unpopular president with Machiavellian tendencies, and with the unprecedented legal muck of the White House, there are a lot of parallels to the 1960s and '70s, particularly the civil unrest and another authoritarian character at the White House's helm. It is some sort of acute, unpleasant déjà vu. Your critically well-received *Song of the Shank* dealt significantly with themes of race, art, class, and religion from the Civil War and Reconstruction. Do you feel more of the new or more of the old in this moment? What world, do you, as an author of historical fiction, an artist, and father, think can emerge from the current challenges?

J.R.A.: I feel both the new and the old in every moment. As William Faulkner famously wrote, "The past is not dead. The past is not even past." One reality is that the human animal is morally flawed. Nothing will ever change that. As an American, I feel there is the troubling reality of the many things I talked about earlier. Despite it all, I am an optimist because I know that life offers so much that is joyous and beautiful. And I also know that we will continue as a species. As Faulkner put it at the end of *The Sound and the Fury*: They endured. We will endure. I will tell you that after the election last November, many of my students at the University of Virginia were devastated, crushed, depressed, distraught, crying. What could I do to comfort them? I knew the answer. I sent them Faulkner's Nobel Prize acceptance speech.

And here's the thing: I lived in New York when the World Trade Center attacks happened in September 2001, and I taught MFA Writing students at The New School, which was only a few miles from the World Trade Center. The university and much of Manhattan beneath Fourteenth Street was shut down the week after the attack, so during that week, I thought a lot about what I would say to my students once class resumed, thought about what I could say to them to let them know that their writing and art still mattered. I decided to give them Faulkner's Nobel Prize acceptance speech, which is a powerful piece of writing. I cry whenever I read it, in the same way that I cry whenever I hear the voice of Dr. Martin Luther King Jr delivering his "I Have a Dream Speech" and some of his other speeches. The words transport me, the words are transcendent, they are all "up in my body" as Miles Davis says in his autobiography of what it felt like to hear Bird and Dizzy playing for the first time. "Music all up in my body." I live for all that is music.

For me, my writing is always about music in one way or another, especially as a way of living in the world, moving about in the world, and as a way of seeing what's actually there. Of course, words on a page never have the immediacy of music or oration, such that you have to do other things to make the work interesting, which is largely about the paradoxical process of both writing the world as is (what Henry James called the "disappearance of the author"), and, at the same time, getting yourself on paper, telling a story that only you can tell in a way that only you can tell it. That's why it can take a while to develop stories that compel you, that draw you in and demand to be written.

So, for example, I wrote a novel about Blind Tom because he was a figure from the historical past whom I found tremendously interesting for a number of reasons. That is, I wrote about him because he interests me, not because I write historical fiction. (In fact, I don't write historical fiction, a particular genre which is fine in and of itself but which I have no aesthetic interest in as a writer.) And in the book of stories I'm presently working on, *Fat Time*, I'm writing about some other figures from the historical past — including Jimi Hendrix, Jack Johnson, and Miles Davis — because they interest me for one reason or another. But I'm also writing stories set in America now, and in Africa now, even as I write stories set in a speculative future in both America and Africa.

As a father, one has to be hopeful about the future. In fact, I fully believe that my children will live enjoyable and rewarding lives. I'm doing everything I can to make that possible. As a father, one also recognizes that my children will face the same specter of race that I have had to face. It's impossible for them not to. So the best one can do is prepare them for it, and be sure that they have the "equipment for living" [Kenneth Burke] that they need. One can only hope that they remain emotionally and spiritually whole as they engage with and navigate through the many absurdities of race (or gender or class). I say that because I know what damage this has done to me, and to so many others. The battle is wearying, so much so that when I retire from teaching in ten or twelve years, I will leave the country and live elsewhere, most likely somewhere on the African continent, most likely in South Africa. All of the African continent is a special place to me with many heartbreaking realities, but also with an energy and an impulse for life that I feel nowhere else.

My story "Heads" is in the current issue of *Oxford American*, their annual music issue. In the piece, I imagine a friendship between Jimi Hendrix and painter Francis Bacon.

P.H.: Is "magic" real? From *Harbor and Spirits* to *Stellar Places* to *Song of the Shank* to "Heads," the reality is there inviting comparisons to the realism of Faulkner and Ralph Ellison, but magic jumps from your pages in language, scenes, and happenings. Is that art, or is it observation?

J.R.A.: Life is rich in myriad ways, far richer in fact than what we often see or feel. I try to capture the thickness of life in my work. I think about narrative in terms of the African sea of time where the past, the present, and the future exist all at once. At the same time, I think in narrative in terms of African cosmology, circles within circles, where life is a swirling continuum of the real and the metaphysical, the supernatural. For these reasons, I reject limiting terms like "magical realism." The real is always more than real. It is fat time.

Dr Jeffery Renard Allen interviews George Clinton of Funkadelic

So, there it is, the American Bard wielding his great instrument of cleansing in the one hand. Tearing down old, staid structures and allowing the light to come through the afternoon branches of evergreen pine needles and to bounce off the demure blues and greens of the lakes, allowing humanity to breathe big, puissant breaths unencumbered by the recalcitrant realities of our current America, which is really the old America come up moribund from the ground. American Bard. Do that thing. Do it hard. He's just beginning. Beginning.

With the work that has taken Allen around the world and the African continent, the future seems clear for those willing to look back on this period from the perch of 2117. The trajectory is clear for those clear-eyed and inviting hope and change in a moment wrought with bitterness, anger, resentments, and a deep depression. In his work with the Norman Mailer Center and Writers Colony, Allen has worked with a number of emerging writers from the African continent, including A. Igoni Barrett, Victor Ehikhamenor, Yewande Omotoso, and Samuel Kolawole. For the 2012 Pan-African Literary Forum, Allen organized a national reading tour for South African poet Keorapetse Kgositsile.

And indeed the struggle is beautiful. It is sweet. It is inspired. It is blessed. That seems to be what Jeffery Renard Allen's body of work would suggest: the metaphysical properties and beauty of light work. The hammering of words, ideas, and visions firm in hand channels the bursts of lights coming from visions previously unseen. The harmonic convergence of his work is beautiful, an incomplete symphonic piece is underlain with rhythms and harmonies, taking inspiration directly from Tom Higgins, Miles Davis, and Jimi Hendrix, American masters. It is a new song for the new day. From here to over there, yonder, where imaginations are fertile, and the land is plenty and willing.

2/3/18

POET LAUREATE OF THE LAND, MESSENGER OF THE PEOPLE

JAKI SHELTON GREEN, NORTH CAROLINA POET LAUREATE, HUMAN ACTIVIST AND FUTURE US POET LAUREATE

Poet Jaki Shelton Green. Courtesy of Jan Hensley.

Wealth is oftentimes hidden in plain sight. Think about it — Apple iPods and iPhones are everywhere. They are as commonplace as blue skies and sunshine. Apple Computers, however, has a $599.70B market capitalization and is the most profitable company in the world, with profits at $57.3B. There you go — *right in plain sight.*

It is no less with the spiritual and creative wealth that buttress our nation and world culture, era after era. Think of Pulitzer Prize poet Gwendolyn Brooks, Maya Angelou or Muhammad Ali and what they have meant not only to our country but to the world. The world we live in is not possible without these ancestors underwriting the struggle with such *savoir faire.* Their body of work and words are emblematic of the American citizen on the highest possible frequency. They literally represent and remix the struggle into sweet poetry. Or, as Movement Be founder Nate Howard has said, "Their poetry really changed society. It's how we change the world... And it's not entertainment." Only, I would add, these assets are *priceless.*

When it comes to the literature and advocacy of our flowering global renaissance, American poet and Duke University professor Jaki Shelton Green is North Carolina's ubiquitous, though not exclusive, treasure. *She is a national treasure hiding in plain sight.* In nearly six decades of work, she has mentored hundreds of authors, poets and women across the country and globally. Her poetry has appeared in the *African American Review, Essence Magazine* and *Ms. Magazine,* as well as dozens of literary journals, trade magazines and periodicals. She is a 2014 Pushcart Prize Nominee, the 2009 North Carolina Piedmont Laureate and in 2003 the recipient of the North Carolina Award for Literature (the highest award the state can bestow for significant contributions in science, literature, fine arts, and public service). I could go on to list countless awards and acknowledgments, from her most recent with Duke University going back to appointments in the 1960s, but that would not be worthy of her electric alkaline poetry.

Griot Jaki Shelton Green does not measure her success by such programmatic indicators. *"Success?,"* she sings in the sister sass and airy melody of her voice, "Success based upon hallowed standards is not something I aspire to or want to participate in. Poetry is about so much more — it is about the work we do here on the planet. It is about crafting quality work and saving lives, elevating lives. It's about the spirit. The serious writer who wants to work with an editor, the serious artist who wishes to workshop her work. My measurement of success is creating someone who is serious about the writing process. This is editing. This is refinement and curation of the spirit."

However, the accolades are unending. In 2014, Green was inducted into the North Carolina Literary Hall of Fame. She has authored *Dead on Arrival* (Carolina Wren Press) and seven other poetry collections. Her poetry has appeared in *Callaloo, Cave Canem African American Writers Anthology, Home is Where: An Anthology of African American Poetry from the Carolinas*, and *Iodine Poetry Journal*, among many others.

The operative word for her is dynamism. Her readings are electrifying. She is a presence at the podium, a meld of panache and humility that embraces every audience, regardless of its orientation. She is North Carolina poetry's Billie Holiday.
— The North Carolina Hall of Fame

i know the grandmother one had hands
but they were always in bowls
folding, pinching, rolling the dough
making the bread
i know the grandmother one had hands
but they were always under water
sifting rice/ blueing clothes
starching lives...
— Jaki Shelton Green, "i know the grandmother one had hands," *Breath of the Song*

Some of Jaki's other publications include *Feeding the Light*, *Masks*, *Dead on Arrival*, *breath of the song*, and *Conjure Blues*, which was cited as one of two Best Poetry Books of the Year by the *Independent Weekly*. She has performed her poetry and conducted workshops and residency programs throughout the United States, the Caribbean, Europe, and Central and South America.

Rooted in hypnagogic logic and deeply seated in the tradition of Jayne Cortez, Quincy Troupe and Ntozake Shange, Jaki Shelton Green's verse narratives pay homage to the orphic ethos of the mythmaking South with all the viscous verve of Van Gogh with a palette of syllables, images and words blurring through our senses like the thick, sleek wax of magnolia leaves... Her poems are totems and tomes; they are percussive, convulsive and constructive.
— Tony Medina, author of *Broke Baroque*, *The President Looks Like Me & Other Poems*, and *An Onion of Wars*.

In her time, ancestor griot Maya Angelou set the tone as one millennium ended and another began with her poem "On the Pulse of Morning" at William Jefferson Clinton's inauguration. Her tenure as America's Griot and as a living national treasure also ran through a number of presidential terms. She was awarded the 2010 Medal of Freedom in the East Wing of the White House her ancestors built, by the president who was the full realization of visions written by her and her Harlem Renaissance coterie nearly one hundred years ago. One might argue that Queen Maya Angelou's tenure as America's Griot was more spiritually and artistically powerful, more culturally relevant, than the tenure of the seven presidents in her term who are limited by the 22nd Amendment of the United States Constitution. As the first African American woman to win a Pulitzer Prize, Gwendolyn Brooks set the pedigree for Toni Morrison and Ta-Nehisi Coates. Likewise with the people's king, ancestor Muhammad Ali, the immortal fighter who will forever float like a butterfly/sting like a bee... before hip-hop was even a cultural catchphrase. He is the Greatest of All Time for did he not pound the enemies of racism and systemic discrimination into submission? I submit, upon the life of Cassius Clay, he did.

She helps people work with the craft of their soul. Women will go on retreats to the beach and they deal with what it means to be a woman in this society. She helps people refashion and build themselves up. She is dealing with the matter of life and the repercussions living has upon our souls and bodies. She recognizes that poetry is a spiritual exercise.
— Richard Krawiec, Instructor of Advanced Fiction at University of North Carolina at Chapel Hill

It is no less with Queen Poetess Griot Jaki Shelton Green, whose work is seeded and nourished within thousands of students who are nurses and postmen, rich folk and poor folk, mechanics and poets, professors and students, Black and white brothers and sisters, strivers and achievers, home-makers and attorneys, doctors and janitors... everyday people who do what they do with the song of poetry informing their work, the melodies of love, hope and faith in the details to which they attend. They have been touched immaculately by the lyrical *je ne sais quoi* of a master supreme poetess.

Indeed, she is poet laureate for the people, by the people, of the people, an American Griot and treasure. And it seems she need only be anointed by the One as she is not interested in the accolades that are heaped higher than the biblical towers of Babel. In the timeless tradition of our Griots, our people and the earth, she is the messenger

of this land in the traditional call/response form of our
African Americanized language:

> who will be the messenger of this land
> count its veins
> speak through the veins
> translate the language of water
> navigate the heels of lineage
> who will carry this land in parcels
> paper, linen, burlap
> who will weep when it bleeds
> and hardens
> forgets to birth itself...
>
> we are the messengers
> new messengers
> arriving as mutations of ourselves
> we are these messengers
> blue breath
> red hands
> singing a tree into dance

3/10/17

Since writing this piece godmother Jaki Shelton Green has
become the Poet Laureate of North Carolina.

DEAN OF AMERICAN SPORTS SMASHES RACISM IN ITS UGLY MOUTH

DR HARRY EDWARDS, INTELLECT, AUTHOR AND ONCE IN A MILLENNIUM CHANGE AGENT

Dr. Harry Edwards by Jai Lennard ©

If you think about it, fusing sports and protest is as old as modern America. Jesse Owens did it in his own quiet way — long before there was Usain Bolt of Jamaica — by performing at such a high level at the 1936 Olympic Games in Berlin that he left historic cleat marks all over

Adolf Hitler's face. Jackie Robinson broke the color line in America's national pastime, Major League Baseball, ingesting the Klu Klux Klan and the toxic racism of an entire nation to create a vision of a future that heralds the coming of George Springer of the Houston Astros as the greatest to ever play the game. There was the towering Bill Russell, long before he handed the iconic LeBron James the Bill Russell NBA Finals Most Valuable Player Award. In Southern California, a young SharkHeart (aka Christian Howell) studies Michael Phelps's, Reece Whitley's, Caeleb Dressel's and Cullen Jones' every stroke with an acute interest. And then there is the immortal warrior king of the twentieth century, Muhammad Ali, the undisputed Greatest of All Time.

However, fusing those thoughts together in an academic discipline was the work of a singular force. The sociology of sports was a thesis of Dr Harry Edwards at Cornell University. Through activism, he burnished the universal appeal of Black athletes with the frame of a man who stands at the height of 6'5" and probably weighs in at 240 to 270 lbs — a man who could be confused with a prize fighter, say George Foreman's sparring partner or the genetic precedent to Marshawn Lynch doubled (he later corrects me — he was 6'8" and 280 lbs back in the day). But he was Professor Emeritus at the University of California at Berkeley. That takes imagination. "Leadership," "vision," "singular focus," "innovator," "freedom fighter," "creativity" and "perseverance" are all characteristics that pique a persona unique to the American character, particularly as we are just getting geared up for this here twenty-first century. If Barack Obama is George Washington for the twenty-first century, then Dr Harry Edwards may be the Benjamin Franklin, underwriting treatises and fusing all sorts of magical social phenomena with a singular focus with purpose.

Aside from music and Hollywood, sports is the pastime that defines American culture. And if you believe a young professor Barack Obama, African American culture is American culture.

You could say American culture is the world's culture. So, you could say Black American culture *is* world culture. Matter of fact, you could say American culture is America's most valuable export. By inference, you could say that this export is responsible for the immigration of millions to America from around the world. As a matter of fact, as Muhammad Ali once said, "I am America. I am the part you won't recognize. But get used to me. Black, confident, cocky; my name, not yours; my religion, not yours; my goals, my own; get used to me."

Muhammad Ali, Magic Johnson, Superman, Michael Phelps, Captain America and Michael Jordan. What's more American than that? Marvel's *Black Panther*? Who in the world does not want to be these icons of American culture at some point? What All-American little boy or girl doesn't dream of being the Man of Steel, Wonder Woman or Michael Jordan at some time in their young lives? "Hero" is not Black or white. For little brown- and peach-skinned children, and every skin pigment in between and beyond, "hero" is the light. And Black is the absorption of all of the lights. Black is how to be everything that is great, that is America. Athletes are the modern-day gladiators of the American empire with one foot in reality and another in our collective imaginations. Everybody wants to be like Mike. Every little boy and girl is in their driveway practicing their tomahawk dunk. Those afros in California, Chicago, Dallas, Milwaukee, and New York? Those are Kaepernick afros. These days, everybody even wants to be Muhammad Ali. Even President Obama looked up to the icon and said, "A man who fought for us. He stood with King and Mandela; stood up when it was hard; spoke out when others wouldn't."

Everybody, however, does not aspire to be the president — at least not these days. But all millennials will tell you that they aspire to be LeBron James, Michael Phelps and Usain Bolt. Where does this power to influence a generation to resistance, revolt and self-affirmation come from? Yes, it is underwritten like a private placement memorandum by the Dean of American sports, Dr Harry Edwards. This year marks the fiftieth anniversary edition of his timeless classic *The Revolt of the Black Athlete*, where he gives the secrets of how an underachieving junior college student went on to attain a Woodrow Wilson Fellowship to Cornell University, earning both an MA and a PhD, before later joining the sociology faculty at the University of California at Berkeley. He writes:

I. Follow your bliss
II. Cultivate the habit of high expectations of yourself and of every effort
III. Respect the challenges and demands of your calling by learning to dream with your eyes open.
IV. Learn to "behave as it."
V. Commit to a strategy, practice, and disciplined program of hard work.
VI. Persevere, stay on course by employing a strategy of "living in anticipation of tomorrow"
VII. Learn and abide by the work-rest cycle of your mind and body.

That "blueprint" for academic achievement and success is why it is critical to not only understand but also appreciate the cultural shift that has taken place in the American culture of sports since the 1960s and into the twenty-first century. Not so long ago, community activists would bemoan "the multi-million-dollar corporations" that were running on the field of dreams, hardwood floors, and football fields but not giving back to their communities. Now, those metaphysical warriors have come home and are the beacons of light. Colin Kaepernick's sacrifice is the most chilling and selfless as we witness a supremacist US president lead an NFL league of coward owners to their own tragic downfall. No wonder Adam Silver's NBA is poised to surpass the NFL as the *dejour* sport of America and the world.

It is not so hard to think about when you consider the impact of the NBA, NFL, boxing and MLB on global culture. Where music doesn't sway a soul, American sports will fill in the gaps with thunderous dunks, suffocating three-pointers, knockout punches, flamboyant touchdown dances or home runs. So, just what is American sports? Is it a piston, a mass market meditation on American capitalism where "eat what you kill" is the unofficial edict? Isn't Michael Jordan's near sociopathological competitiveness celebrated as a virtue with at least the same glee as the fictional Gordon Gekko of Oliver Stone's *Wall Street*? Is American sports a metaphysical field for Black souls and Black bodies, the spirit of the American promise to seek completed liberation from the ideology of racism? Or is it perhaps a metaphysical plane upon which we all focus, meditate and come together for a common American cause?

When you think about names such as Muhammad Ali, Bill Russell, Jim Brown, Arthur Ashe, Althea Gibson, Billie Jean King, John Carlos, Tommie Smith, Wilma Rudolph and Jackie Robinson, there is a direct correlation between competition at the highest levels and the movement of the needle of social justice to the total and complete liberation of all Americans. The Michael Jordan-era was a respite from this sort of expression. It was the "Republican wear sneakers too" respite. Or, if you will, the Charles Barkley-era of "I'm not a role model" getting paid Black athletes.

Sure, it was a lot of fun to watch but we now find that the prison-industrial complex was made whole in that era. Michelle Alexander, in her American opus *The New Jim Crow*, has called it an era of "neo slavery."

Athletes such as Colin Kaepernick, Dwyane Wade, Kevin Durant, Carmelo Anthony, Chris Paul, Stephen Curry, Michael Phelps, Richard Sherman, Marshawn Lynch and LeBron James reject that notion. They play for a cosmic, universal cause for common humanity headed by a certain Dean of American Sports. Colin Kaepernick's sacrifice at the height of his athletic prowess, the prolonged financial fasting and social castration, are so familiar to a young Muhammad Ali at the height of his powers. He is, however, Muhammad Ali 2.0, with such acts as a pledge to donate $1 million of his salary plus all royalties received from the sale of jerseys and $100,000 going out for each month for the past ten months.

I spoke with Dr Harry Edwards by email, phone and voicemail over the course of the month and he is as impassioned by the cause for complete American liberation as his 1969 treatise *The Revolt of the Black Athlete*. His organization and implementation of the Olympic Project for Human Rights and the Black Athletes' Revolt at San Jose State University holds up and applies today, because it is the thesis that underwrites our current moment. In *The Revolt of the Black Athlete*, he stipulates five guiding and strategic imperatives to heightening potentials for the achievement of protest movement goals (imperatives derived in substantial part from his MA/PhD studies under professors Robin Williams and William Foote Whyte at Cornell University).

My questions can be whimsical and even light but I want to capture the essence of a man heavy with cosmic consciousness and the burden of knowing a singular outcome when everybody else is afraid, when everybody is stepping away from the center of the fire.

Patrick A. Howell: Colin Kaepernick is the cracker jack or, perhaps he is the TNT powder, of this generation. Is his the metaphysical jump-point generations will use to open a new window to a collective peace or will he and his sacrifices fade into obscurity?

Harry Edwards: Kaepernick will be remembered as a timely, relevant, and courageous "athlete activist" in the mold of Ali, Smith, Carlos, Ariyana Smith (of Knox College and the first athlete to protest the summary execution of Mike Brown of Ferguson, Mo.), etc. because he so well projected the reality and urgency of confronting the violence of racism and injustice in the lives of "people of color" in America. It is precisely for this reason that I pressed for him to be installed in the Smithsonian National Museum of African American History and Culture, right alongside other athletes who contributed so much so courageously and at great personal sacrifice in the struggle to "level the playing field" — both within and beyond the arena.

P.H: What were your accomplishments in college as a former San Jose State discus thrower and basketball player?

H.E.: I set a national community college discus record during my one semester at Fresno City College; I set the school and conference record during my first season at San Jose State (1961) and started at center on the basketball team. I had thrown the discus well past the Olympic Trials qualifying mark during my sophomore track season of 1962 when I was a team captain and dismissed from the track team permanently for trying to organize "Negro" athletes who I felt were being brutally exploited.

P.H.: What is your favorite sport to watch these days? What is the sport you can watch to get outside the work grind of academia and being a thought leader?

H.E.: I watch all sports because that's my business. When I want to just chill, I listen to jazz — Miles, Coltrane, Duke, Ella, Sarah, Billie, Bird, Dizzy, Bud Powell, Monk... traditional, straight-ahead jazz, like I grew up with in E St Louis, Illinois (literally a mile from Miles) that I grooved with throughout my collegiate days, that I now luxuriate in during my senior years.

P.H.: Of all the iconic movement athletes of the Sixties — Muhammad Ali, Jim Brown, Kareem Abdul Jabbar, Arthur Ashe, John Carlos, Tommie Smith — who does LeBron James remind you of most? Colin Kaepernick? Marshawn Lynch? Richard Sherman?

H.E.: LeBron James = Bill Russell. Marshawn = Dwayne Thomas (Cowboys). R. Sherman = Richie Allen (Phillies). Colin Kaepernick = Muhammad Ali.

He is a large man. Big like a tribesman of the Igbo, Ashanti or Zulu tribes. You would think he was an athlete — he is so large. I'll say it again, it's not difficult to imagine him as a lineman and boxer. But he is the one whose mind and actions and direction created a different altogether metaphysical field of play. He is definitely of West African ancestry if you consider his penchant for academic excellence and intellectual pursuits. He knows the system and leverages his knowledge like he is creating an arsenal of weapons against the system of American racism and institutionalized discrimination. In fact, he has created the artery of his own system within the body of America.

Nigeria and Ghana — that's what we call those tribes these days (Zulu is Southern Africa though). Yeah, he's got that swag. It ain't gangster hip-hop. It's crunk though, like Miles or Thelonious or Coltrane jazz. It's from outside the norms of conventions, improvisational and inspired. And it is real. He smashed racism in its ugly mouth with a metaphysical fist. The jab began with a wind up in the late 1960s and he stepped through with a follow-up upper cut in the 2010s. The system is buckling. This is spirit work. Nobody drew the parallel from sports to social activism until Dr Edward's 1971 thesis, *The Sociology of Sport*.

9/18/18

HARLEM'S LAST POET

ABIODUN OYEWOLE, POET AND ARCHITECT OF HIP-HOP CULTURE

© *Chester Higgins Archive*

I wanted to say something beautiful
how we turn garbage into gold
how we made a swamp fertile land
how we turned a curse, into a blessing.
— Abiodun Oyewole, "Something Beautiful"

If God spoke with a voice, it might sound like Last Poet Abiodun Oyewole's. The authority. The metaphysical fire that fires passions. Wisdom fleshed with tenor. A strength. The off-world fire that burns wood of life within the fire. The gruff. The grizzle. The song. The power. The knowing. The innocence.

Last Poet Abiodun Oyewole wrote *Something Beautiful* in 2014, released through 2Leaf Press. But who knows? Perhaps the way things can work in another epoch, in another time; he wrote *time* with that poem. Perhaps, Last Poet Abiodun is a seer. Perhaps he is a griot in the tradition of our ancestors. Perhaps Last Poet Abiodun Oyewole speaks a living breathing word and perhaps he spoke of these current times before they became our current time. Last Poet Abiodun Oyewole wants to say something beautiful but bad feelings and unresolved history seem to be getting in his way. Perhaps, he sees what is the real, and like x-ray vision, looks through the bone to the granular marrow of our lives.

I wanted to say something that would make us stand up and be proud
with the sun shining on our faces and in our hearts
I wanted to say but the day wouldn't let me
and the skies were too gray
the air were choking my dreams
and all the smiles on the faces of people had turned to frowns.

Are we so loving that we love what hates us
that we love what breaks us
that we love the pain that twists our minds into creatures we can't even recognize
Are we so strong that we play being weak?
— "Something Beautiful"

Abiodun Oyewole is a founding member of the Last Poets. The Last Poets and Gil Scott-Heron cleared a path for the birth of hip-hop. Kids in the Bronx and Harlem like Grandmaster Flash and DJ Kool Herc took their cues from the work of the Last Poets. The Last Poets are the bridge from the Harlem Renaissance to hip-hop. How appropriate the name then, *the Last Poets*.

Abiodun published his first poetry collection, *Branches of the Tree of Life — The Collected Poems of Abiodun Oyewole, 1969-2014* in 2014. But Abiodun has been doing this a long, long time — honing his craft and perfecting the spirit of words that live. I tell him something that Jaki Shelton Green, Poet of the People, told me. She had just seen the critically acclaimed film *I Am Not Your Negro* about James Baldwin and through a series of revelations came to the conclusion that the only obstacle Black folk have to their complete liberation is themselves.

"She is absolutely correct." Abiodun bellows in baritone, "We are the folks we been looking for. That was a mantra. That's always been my mission. That was always my mission and the mission of the Last Poets but we just got funky with it." The group's message, deeply rooted in Black Nationalism, quickly became recognized, emulated and canonized within the African American community. The Last Poets, along with Gil Scott-Heron, are credited as having had a profound effect on the development of hip-hop music. Their pioneering work foreshadowed that of later, hard-hitting hip-hop like Public Enemy, Tupac Shakur, and Kendrick Lamar, blending consciousness with beats in rhythms irresistible.

As he speaks, Abiodun Oyewole's voice is earthed with granular knowing, and how a soul speaks itself into greater being, speaks for a whole generation. What he knows is the power of language, language that speaks from the soul of man. He knows, as a last poet, as a thirty-five-year resident of Harlem, how language and sounds have and will change the world. He knows the soul of America. Somehow our conversation turns to the first one hundred days of the 45th President and he's got something for that too, "Am I the only one who noticed that Barnum and Bailey's is closing its doors at the same time Donald Trump was elected?" The P.T. Barnum and Bailey Circus closed in May 2017 after 146 years. P.T. Barnum was an American politician, showman and businessman who founded the Barnum and Bailey Circus. He is widely and incorrectly credited with the phrase, "There's a sucker born every minute."

Abiodun continues, "It's like we can't have two circuses going at the same time! Trump is a self-destructive brat, suffering from a heavy dose of immaturity. But he is like so many of his kind where we helped them be children. We enable their behavior. But Trump is the worst of them. He got that new toy called 'executive order' and man, does he like his new toy.

"It's very sad that this country has allowed this character to become the president. He's not very smart. He's a con artist. I guess he has to be smart to do that. It's a bad example about what this country is to be about.

"I honestly believe that something good is going to come out of Trump. You have to have a balance. I do believe there will be a balance. I don't know what angle it will come in. I do see us coming together as a people. We actually come together and make it possible for some change by galvanizing. We have power. I do expect us to have that fortitude. Our strength is unquestionable."

Every Sunday Abiodun does "sit ins" with poets, singers, dancers and musicians. He has been doing it for thirty-nine years and says, "I do it because there is a need for us to come together and have communion. I have been doing it primarily for poets. Since I have a reputation, I believe it is an obligation of mine to share and enjoy. There is a need for this kind of work. Poetry has become a major voice in the world."

I ask Abiodun some more of my questions.

Patrick A. Howell: Will you talk with me about the Last Poets being founders of hip-hop?

Abiodun Oyewole: The Last Poets were born May 19, 1968, Malcolm X day. Charles Davis was my American name. I had an African name but I wasn't using it yet. In 1968 we came and performed at the commemoration of Malcolm X's birthday. There was a lot of revolution activity at that park in Harlem and it was crowded. The park was very crowded. David Nelson went about searching for a name for us. Gylan went looking for a place we could operate from. I was young and bold and didn't know much and was willing to be a part of this. I was totally messed up by the killing of Dr King. I realized we were in grave danger. I realized that anything we did as a people for total liberation would put us in grave danger. I really respected him [Dr. King], even though I was not about the turn the other cheek thing.

We came to own a place — the East Wing. We got our name from a South African poet named K. William Kgositsile . The poem was called "Walk in the Sun." In the poem it states: "This wind you hear is the birth of memory. When the moment hatches in time's womb, there will be no more art talk. The only poem you'll hear will be the spear point pivoted in the punctured marrow of the villain, the timeless native son dancing like crazy to the retrieved rhythms of desire fading into memory."

David Nelson (co-founder of the Last Poets) added, "Therefore, we are the Last Poets of the world."

Ten years ago when we went to South Africa every one of the two thousand of the students at that school in Johannesburg knew who the Last Poets were.

P.H.: The last conversation we had — you had some tough words for Donald Trump and the state of America. You said, "For people that have faith in that system — they are going to suffer." Marvin L. Mills, an emerging hip-hop artist, had a thesis he published to critical acclaim called "Is There a War in America?" Are we at war in America?

A.O.: Yes we are at war in America. It's a spiritual war and it's been going on for a long time. It has picked up steam recently but we have always been at war. That war will continue until we realize we are one race — the human race.

There is a war spiritually — we have to use our spirits to fight. We are getting shot in the streets but we have to fight. We are still under attack by a very evil character who does not respect life. But I still have faith in people. But it's going to take a moment.

P.H.: Tell me about your new song "Pelourinho." It seems that song is about healing, truth and peace. Pelourinho is the historic center of Salvador da Bahia in Brazil, also known as the Pelo. It is a historic neighborhood in western Salvador, Bahia. Can you talk about that song, its inspiration?

A.O.: It was the first time I worked with a drone for the shooting of that video. It looked like a toy and it was deep.

"When the light is clear I know how beautiful I will be" — that is really the summation of all of our lives. We have worked towards a goal and we want that to be the salvation of our souls. So we don't have to be alert about danger. And we would like to live in a place where we don't have to live in fear. When we consider what Black people have been through, with systemic discrimination, with the abuse, the mis-educations, the cruelty — it is amazing. We want to arrive at a point where we and our ancestors understand our glory and celebrate it. For everybody, but particularly for our people.

That is why I consider myself a revolutionary.

4/29/17

THE NEW POWER GENERATION

INGRID LAFLEUR, DIRECTOR OF AFROTOPIA, FORMER MAYORAL CANDIDATE, REAL WORLD VISIONARY & BITCOIN ACTIVIST

The solutions to the problems that have developed during our time in power will most likely need to be solved by those who aren't conditioned to see through our lenses.
— Baby boomer Richard Krawiec, American author and publisher of Jacar Books

What is politics? Perhaps it is the social metrics of mass manipulation and demagoguery of citizenry for the purposes of personal gain? Or is it an endeavor of selfless service? Is it the marshaling of higher ideas into pragmatic policies that are enacted legislatively? Is it a call to design, curate or marshall economic, cultural and social resources for the benefit of all? From the many come one? Is it power "by any means necessary"? Is politics big corporate donations and private $10,000 plated dinners? Is politics good or is it great? Does one quality necessarily negate the other? Is politics colluding with hostile foreign governments, billionaire buddies and world powers to satisfy personal agendas and multiply wealth for cronies and family?

Is politics the ultimate Machiavellian conman's game?

Resist: resist, resist and resist. Then, reset, re-juice, rejuvenate and revolutionize. Oh, and organize, volunteer and vote! This is how Ingrid LaFleur continues to bring a spirit of renaissance and renewal to the Detroit communities she loves. She has dared to dream of a new future, a new way and a perfect beauty. But more than dream, she has harvested the sweet fruits of cultural revitalization, bringing bright futures heretofore only imagined in Octavia Butler novels, Earth, Wind and Fire opuses, Candidate Obama's speeches and President Obama's policies. She is a conjurer with unlimited resources as she shapes light energy into film festivals, workshops, TED discussions and mayoral bids that capture imaginations and enliven spirits.

"I have always been the eccentric Black girl," said LaFleur in a *USA Today* interview in 2015. "Afrofuturism is such an expanded idea of Blackness that, for me, it has been a comfortable place to be in." She graduated from

Renaissance High School in Detroit, Michigan before attending Spelman College in Atlanta and New York University.

Ingrid LaFleur is part of an ongoing trend around the nation that includes names such as Pasadena City Council member John Kennedy, former Secretary of Housing and Urban Development and former San Antonio Mayor Julian Castro, former Council member and Vice Mayor, City of Long Beach Dr Suja Lowenthal, Congresswoman Tulsi Gabbard and California Senator Kamala Harris — a group of unconventional candidates with various hues of beliefs and backgrounds commonly united around creative governance that is as pragmatic as it is visionary.

These candidates and elected officials join Atlanta candidates Jon Ossoff and Khalid Kamau as part of a new vanguard in progressive values and forward vision to move the country from its current malaise of toxic politics. Jon Ossoff for example was buoyed by $8.3 million in donations from small Democratic donors from around the country. Donors were eager to make a statement about their feelings about the new president and his administration. Both Georgia races were seen as referendums on the current political environment.

As North Carolina's Richard Krawiec, an enlightened man, recently noted on Facebook:

Angela Davis, Che Guevara, Malcolm X, Dr King, Audre Lorde, Nina Simone, Abbie Hoffman and almost all the other leaders in the fight for progressive causes in the 1960s were in their twenties and thirties (some like Dr King, Malcolm X dead before they hit forty) when they were leading the national movements for change. It's time for us Baby Boomers to give up control, step aside, and let younger activists, with fresh ideas, take their place as leaders of the movement while we take on more support and advisory roles. The solutions to the problems that have developed during our time in power will most likely need to be solved by those who aren't conditioned to see through our lenses.

I have always believed young people must take the reins of leadership early. Martin Luther King, and for that matter, Jesus Christ started their ministries at the age of twenty-five. After graduating from Howard University School of Law, I came home to run for president of the Pasadena Branch of the National Association for the Advancement of Colored People. I wrestled the post from someone in their eighties. My victory, at the age of twenty-five, was not easy! Eliminate the fear!!!
— Pasadena City Council Member John J. Kennedy

On February 28th, the arts professional and visionary Ingrid LaFleur announced her 2017 bid for mayor during a party at the headquarters of art collective O.N.E. Mile during the Detroit is the Future event, calling herself a "concerned citizen" with an in-depth understanding of the city's needs. She is running against the establishment in the form of incumbent mayor Mike Duggan. She is also running against political royalty in the form of Andrew Young, Coleman Young II, State Senator and son of former Detroit Mayor Coleman A. Young. In her launch bid, the founder of AFROTOPIA said she would base her campaign on "uniting, healing, and inspiring Detroiters while bringing humanity to government."

Despite the rigors of a demanding schedule and the high tides of an unconventional candidacy, Ms. Ingrid LaFleur was kind enough to take the time to answer my questions thoughtfully and with equal measures grace, reality and inspiration.

Patrick A. Howell: Does the same drive or inspiration run through AFROTOPIA that runs through your bid for mayor?

Ingrid LaFleur: Detroiters inspired AFROTOPIA. Detroiters inspire my bid for mayor. Because I love Detroit so much, I understand that it is the people and the culture they produce that makes the city so warm, welcoming, and uncommonly pleasurable. That's why I decided to challenge our political aesthetic, to ensure that every Detroiter, especially the youth, has a healthy, enjoyable relationship with the city. I want adults and children alike to imagine themselves having a prosperous life in Detroit that actually comes to fruition.

P.H.: Do you feel Generation X or the Millennial generation have a particular take or position that is not represented in civic politics?

I.L.: A major concern for these two generations is the ability to self-sustain and be empowered. It becomes a difficult goal to achieve when economic opportunities for advancement are few and far between. I want to note that I am specifically speaking about the current socio-economic system in which we exist that privileges whiteness and heterosexual men. For this reason, it is important to develop a new framework for city governance in a city where the majority of the citizens are Black women.

P.H.: Do you have a particular connection or insight into the community that is not currently met by the current mayor?

I.L.: I am a born and raised Detroiter. My father taught me to appreciate the beauty and life of this city way beyond the surface. My connection to the neighborhoods and the creative, cooperative communities that exist within Detroit is intimate and compassionate. That makes me completely invested — intellectually and emotionally — in making sure Detroiters are provided for. This provision includes the safety of every citizen, accessibility to fresh food and air, clean water, affordable housing, recreation, and wealth-building opportunities. Another underestimated but significant aspect of revitalizing Detroit is, quite simply, beauty. There are many parts of Detroit that are clean and beautiful but there are far too many that are physically strained. I care so deeply for Detroit that I want the city to be clean and beautiful for everyone no matter where they live, no matter what their socio-economic status. A beautiful city instills pride and joy, which leads to a strong and caring relationship to Detroit. Beauty is one of the many ways to inspire citizens to participate in city government, which ultimately is the goal. It engages the minds, souls, and imaginations in a real and vital conversation. Voices of the citizens not only should be heard but also reflected in the policies and initiatives the city implements. However, city government must be trusted in order for people to feel that their voice makes a difference. Right now trust in government is low and that affects participation on the level we truly need in order to revitalize the entire city. I'm hopeful that the trust I've gained throughout the city can become an effective bridge for co-creation.

Perhaps politics is *the art* of what is possible?

In 2017, the millennium is still young. Think of 1917, one hundred years ago: America was joining World War I and was not even a world power. The United Nations did not exist. World War II — perhaps the beginning of the "modern age" — had not occurred. America was just at the beginning of transforming from an agricultural society into an industrial one. Televisions, never mind cellphones and computers, were not yet invented. Liquor was not yet legal — as a matter of fact, prohibition was not yet a US Constitutional Amendment. Woodrow Wilson was president and Hollywood was two years old, with *The Birth of a Nation* only coming out in 1915.

2017 is young in the thousand-year history of a millennium and a new century. What history will be reported in 3017? That is dependent upon decisions, innovation and bravery inherent in the current moment. Unconventional campaigns and candidacies such as Ingrid LaFleur's are a harbinger of the new future that continues to take hold in this reality.

The US Constitution expresses American politics as:

We the People of the United States, in Order to form a more perfect Union, establish Justice, insure domestic Tranquility, provide for the common defense, promote the general Welfare, and secure the Blessings of Liberty to ourselves and our Posterity, do ordain and establish this Constitution for the United States of America.

Beyond the 24/7 vitriol and hyperbole of corrosive politics, social and mass media, this is the reality of a governing document in both form and inspiration. Further, the great seal of the United States of America reads "*Novus ordo seclorum*," or "New Order of the Ages."

Just keeping it 100, however, these edicts were made in a time when tens of millions were enslaved, murdered and terrorized — a national legacy that is still unfolding nearly four hundred years later. However, as has been suggested by some of America's most successful visionaries, legislators and statesmen, America stands as a nation of *ideas* and we Americans are working towards higher ones. Forward and progressive politics mean the future will not be delayed, sacrificed or stunted for the past. It means clear eyes fixed on the horizon.

Nobel Prize-winner Toni Morrison has said of the politics of art:

> All of that art-for-art's-sake stuff is BS. What are these people talking about? Are you really telling me that Shakespeare and Aeschylus weren't writing about kings? *All good art is political!* There is none that isn't. And the ones that try hard not to be political are political by saying, "We love the status quo." We've just dirtied the word "politics," made it sound like it's unpatriotic or something.
>
> That all started in the period of state art, when you had the communists and fascists running around doing this poster stuff, and the reaction was "No, no, no; there's only aesthetics." My point is that is has to be both: beautiful and political at the same time. I'm not interested in art that is not in the world. And it's not just the narrative, it's not just the story; it's the language and the structure and what's going on behind it. Anybody can make up a story.

Ingrid LaFleur is the future deciding it will continue to assume the mantle of leadership and responsibility in the present. Hers is literally the "art in the world" that Morrison articulated. It is an ascendant and cosmopolitan view of the world. It is deciding to step forward and have the courage and conviction of ancestors who came before and continue to come into our own.

Ingrid LaFleur's campaign is a strong indication that tomorrow's folks have come to pull us into the future. Sculpt, paint, draw, write, envision, curate, compose, campaign, code and yes, vote. We will stand upon that plateau of blood, sweat and tears, look to the horizon and take those strides of faith and belief. You may find the future is there, Cheshire grin, with open arms. Or, maybe, she's just there waiting patiently.

4/17/17

Currently, Ingrid LaFleur is traveling throughout Africa conducting research on modes of governance and community-based economics, with a particular interest in Rwanda. She began The Afro-future Strategies Institute, a creative thinktank that researches the future through the lens of Africa and the African diaspora on how to incorporate the principles and cultural production of Afro-futurism into the development of a business or project.

BLACK MAN JUJU

TYEHIMBA JESS, PULITZER PRIZE WINNER, POET AND TEACHER

Tyehimba Jess, photo by John Midgley

Juju or juju (French: joujou, lit. "plaything") is a spiritual belief system incorporating objects, such as amulets, and spells used in religious practice, as part of witchcraft in West Africa. The term has been applied to traditional West African religions.

There are Black men and women of the old West African tribes, the ancient empires, still performing this ancient artform at its highest levels. However, they are now called Pulitzer Prize winners. Their originality is unquestionable. *They are connected to the source* — their mastery of their high art is celebrated and lauded. They don't use objects in the ultimate manifestation of their craft. Gone are the amulets, bones, stones and rooster blood. Maybe they use pens, 8x11 yellow ruled, bound paper, a laptop or a notes app on their smartphone. Mostly, however, they now confer their work on skulls and within souls.

They still use the drums — djembe. They will invade your dreams. They will craft realities heretofore impossible. They put their magic on American democracy, within capitalism, and sew it into Christian traditions. It has taken centuries to perfect their craft but the spells which they weave in rhythm, rhyme and meter and, sometimes, melody are everywhere. Sometimes they just put it in a word — these so called poets, novelists or essayists. They place that word on a page in such a way that it disrupts your thoughts or stops your heart. Maybe it makes you feel like you can fly to the heavens. Or, just lay down and die. Or, just want to cry, wallow in misery. That's juju, when the world is in a word and that word carries the power of spirit.

The term *juju* is commonly used to refer to the feeling of something. For example, if a person feels offset by an object or place, they would say that the object or place has "bad juju." In the modern age, we take some creative genius, splash in some cool, take some marketing and branding savvy, dress it up real contemporary and call it, say, a Pulitzer Prize. It's how we do what we do.

George Walker became the first African American to receive a coveted Pulitzer Prize for Music in 1996 for his work *Lilacs*. Walker, who is noted as one of the greatest composers of his time, was also the first African American to graduate from the Curtis Institute in 1954, then received a doctorate degree from Eastman School in 1956 and became a tenured faculty member at Smith College.

Gwendolyn Brooks became the first African to win a Pulitzer Prize for Poetry in 1950 for her book *Annie Allen*, which chronicles the evolution of a young Black girl into womanhood. Brooks, a literary giant who focused much of her work on documenting the lives and struggle of African Americans and migrants, was also the first Black woman to serve as the poetry consultant to the Library of Congress.

Then there is the immortal playwright August Wilson. Also, there was recently Kendrick Lamar of Compton (or Bompton). There was also Colson Whitehead and his *The Underground Railroad*, of which Oprah Winfrey said, "Every now and then a book comes along that reaches the marrow of your bones, settles in, and stays forever. This is one. It's a tour de force, and I don't say that lightly."

And so there is Tyehimba Jess. Does that name mean anything to you? It ought to. Gwendolyn Brooks, Colson Whitehead, Suzan-Lori Parks, Kendrick Lamar all share space in rhythm, rhyme, melody, harmony of this juju spirit. *Olio* is Tyehimba's juju. Much as "Damn" is Kendrick Lamar's. Much as *Annie Allen* was Gwendolyn Brooks's. He is also the winner of the National Book Critics Circle Award for Poetry and PEN/Jean Stein Book Award. When we spoke, he was in the midst of his national tour with stops in Exeter, South Carolina, D.C. and San Francisco. He thoroughly enjoys doing these readings — he loves putting poetry into the world.

This juju man is a juju light worker at the highest possible frequency. Part fact, part fiction, part meditation, part dream (at times, American nightmare) — Tyehimba Jess's much heralded and celebrated second book of poetry blends sonnets, story and narration to look at the uncelebrated lives of African American performers from

1861 to 1918, before and after the Civil War and up to the end of World War I, as an American Empire was coming into its own. *Olio* is an effort to understand how they came together, formed their own resistance, survived, thrived co-opted, and sometimes defeated attempts to minstrelize them:

> So, while I lead this choir, I still find that
> I'm being led I'm a missionary
> mending my faith in the midst of this flock
> I toil in their fields of praise. When folks see
> these freedmen stand and sing, they hear their God
> speak in tongues. These nine dark mouths sing shelt

Patrick A. Howell: First off, congratulations Tyehimba on your 2017 Pulitzer Prize for Poetry. You are sharing some rarified company with the likes of Gwendolyn Brooks and her 1950 work *Annie Allen*. Rita Dove and her 1987 *Thomas and Beulah*. Toni Morrison and *Beloved*. Duke Ellington, Thelonious Monk and August Wilson were all awarded the Pulitzer posthumously, a virtual who's who of American culture. What, if any, has been the change in reception to you and your work since being awarded?

Tyehimba Jess: No real significant changes other than feeling honored to have the prize, feeling surreal about it. The best thing about it was living in Chicago [for the first time] since 2002. I spent a year in Chicago on sabbatical and [I was] there on the 100th anniversary of Gwendolyn Brooks's birthday. That was great and pretty cool. I remember going to her funeral and I also remember seeing her in real life and being in awe of her mastery of the language. I think it was kind of karmic to be back in Chicago when they announced that award. It was her hundredth birthday this year [2017]. She is out of Chicago and she writes a lot about Chicago. To win on the 100th anniversary of her birth was special for me.

P.H.: Also, do you have a particular relationship with previous Pulitzer Prize winner Yusef Komunyakaa?

T.J.: I would say primarily my relationship with him is I saw him read a couple years after he won the Pulitzer and seeing him read was a revelation to me. I used to run around with *Neon Vernacular* kind of grooved to my side. [Laughs] I have always been in awe of his work and then I finally got to meet him when I was in graduate school and I would see how he rolled and see how he handled himself. He has always been a model of class. But also, one thing Yusef is about is the image and reading his work has really pounded the importance of imagery through to me. His work is so vivid and so electrified. He's been an inspiration for years.

P.H.: You relocated from Chicago to Brooklyn earlier last year. Currently you are teaching at Staten Island College. Detroit, where you were born, is also another city with a strong Black culture. All cities are epicenters of Black American Culture aka American Culture. I note your work with Sterling Plump, whose teaching focused on the era of the Harlem Renaissance and Black Arts Movement. How does the Black culture, ethos, spirit inform your work? Specifically, I recall a quote by Toni Morrison in which she said, "I'm writing for Black people ... I don't have to apologise." Further, she has noted in "Playing in the Dark," her 1990s literary treatise:

The habit of ignoring race is understood to be a graceful, even generous, liberal gesture. To notice is to recognize an already discredited difference. To enforce its invisibility through silence is to allow the Black body a shadowless participation in the dominant cultural body. According to this logic, every well-bred instinct argues against noticing and forecloses adult discourse. It is just this concept of literary and scholarly moeurs (which functions smoothly in literary criticism, but neither makes nor receives credible claims in other disciplines) that has terminated the shelf life of some once extremely well-regarded American authors and blocked access to remarkable insights in their works.

Is there a social agenda agenda, spiritual work, a hope, a mindset that informs your work? Are you just reflecting voices that came before you?

T.J.: I think there is definitely the idea of reclaiming, as Maxine Waters would say, reclaiming our time, reclaiming our history, reclaiming voices from the past, reclaiming narratives of the past that still inform the way we encounter race today.

I am interested in exploring the spirit of these many folks in *Olio* who were dedicated to the idea of bringing their art to a larger population. I want to explore the many types of conflicts they had to work with regarding race and they were only able to come through sheer grit and talent. I am dedicated to the idea of telling their stories in unique and layered ways.

P.H.: In *Olio*, your Pulitzer Prize-winning effort (and only second outing as a poet), you reference the work of Edmonia Lewis, Henry Box Brown, John William Boone, Fisk Jubilee Singers, Ernest Hogan, Blind Tom Wiggins, George Walker, Bert Williams... and one of my all-time favorites Paul Laurence Dunbar. How do you approach your work? What is your process? How do you create such intimate portraits and caricatures of those in the times before our times? Why focus on the ancestors and their lives — what about those who are in the future and the genius of our current poets? What do you know about the world of our ancestors because of your work with *Olio* that most do not consider?

T.J.: Writing the book was a discovery for me because I didn't know about many of these people. I didn't know about many of their histories. It was for *my* edification. I was able to explore the histories of people that I'd only understood in a rudimentary fashion. It was gratifying to be able to explore their lives and to find new ways to bring them onto the page. Insofar as how my research and my writing process goes, it is heavily informed by a lot of research. That means seeking out as much information as I can, as many archives as I can, about the folks that I am interested in. Then I build a structure of poems that explore, in a meaningful way, the core issues of their lives.

Countee Cullen is one my favorite all time poets, specifically his poem "Any Human to Another" and that passage:

The ills I sorrow at
Not me alone
Like an arrow,
Pierce to the marrow,
Through the fat
And past the bone.
Your grief and mine
Must intertwine
Like sea and river,
Be fused and mingle,
Diverse yet single,
Forever and forever.

P.H.: Of the artists you honored in *Olio*, is there a particular figure or work of a figure that is your own personal Kanye West, Michael Jackson or Beyoncé... someone whose work speaks to you and your work consistently, decade after decade? Is there somebody who constantly inspires you to take it to the next level, go places you have not been previously?

T.J.: All of them do. All of them were fascinating because they had to work in what was called the nadir of American race relations, at the height of public lynchings in the United States. (Although we still have lynchings today that are executed in a different kind of form.)

They were all superstars in one way or another. Scott Joplin, creator of ragtime. Edmonia Lewis, the most successful African American artist of the nineteenth century even though she had to leave the country. The McCoy twins (Millie and Christian), who were able to persevere through slavery and the violation of their bodies countless times but were still able to maintain their integrity, buying plantations for their entire families. John Williams Boone, who could play any song that you wanted back to you at the drop of a hat. He built his career around another fascinating individual who was autistic and blind and was able to find a way to express himself past those obstacles, Blind Tom Wiggins. Wiggins was forced to endure the ownership of the same white family for his entire life while they exploited his piano playing for a million dollars in profit. Sissieretta Jones was a badass opera singer who was at the top of her field and really, really cared about people around her. She died in relative obscurity but sought to maintain her integrity. The Fisk Jubilee Singers were nine youngsters, late teen and early twenty-year-olds who spread the spiritual and gospel of Black voice across the globe for the first time. They were messengers, they were evangelists of the free Black voice in the early 1870s. Every spiritual singer today owes them a debt.

They are all fascinating individuals. Bert Williams and George Walker — they were working through a conundrum. They were trying to work out of Black caricatures of the comedy industry and minstrel show in order to create three-dimensional characters. They used their resources and their name to make the first independent Black theater productions in the country. They were not just clowns. They were trying to make more honest portrayals of their people. Henry Box Brown, who put himself in a box and escaped from slavery. He literally came out of the box — a two and a half by three foot box — singing. And when white folks came from the South and tried to drag him back into slavery, he said "Nope, I'm going to England. Peace y'all!" He went to England and started a whole other career as an entertainer and abolitionist. He spoke out for Black slaves in the United States. Fascinating!

All these folks! Paul Laurence Dunbar and Booker T. Washington. Paul Laurence Dunbar was the first Black poet to make a living off of his poetry. He had elegance and grace and power and a seething ministerial awe in all of his work. He had control and mastery of form. And then Booker T. Washington was a conflicted figure but a human dynamo who was also kind of operating with a mask on. One mask he would show to the white establishment. Another mask he would show to his people. And a few other masks in between. [Laughs]

P.H.: Is it our people's creativity? Is overcoming the struggle? Is it a little bit of both? What is the commonality in all of it?

T.J.: I think that the folk in *Olio* clearly had more to struggle against in their careers and in their lives. But I think that one crucial way they did it was through their creativity. One of the missions of the book is to look at Black creativity at a particular time when we really don't think about our capacity to be creative. This is the first generation that tasted freedom. The question is, how were they interested in exploring their creativity through their freedom? Creating for their own edification and not for that of a master for the first time in their lives? What is that like? What forms does that take?

There was this explosion of Black creativity — and the folks in *Olio* are just a small chunk of the huge population of Black musicians, actors, artists. And we are still wrestling with many of the same questions they were dealing with — how do I comport myself? How do I wrestle with these difficult decisions about the maintenance of my craft and my life? How do I navigate the shallow, rocky shoals of prejudice and racial hatred through the nineteenth, twentieth and twenty-first centuries? How do I maintain a vision for my art that I can be proud of, that I sincerely love? How do I protect that and work in this inferno of America's racial animus?

P.H.: Jess, you are growing in your influence as a professor, teacher and poet. You have the ability to not only reflect American culture through your own unique prism, but to set the tone. In politics, they say the pendulum swings from left (Obama and the Democrats) to right (Trump and the Republicans)... I see a slight overcorrection from left to alt-right... also, there are clearly two Americas dealing with the legacy of slavery. I believe there will be an over correction to alt-left in the near term. In the vision of Tyehimba Jess, what does the future of America portend for its citizens? What do you think your children or those in the world to come will say of our times? In the year 2117?

T.J.: When we are talking about 1917 we are talking about a Black population in the rise of an empire. World War I was the cataclysm that made the United States a true world power. Right now, one hundred years later, we are looking at the decline of that world power. The current administration and the preceding overextension of American empire, the corruption of every branch of government, etc. How we will be seen one hundred years from now will depend on how we hold steady to the principles we proclaim in the best of our art, in the best of our political, social and artistic action. Hopefully, we will make choices that will inspire future generations to look within themselves and search out the most honest and original expressions of themselves that look along the long arc toward justice.

12/3/18

LIVING LEGEND

ISHMAEL REED, SATIRIST, AUTHOR AND NAGGING GADFLY TRUTHSAYER

Ishmael Reed in 2015 by Kathy Sloane

Through the need to suppress a variety of Black voices, the literary and cultural establishment engage in one-at-a-time-ism. So the establishment still tries to control the direction of Black culture by creating tokens, a remnant of the old Colonial strategy which relies upon a few gifted assimilated natives to tell the colonial office which natives are reasonable and which are unruly.
— Ishmael Reed

"Living legend" — two words that when put together conjure many ideas. But what is a living legend? The Merriam-Webster dictionary defines a living legend as "a person who is famous while still living for doing something extremely well." In the Macmillan dictionary it is "someone who is extremely famous during the time that they are alive." Surely a living legend is more than that?

My definition of a living legend is an individual who has lived fearlessly, puncturing the cosmetic veil of a reality thick with superficiality, without concern for their own wellbeing. Dr. Martin Luther King was a living legend. So was Malcolm X. Muhammad Ali. Of living legends who are currently *living* there is Nikki Giovanni and Colin Kaepernick, to name only two. "Living legend" is second cousin to "martyr". Both define a person with the willingness to speak, live, and be the truth no matter the potential consequences.

Ishmael Reed — poet, playwright, activist, essayist, songwriter, editor, publisher, novelist, Pulitzer nominee, two-time National Book Award nominee, and author of over thirty titles, including the 1972 novel *Mumbo Jumbo*, described by literary critic Harold Bloom as one of the five hundred most significant books in the Western canon — is a living legend. Some of the most celebrated work in African American culture — Colson Whitehead's 2017 Pulitzer Prize and 2016 National Book Award winner *The Underground Railroad*, for example, or the 2016 Booker Prize winner *The Sellout* by Paul Beatty — would not be possible without the verve and vision of Ishmael Reed.

I asked Reed a few questions about American culture and his work past and present.

Patrick A. Howell: While so much has changed in American culture, so much has remained the same. We live in a time divided between the movement of Afrofuturism and the eighteenth-century America that gave birth to the Declaration of Independence, the Constitution, and so many of our current contradictions and idiosyncrasies (a nation of "freedom" and "justice" founded on the perversion of those ideas). At times, it seems we will be permanent prisoners of this past. At others, it seems we surge into a future of unlimited potential. What insights can you offer to artists of all kinds who want to create a better future?

Ishmael Reed: More tools are available to writers than any time in history. For the first time, a writer can keep his work available for decades. As for me, right now, I'm looking at artists who opposed totalitarian regimes like the one that is operating now. My most recent play, *Life Among the Aryans*, was based upon Brecht's experience under the Nazis. The Nazis denied his staging a performance of the play and so he sponsored readings, which is what we did in June at the Nuyorican Poets Cafe.

Blacks, browns, and others are faced with administrations that have openly argued for their benign extermination, which explains Katrina, Flint, Puerto Rico, as well as policy positions proposed by the administration. *Buzzfeed* recently found a link between white nationalists and president Trump's administration. So, instead of the kind of euphemism that Lee Atwater proposed (as Jesse Jackson said, "The bus is us"), spokespersons for this administration such as Richard Spencer advocate "non-violent ethnic cleansing".

Black fiction is at the crossroads. Before the 1960s Black fiction writers were imitative. They were guided by the modernists — Eliot, Hemingway, and Faulkner. The 1960s saw Black writers expand their sources. Some studied Arabic. Others African languages. The Black Arts Movement spearheaded this cultural direction. Groups like Umbra and the Watts Writers Workshop. In the late Seventies there was a return to imitation.

But the Afrofuturists, John Keene (whom I first published when he was a student at Harvard), and many others have picked up where the Sixties took off. Hip-hop is an offspring of Black arts, especially Tupac, who mentions me in a song. In music you have Sun Ra, Cecil Taylor, Archie Shepp, David Murray, and others.

I did a workshop for the Givens Foundation. Most of my students were Black women. They were writing science fiction. My approach to achieving longevity in a country that is mostly hostile to my work is what in basketball is called a full court press. I write novels, poetry, plays, songs, and play jazz piano. Because of my collaboration with David Murray and Kip Hanrahan, Taj Mahal, Bobby Womack, Jack Bruce, Macy Gray, Cassandra Wilson, and Little Jimmy Scott have all done my songs. Composers like the great Allen Toussaint have set my songs to music.

P.H.: Your work expands to a period of time that passes from the Harlem Renaissance to the Black Arts Movement to hip-hop culture to Black Lives Matter. Early on in your career, you worked with writers such as Langston Hughes, Amiri Baraka, and Walter Lowenfels. You have interviewed Ralph Ellison for the *New York Times*. Where do you see the African expression in universal art right now? Is there a new movement underway? Or is the culture stagnant?

I.R.: Black culture never stands still. As I said in Darius James's film *The United States of HooDoo*, Neo-African religion had to always be one step ahead of the law. The same can be said of Black culture in music and writing. Novelist Martin Delany's mother had to leave Virginia because she was teaching her son how to read and write. Through the need to suppress a variety of Black voices, the literary and cultural establishment engage in one-at-a-time-ism. So the establishment still tries to control the direction of Black culture by creating tokens, a remnant of the old Colonial strategy which relies upon a few gifted assimilated natives to tell the colonial office which natives are reasonable and which are unruly.

An example: Robert Boynton informed the neocon establishment, of which he is a member, that a new group of Black writers weren't pestering people with "victimology." The kind of people who denounce Affirmative Action after having benefited from it. He then listed those writers whom he cast as unruly. This was the role of the Indian agent who went back to the military and told which savages were reasonable and which weren't. Or an informant in India doing the same thing for the East India Company. I debated Boynton at the Nuyorican Poets Cafe. He knew nothing about Black intellectual history. For that you'd have to read *Transformation of the African American Intelligentsia, 1880-2012.*

This is an example of what I call the Occupation of the Black Experience. Men who have never been racially profiled or red-lined are more likely to get their script ideas, novels, and TV projects about Blacks green-lighted than Black writers. I guess I'm unruly. Paul Devlin, Henry Louis Gates Jr's former employee and collaborator, said that with my recent novel *Juice!*, which uses the hysteria surrounding the O.J. [Simpson] phenomenon as a backdrop, I'd gone too far — a rare glimpse into the restrictions placed upon Black writers by the establishment. My answer was to title my next book of essays *Going Too Far.*

P.H.: Aside from razor-sharp wit and intellect, there is little connecting your eleven novels. What is your creative process? How do you know when you have an idea that will fit into a body of work as eclectic as yours?

I.R.: One can find inspiration from many sources. The idea of *Japanese by Spring* originated in a news item that claimed the endowment to a major university was traced to Japanese mob, the Yakuza. *Flight to Canada* began as a poem. *The Terrible* series began when I heard someone at party mention that there was a Black figure, Black Peter, in the Dutch Christmas, and by coincidence I was invited to the Netherlands shortly afterwards, where I witnessed the arrival of Saint Nicholas and Peter on a barge that floated into Amsterdam with crowds looking on. I took photos of the ceremony, which are in my archives at the University of Delaware. I've published *The Terrible Twos* and *The Terrible Threes* and I'm working on *The Terrible Fours*, excerpts of which have appeared in *Artbyte Magazine* and *Black Renaissance Noire*. *Conjugating Hindi* began from an appearance at an Irish conference held at the University of California — a heckler questioned my criticism of Lord Mountbatten, who was Viceroy of India. It is also a follow-up on *Japanese by Spring* which freed me from the restrictions placed upon Black artists in this country. I have difficulty getting my op-eds printed in this country. And so within the last half year I've had articles published in Spain's leading newspaper, *El Pais,* and the left-leaning Israeli newspaper *Haaretz*. I have an op-ed coming out in a London newspaper. I can't be stopped.

P.H.: Why does Tennessee feature prominently in your work? You wrote "Chattanooga" in 1980, writing:

> They're all right
> Chattanooga is something you
> Can have anyway you want it
> The summit of what you are
> I've paid my fare on that
> Mountain Incline #2, Chattanooga

I want my ride up
I want Chattanooga

I.R.: Chattanooga was the scene of many family tragedies, including the schizophrenia suffered by my grandmother, which was passed down to my oldest daughter. My grandmother's husband was murdered by a white man under strange circumstances. According to my mother, she visited him in Chattanooga Erlanger hospital, where I was born, and he said that he overheard a doctor say "Let that nigger die," and when I got the death certificate, it noted that he died from shock. The white man who stabbed him of course walked. I haven't been able to locate notes of the inquest. My mother called the murderer a liar during it. Since she and my grandmother worked for a wealthy family in the mountains, she had white people form a buffer between my family and the dyed-in-the-wool racists of the kind that you still find in the South. The murderer said that my grandfather came at him with a knife, yet the undertaker said that the knife was unopened. There was no note of his 1934 murder in the Chattanooga newspaper. I got the name of the doctor from a book about Erlanger hospital. The book mentions that there were segregated practices in this hospital during the 1930s. There was another cold case. His sister Rita Hopson was murdered by some Klansmen in Anniston, Alabama. Of course, my stepfather and mother couldn't wait to get out of Chattanooga in the 1940s.

Things have changed though. I was welcomed back to Chattanooga a few times. During the first, there was an empty auditorium because the Klan had launched a terrorist attack that included the shooting of nine Black women. During the second trip I was hassled by a cop as I stood outside of a gift shop on Lookout Mountain, but he toned it down when he noticed I was in the company of some of Chattanooga's leading Black citizens, including the Robinson sisters, whose father Walter Robinson was a Republican newspaper editor and had the power to elect mayors and challenged the Klan after they left a coffin on his doorstep — the cop calmed down and gave us an escort. There are streets named after Black heroes on the mountain said to be the creation of Black soldiers who accompanied General Grant. My most recent visit at Chattanooga State [Community College] was pleasant. They requested that I read "Chattanooga," a poem that has some fans in the town and makes the Chattanooga papers from time to time. My brothers were raised in Buffalo yet followed Chevrolet jobs to Nashville where they and their families live very well. Nashville Blacks have always been industrious. Their answer to segregated buses was to start their own bus company. I was refused entrance to Chattanooga's main library. Now they carry my books. Chattanooga is one of the most beautiful cities in the world.

4/14/18

THE FUTURE OF THE FUTURE

YTASHA L. WOMACK, AUTHOR, ACTIVIST AND INFLUENCER

Ytasha L. Womack is a critically acclaimed author, filmmaker, dancer, independent scholar, and champion of humanity and the imagination. Her book *Afrofuturism: The World of Black Sci-Fi & Fantasy Culture* (Chicago Review Press), a 2014 Locus Awards Nonfiction finalist, is the leading primer on the exciting subject which bridges science fiction, futurism, and culture. Learn more about her at ytashawomack.com.

Patrick A. Howell: I have often thought of one's principles as being both peace and technology because they enable the human spirit to reach its highest form. Having recently read of language being the first and most fundamental technology, it was interesting to see your identification of "race" as a technology. How does race being a technology affect the United States of America, as well as global culture?

Ytasha L. Womack: Race as a technology is a recognized aspect of Afrofuturism. We all know that race was created and yet our society maintains these categories as existential states of permanent existence. Race or the notion of being Black or white specifically was created to justify the transatlantic slave trade. The caste system that resulted was encoded through law and violence. People in our society have fought very vigilantly to change the system and recognize our shared humanity but the idea of separation continues to exist.

How race functions varies from country to country and sometimes is defined by who colonized the nation centuries ago, the nature of enslavement or colonization, and the reconciliations, if any, that followed. Race is closely related to access, and as access for people changes, race as we discuss it changes as well. Race, like many identities, including gender, religion, etc, is more fluid than we know. This fluidity is attributed to the fact that it was created in the context of limitation and individuals are constantly negotiating their relationship to it. Technologies are created to serve a need or function and discussing race in that context is a reminder that it is, in fact, a creation.

P.H.: You wrote *Afrofuturism: The World of Black Sci-Fi & Fantasy Culture* in 2013. With Octavia Butler, Janelle Monae, and Renee Cox there was already the blueprint for "Afrofuturism" but it was not until your book that there was a cogent embodiment of those concepts in a literary treatise.

Y.W.: The book did help synergize people who were interested in Afrofuturism but weren't familiar with the term. I've always seen Afrofuturism as universal so I'm not completely surprised by people's enthusiasm about it. I just feel that naming a subject is empowering and helps point people to works and histories that remind them they aren't alone in their contemplations. My book isn't the first writing on the subject. There were quite a few essays in academia. However, my book is a leading primer that I wrote largely to create bridges for people who approached Afrofuturism in a range of ways but, for the most part, didn't know they were Afrofuturist or that such a thing had a body of work behind it.

P.H.: A trailer for the blockbuster film *Black Panther* featured an image of your book. I see the influence of *Black Panther* as having the ability to shift mainstream culture away from alt-right and back toward alt-left. Are you a futurist? Can you create the future? Do you have any actual superpowers?

Y.W.: Someone once told me that my superpower was the belief in possibility. I thought that was a pretty wack superpower at the time. However, now I think there's a virtue in optimism. To quote Rev. Jesse Jackson, you can't move forward with cynicism. As for the future, people collectively create futures every day through their thinking and actions. Many of us are just not cognizant of how our thought and actions (or lack thereof) shape the world.

P.H.: As a filmmaker, your vision and its manifestation create realities in other folks' minds. Do any agendas — social, spiritual, visionary — color you and your work now or in the next decade?

Y.W.: As humans we're hardwired to engage in stories. I like telling stories that remind us of our own humanity, resilience, sense of purpose, and the value of community. I like sharing histories and present actions that reflect that as well.

P.H.: What is imagination? Is it a real space? Or is it a private hallucination? Are we, the children of slaves, kings and queens, the imagination of our ancestors? Is there a collective experience of imagination that informs your work?

Y.W.: The imagination is as real as the dreamer wants it to be. I think Rasheedah Phillips's work in *Black Quantum Futurism* is really interesting because it looks at African traditional and diasporic perspectives on time as it relates to quantum physics. Essentially, her work is a reminder that our current take on linear time is a perspective we've all been conditioned to work within. Our current perspective on time as linear is like looking at the ruler as the object it measures.

P.H.: Politically and socially, America is in a position with the KKK, alt-right, and relics of the 1980s setting a tone a lot of us did not foresee for the twenty-first century. What does futurist Ytasha Womack see in the distant future?

Y.W.: People can create whatever they want to create if they believe they can do so. I think it would be great for more people to give thought to the kind of world they would like to see and to really envision what that world looks and feels like. Personally, I like creating spaces that value humanity. Perhaps we should give more thought to thinking about valuing humanity and what that means. Many people put energy into what they don't want instead of into what they do want. They put a lot of energy into fear and frustrations. Having a vision and taking steps to bring it about is important.

4/2/18

AMERICAN POET AND AFRICAN CULTURALIST BUT BESPOKE AND AMBIENT

E. ETHELBERT MILLER, LITERARY ACTIVIST AND NATIONAL DEAN OF POETRY

Ethelbert close-up. Photo taken by Rick Reinhard at Sheridan Circle

Ethelbert Miller is an amicable, eloquent, Ambassador of the People's Poetry. His voluminous knowledge of literature is only matched by his voracious appetite for verse and his seemingly endless desire to share The Word with all humanity. We're fortunate to have such a Griot in our midst.
— 2017 Pulitzer Prize-winning poet Tyehimba Jess

Consider the person who decides to secure a box, place himself in it and mail himself out of slavery. The ability to make a way out of no way is perhaps imprinted on the souls of Black folks.
— E. Ethelbert Miller

Want to talk about poet Langston Hughes? Maya Angelou? Want to speak with a beloved friend of June Jordan's? Want to speak with one of those direct living legacies of poet and griot Amiri Baraka? I mean who gives deference to the Def Poetry Dean but Mos Def? Yes, call the Dean of American Poetry, E. Ethelbert Miller. He'll hear you out. Yes, talking with E. Ethelbert Miller is like listening to the cosmos: they hear you — an elegant vacuum of Black knowing, eternity in a body that is knowing and all-encompassing. After nearly thirty years of teaching, writing poetry and lecturing, the Dean of American Poetry does not just speak of ideas, poetry and justice, he has transformed his very being into an instrument of, for and to those higher ideas. E. Ethelbert Miller is an American poet and African culturalist.

I sent the Dean of American Poetry a few poems and he sent me back comments that were basically: "Start over, it doesn't sing. What Black?" They were final words, knowing too. They were kind and temperate but definitive. Because what's the point in arguing with a Panamanian septuagenarian Black Arts Movement devotee, a scion of the Harlem Renaissance, a friend of June Jordan's, the Def Jam poet trumpeted by Mos Def, he who critiques not only Ta-Nehisi Coates but his daddy, Paul? He who moderates Chimamanda Ngozi Adichie? The author of nine books of poetry, two memoirs and the editor of three poetry anthologies? The one after whom September 28, 1979 was declared forthwith E. Ethelbert Miller Day by Marion Barry, the mayor of Washington D.C. American Poet and African Culturalist, "E. Ethelbert Miller Day" edited me? Naw Black. That's blessings. Benedictions. So, I take the blessings and I absorb them into my being. In doing so, I am refined. Long live the Dean of American Poetry.

When we sit still with the music of the ancestors' soul sound prompting spirit fingertips, beating hearts into a symphony of djembe, the rain's pitter patter and kettles drums. And you know what I found E. Ethelbert Miller? On this brotherhood of the Dean of American Poetry to a nation of poets? I found, as Mos Def did, "Freedom":

> after word spread
> about emancipation
> some of us went to
> the end of the
> plantation and looked
> for our children to
> return. freedom don't
> mean much if you can't
> put your arms around it.

But let's talk with the Dean of American Poetry and see what he has got to say about the current state of global affairs. He is former chair of the Humanities Council of Washington, D.C., and has served on the boards of the AWP, the Edmund Burke School, PEN American Center, PEN/Faulkner Foundation, and the Washington Area Lawyer for the Arts (WALA). His speak is quiet and respectful, pregnant with all the possibility of the bright new age birthing from the old decrepit hierarchy. So speaks the Dean.

Patrick A. Howell: When we spoke earlier this year, after you had presented on poet June Jordan at the Medgar Evers College in Brooklyn, you said something that struck me and prompted this article. You said, and I am quoting as best I remember, that African Americans are some of the most creative spirits on the planet. What did you mean by that?

E. Ethelbert Miller: The ability to overcome oppression, to pursue freedom, to survive daily in a hostile environment, often requires a considerable degree of resiliency as well as creativity. Consider the person who decides to secure a box, place himself in it and mail himself out of slavery. The ability to make a way out of no way is perhaps imprinted on the souls of Black folks. To the extent that America "invented" the Negro, Black survival in America has been dependent on invention.

This is evident in our cultural footprints. Our art, especially our music and literature, has at times been difficult to define. Consider the inability of music critics to define and understand the first notes of bebop. How does an ear prepare for the coming of Charlie Parker or Ornette Coleman? Didn't August Wilson change American theater? Where does one place the contemporary literary genius of Olio by Tyehimba Jess? His collection of poems this year was awarded the Pulitzer Prize. The intellectual heft of this book represents the brightness of a new Black literary generation. One could see this coming from simply measuring the arching reach of the Cave Canem organization founded in 1996 by Cornelius Eady and Toi Derricotte. Today, we see African American poets beginning to dominate the genre of poetry as if it was the NBA.

In just the last few years American literature has been "spiced" by the work of Natasha Trethewey, Tracy Smith, Greg Pardlo, and Terrance Hayes. In film, as well as the visual arts, we find not one but many African American artists changing the landscape. It is also impossible to place all these artists inside one silo. This is not a rebirth or renaissance. It is simply the removal of the veil that was once placed over Black culture in America. Our artists have more visibility as a result of social media; in much the same manner we are able to document more incidents of police brutality because of a cell phone. Black people are no longer the children of Ellison. In many ways Barack Obama was our George Washington. Now comes the flowering of a new America and for some — the fear of a Black planet. Today's creative Black artistic energy must protect us from what Langston Hughes prophetically called "the backlash blues." This is what now stands between Trump and a hard rock.

P.H.: In your work, in your teaching and speaking, in your consciousness, there is connectivity, there is peace, a gentleness and a precise relationship with truth. These qualities seem to be absent in our current national discourse, leadership and cultural norms. What is "Literary Activism," a term you have used to refer to yourself and which has been attributed to you widely, even having September 28, 1979, memorialized as "E. Ethelbert Miller Day"?

E.E.M.: Forty years of working at Howard University turned me into a literary activist. In the early 1970s I was a research assistant to literary critic Dr Stephen Henderson. I took a couple of classes from him during my senior year at Howard. After I graduated I helped him interview various writers. Among them were Sterling A. Brown, Owen Dodson, Frank Marshall Davis, Julian Mayfield and many others. As director of the African American Resource (starting in 1974) I understood the importance of documenting and preserving history. For decades I conducted video interviews, I also hosted several radio programs that provided me with a way of sharing information with the community of Washington. I coined the term literary activist because it defined the many things I was doing. I was not just a poet or writer. In 1974, I founded the Ascension Poetry Reading Series which gave a generation of poets their first readings and stage.

Being a literary activist means helping to promote other voices. It means encouraging the person who might only have one poem. It means going into senior citizen homes, schools and prisons and discussing poetry as well as listening to it being recited. Today I edit (with Jody Bolz)

Poet Lore magazine, which is the oldest poetry magazine in the United States. It was founded in 1889. Editing this magazine for almost fifteen years has given me a vehicle in which I can help writers reach an audience. Editing a journal keeps one in touch with the pulse of the national literary community. At one time I sat on the boards of many literary organizations. In a small way I've helped shaped cultural policy and strengthen literary institutions. I take pride in having received two awards. On February 27 2007, I received the Poets & Writers Barnes & Noble Writers for Writers Award and on March 31 2016, the Association of Writers and Writing Programs gave me their George Garrett Award for Outstanding Community Service in Literature. Serving the literary community instead of simply sitting down and writing everyday often requires a considerable degree of sacrifice.

As a literary activist I've also spent time giving workshops and talks. For several years I was a core faculty member at the Bennington Writing Seminars. Today I teach an online memoir class for the University of Houston-Victoria. But maybe the key aspect of being a literary activist is the emphasis I place on preservation. I'm deeply grateful to George Washington University and their Gelman Library for housing my personal archives. At last count I believe the collection consisted of over 200 boxes. Hopefully, the material I saved will be of use to future scholars.

That comfort with words came from my father. As a new mother, I see that what we emphasize as important before our children affects their values. In our home my father valued literacy and the ability to both give and receive knowledge from the power of words. Growing up, we frequented trips to the neighborhood library and over dinner were quizzed on current events from articles we read in the New York Times. I grew up watching my father read

entire novels in one night, mentor budding poets and lead writing workshops in prisons.
— Jasmine-Simone Morgan, Esquire, E. Ethelbert Miller's daughter and rising activist attorney in Washington D.C.

P.H.: In 2010, on NPR in a show called, "How Will We Refer to the Next Ten Years," you offered a meditation on the next ten years and predicted a decade not unlike the roaring Twenties and the defining talents of F. Scott Fitzgerald, Langston Hughes and Zora Neale Hurston. You seem to be saying that we are in these times. Aside from literature and poetry, your industry and keep, where else (in what other art forms) do you witness the blooming of this work?

E.E.M.: It's funny looking back at what I said in 2010. I was concerned about those "teen" years of the new century.

Well it looks as if we've elected a child to lead us into 2020. Fear is real. Might we go to war with North Korea before we celebrate Kwanzaa again? Such darkness seems too real these days. I want to be optimistic but I don't want to be a fool. What seems to be blooming is the art of resistance. It's going to be dangerous if we erase the gains made on climate change or race relations. It would be sad if this decade is defined by Trump's ego and personality. Who wants the sky to turn a funny shade of orange? If this occurs, may all the willows weep for me.

4/22/17

THE UNLIMITED POWER OF ART IN MAN

ASKIA M. TOURÉ , POET & CO-FOUNDER OF THE BLACK ARTS MOVEMENT

Askia Muhammad Touré is a poet and leading voice of the Black Arts Movement. His works include *African Affirmations: Songs for Patriots — New Poems, 1994 to 2004* (Africa World Press, 2007), *From the Pyramids to the Projects: Poems of Genocide & Resistance!* (Africa World Press, 1990) and *Juju: Magic Songs for the Black Nation* (Songhai Press, 1972). In 1989, he won the American Book Award for his work with poetry, in 2000 the Stephen E. Henderson Poetry Award for *Dawnsong!*, and in 1996 the Gwendolyn Brooks Lifetime Achievement Award from the Gwendolyn Brooks Institute in Chicago, Illinois.

In 1961, Touré protested the assassination of Patrice Lumumba with Amiri Baraka, Calvin Hicks, Aishah Rahman, Max Roach, Abbey Lincoln, Alex Prempe, Mae Mallory, and Maya Angelou at the United Nations. He is a former editor of the *Journal of Black Poetry*, *Black Dialogue* and *Black Star*. He also participated in the rise of the Black Panther Party and helped write SNCC's 1966 "Black Power Position Paper." The current Resistance finds its roots gripped tightly in Askia Touré's clenched Black Power fists.

These days, he resides and teaches in Boston, Massachusetts, where he was a writer-in-residence at the now defunct Ogunaaike Gallery in Boston's South End. He is currently working on a film about the Black Arts Movement and completing further projects of his writing.

Askia expresses a pride in the next generation of millennials warriors and draws a line straight from the Harlem Renaissance to our current cultural milieu.

Poets like Larry Neal and Askia Touré were, in my mind, new masters of the new Black poetry... Askia had the song-like cast to his words, as if the poetry was actually meant to be sung.
— Amiri Baraka

Patrick A. Howell: Elder Askia Touré, as one of our preeminent poets, National Poetry Month might hold a particular significance to you. What kind of poetry have you been working on lately?

Askia Touré: While having a background of modern lyrical and narrative poetry, rooted in the blues/jazz tradition of Langston Hughes, Margaret Walker, and Gwendolyn Brooks, I found myself drawn to the epic, as a form for conveying specific cultural and spiritual experience. While a young poet, in the Umbra group, and later in John Killens's writers' workshop at Columbia University, I was advised by poet-critic Lorenzo Thomas to explore the works of the Negritude poets, Aime Cesaire and Leon Damas. While "abroad," I discovered W.B. Yeats and the Irish tradition, the Romantic Percy Shelley, and the Chilean bard Pablo Neruda. I was deeply moved by Neruda's Spanish Civil War poems, and the great epic, "Song of the Red Army at the Gates of Prussia." However, my major Neruda influence was his "Canto General," or the General Song of South America. These influences inspired my volumes *From the Pyramids to the Projects*, and *Dawnsong!*. Currently, I'm working on my Nile Valley epic, *Isis Unbound, the Goddess Songs*, which includes my first Nile Valley short stories.

P.H.: As one of the founding voices of the Black Arts Movement and Black Power Movement, you have witnessed jazz at its height and the emergence of hip-hop as a global sound. Where has Black expression been and how has it informed the Black American experience?

A.T.: My view is that Black expression is, or dominates culturally, the "American" experience. African American classical music "jazz" is functionally "American" classical music! Jazz is the "voice" of the Modern-Post-Modern era. Unfortunately, the US is dominated by giant corporations, created and controlled by the Anglo elite, which has never accepted jazz as American classical music. The liberal acceptance of Wynton Marsalis and his mentor Stanley Crouch is a half-hearted motion to reflect the World's recognition of jazz as US classical music.

Jazz, of course, is the music of the descendants of slaves, and therefore could never be accepted by the descendants of the Anglo masters. The 2007 study *This Is Our Music, Free Jazz, the Sixties and American Culture* by Professor Lain Anderson reflects this particularly "American" cultural dilemma.

As for hip-hop, I view it as basically a youth musical expression of the Millennials, Black Arts' grandchildren. Because of African American national oppression, hip-hop was interfered with by white musical corporations and transformed from youthful cultural pride with groups such as Sista Souljah, Queen Latifah, X-Clan, Common, KRS1 and Public Enemy into the degenerate "Gangsta Rap" thuggery, led by Lil Wayne & company. Within the original cultural imagery, young women were celebrated as beauties and "queens," but with the Corporate "intervention," the lumpen "thug" negative was emphasized, and young Black females were denigrated as "chicken-heads, skeezers, bitches and hos." As a prominent Black journalist and novelist pointed out, his teenage daughters complained that nobody sang them any love-songs! A negative "first" for Black urban blues and soul music.

P.H.: Your name is that of a kingdom governor, military strategist and statesman. He was renowned for encouraging literacy amongst his followers in the Empire of Songhai. How has that name impacted your life?

A.T.: My name change developed out of the Black Arts Cultural Revolution. While reaching back to Africa, and the Ancestors, we embraced what we discovered about African civilization and history. I chose the Songhai emperor, Askia the Great, who was a legendary and inspiring leader and ruler of the Songhai empire of West Africa. We rebelled against the culture of our Anglo former enslavers, and sought to get rid of our "slave" — read Anglo-Saxon — names. We hoped to create radical, new traditions among us which we could leave to the younger generations. It was in that spirit that Maulana Karenga and colleagues created the African holiday known as Kwanzaa, which has become a new tradition among our people.

P.H.: Black Lives Matter. I ask you this question listening to a video in which you stated, "Free people don't have to say 'Black Lives Matter.' Free people don't have to say that. That's a known reality. Some of the more perceptive scholars have called this Post Reconstruction two." How do you believe that American Lives Matter at this juncture in world history?

A.T.: This period is potentially entering into the second Civil War and the condition of African Americans and other peoples of colors and mirrors that of African Americans and Native Americans in the 1900s. We are still colonized.

They have just shifted the slavery to the inner cities and prison industrial complex. The urban police in the cities across the country take the same position as the slave patrols. Matter of fact, the way Black people are treated now, they are worse than the slave patrols. Because the slaves were considered valuable for their economic value in picking cotton. Now, an active minority appears to be capable of shooting down.

I think it is critical as a senior activist, it is a number one priority to engage the Millennials to make them aware of their legacy and to talk the history with them. I think that is very important. As we did in the 1990s and 2000s, we will develop institutions whereby we can transform and transfer a lot of experience to the younger generation. They are very receptive, they ask a lot of questions. A lot of our colleagues have sat down with them and we are so proud of them. A lot of them are the children of the buppies but in a lot of cases they went looking for the old folks that were the Black Arts Movement and Black Power Movement. I am so proud of them. We got along instantly. They sort of see us as living legends because they generally know the story of our struggle. We are to them what John Henrik Clarke was to us.

We created the largest Black cultural movement in the history of the United States. We created the Black arts journals. We created over twenty journals of various regions of the United States from the east coast to the west coast. And yet there is no mention of that throughout the literature.

What really disturbs me is that the establishment would not deal with our work because you are dealing with a society that tries to ignore those contributions, but the fact is that the Black literary world would not exist without our movement and has romanticized the Harlem Renaissance. I came from the *Umbra*, a Black magazine which came under the authority and guidance of Langston Hughes. So we always revered papa Langston but what you have now is assimilationist Negroes who would not deal with their own heritage. The movement was basically created by Amiri Baraka, Larry Neal, Sonia Sanchez and myself. Later, there was Nikki Giovanni in Chicago due to *Negro Digest*, Hoyt W. Fuller and Hakeem Donnell Reed and the writers and artists out of Chicago. It went out to the West Coast with Marvin X. Jackmon and Eldridge Cleaver. All across the country we were linked up. Out of New Orleans, it was John Dent. *Umbra* magazine was the message for all of that. We were all in it, in Chicago and Detroit and so forth. We put forth a major movement. These assimilist Negroes were ducking and dodging in the 1960s until now.

4/27/17

RESISTANCE JEDI KNIGHT

SEVAN BOMAR, THINKER AND RESISTANCE LEADER

There is an intergalactic war going on between opposing forces. And you don't have to go to the cineplex in December to see it. It's here now. It is always "here." These forces are outside the constructs of man-made time and place. They are simultaneously within and outside the constructs of galaxies and black holes. Energies are either positive or they are negative. We are constantly building, tearing down, and transforming the constructs of those energies with our being. Everything is ultimately a binary charge between fear and love. Which are you?

Yes, there are dark lords who have mastered their dark craft, sitting high upon world structures of finance, negative power, and politics. In fact, you might say, they aren't all that dark. They appear in the light. They hate nearly everything around them: loyalists, allies, friends, enemies. They maintain their power at all costs. To look at them, you will see serious eyes formed by shadows; brows heavy with the constructs of worry and hatred. You will see lumpy bodies formed by greed and avarice. You will see hulking frames of these men on devices saying they own the world. They are brash, trying to convince and connive. Are they really bold, though? Or, are they cowering in the edifices they sought to enlarge them? See, these power structures are merely facades. They are simply a matrix.

Matter of fact, there are two matrices. One is the real matrix and the other is a fake matrix. We have unplugged from the energies of nature — the trees, the sun, insects, birds singing, the musical symphonies of water cascading into other bodies of waters and renewing itself over and over and over again. There is a system outside the system of MSNBC, Fox, Democrats, Republicans, i-Thou, iPhone, stock markets, and the constructs of learning and existence on this man-made system of things. It is infinite. It is the real world. It is the air we breathe. So, take a closer look. In the air we breathe are the elements that have been traveling the cosmos for millennia. Elemental composites of oxygen, carbon, and hydrogen — the elemental composites of our bodies and earth. But there are also elements such as germanium, nickel, uranium, and sulfur, elements on the periodic table of elements.

After spending several months studying not only Sevan Bomar's teachings but also his sites Secret Energy or 2010Resistance.com, after authentically searching for not only him but what could connect the two of us, an invite from LinkedIn is responded to. The connection is not only authentic but strong and immediate. What follows is a transcription of our exchange.

Patrick A. Howell: Sevan, according to my research over the internet, the earliest mention of the Resistance comes from a site, an unembellished ambient energy outside of time, rooted in cosmic knowing, quantum physics, metaphysical exercise, spiritual technology, superfoods, astral projections and this New Age. It seems, that concentrated frequency, the internet which comes at a higher digital frequency than the industrial age of the twentieth century — it seems resistance2010 has broken its boundaries into the currrent reality. The resistance is everywhere and everybody is doing it — manifesting. Are you the author of *The Resistance*, Sevan Bomar?

Sevan Bomar: Yes, I am the developer and author of *The Resistance*, blogging a little over 1,300 blogs in a short period which propelled the site to the #1 spot on Google for the keywords "The Resistance" while it was in active operation. The site is now archived as a cultural classic and repository and its members, which reached 14,000, were transferred to the next site I built for yet more expansion, Secret Energy.

Existence is not only measured by how high you can climb on the ladder, it is also measured by how easily you can come down and assist others with what you have gained in such an ascent.

P.H.: What was the seed for the original idea, the Resistance, which seeded and rooted in your being?

S.B.: The Resistance was developed in conjunction with my book *The Code to the Matrix*, an opus that was divinely inspired and contains a methodical, poetic, and passionate approach to decrypting the English language in order to ascertain a more accurate history/herstory of humanity. The work was self-published and made available to the public for free. It was in some ways a last will and testament, a sort of farewell to the world with my final gesture being to impart it with specific keys to unlocking unlimited potential. I felt it unjust to retreat from humanity without lending them the same tools that allowed me to deprogram my consciousness.

To be clear, I was not suicidal. I left the United States and came to Costa Rica after vividly seeing "behind the veil of reality" for a two-week stint after a sequence of events placed me in a state of heightened awareness. I simply had no desire to engage any longer in such a high level of the illusion. Costa Rica took me in and welcomed me as its child so I made it to paradise. As if to herald the advent of a calling, the book went viral amassing approximately 500,000 reads in three days. Since I had left personal information such as my email address on the final pages of the book, I was overwhelmed with responses of others who had serious inquiries about my discoveries and found their own connection with what was being presented. I came to the notion when questioning myself that I had not done my best in ensuring this information and application was made available to the people since, after all, I had seen my best on other occasions. So I elected to create a platform that revealed the highest levels of spiritual knowledge in the world.

P.H.: Is the Resistance kinetic and telepathic in its nature now?

S.B.: There are some deeper works written by well-educated men that explain what we did naturally and intuitively. These works speak in relation to the process of creating something that is non-corporeal and not bound by the general confines of what we know to be terrestrial. The formula is summed up to the requirement of strong belief and a unified cause in its creation which eventually leads to a knowing. It can then take on the characteristics of its members while maintaining a superlative form. Since we place so much emphasis on spiritual advancement and sovereignty the faction has erected an organic grid of members that serve as waypoints to a collective projection of limitless potential. It is capable of causing undeniable synchronicities that defy practical odds. It is also capable of traversing spaces that so far have been inaccessible to navigate consciously by the average person such as the dream space and the subconscious of others with matching resonance and ideals.

P.H.: As the movement is political and social now, does it retain its concentration spiritually?

S.B.: While in most cases you generally see an erosion of anything that operates on energy over time, it's clear to me that true spirituality does not suffer from those same confines. Our faction and its members grow stronger, wiser, and sure of themselves every moment. I can credit this to that I'm not the central character in the theme here, the person is. The message reminds anyone that comes across it that if we exhaust our energy by placing it into the belief in external things, especially those of a dogmatic nature, we will disempower ourselves. Once a person realizes this they begin the process of freeing themselves mentally, physically, and spiritually. When they do this they have more energy than they ever had so you can see how empowering a transformation like that can be.

In conclusion, one must still have plans for what they will do after they reach a very challenging goal, they must project an even greater vision. That is what we specialize in. The humble origins of the Resistance has now become Secret Energy, an "Open Source Spirituality" network that has a plethora of tools to assist the Seeker including its own university dubbed "The Innerversity." It has grown into Spiritech, a company that employs conscious people and has over 1,100 specialists all over the world actively engaged in bringing awareness in their own unique way while using us as a strong foundation of support. It has even incited me to create solutions for the financial issues that we face in our communities by inventing and manufacturing the world's first water programming device, PhiAqua. *Existence is not only measured by how high you can climb on the ladder, it is also measured by how easily you can come down and assist others with what you have gained in such an ascent.*

Now: get off the *Huffington Post*. Put down this book. Get off your computer. Get off your smartphone. Forget the politics — if that is real, wouldn't you rather be alive? Turn them off because — we can go astral. We can go metaphysical, communicate telepathically, move telekinetically. We can go higher.

Walk into the light of day and smile. Life will happen to you. The sun is shining. Let go. Let it all go. The moon is rising. Just be. The stars you see when you close your eyes are also planets and astral phenomenon. And you are connected to something much larger than yourself.

They — these parasites of the human condition — do not control anything. Particularly the universe that is you. They will try because you, awake, is not in their vested interest. But you simply will not let them.

So, NOW. Just wake. Up. It doesn't get any easier, just better.

2/10/18

GRIOT JALI

QUINCY TROUPE, POET, MEMOIRIST AND CALIFORNIA'S FIRST POET LAUREATE

© Chester Higgins Archive

Griot Jali. He is a West African storyteller, a giant of American and global culture, using words to convey flavor, deeper meaning and all that jazz in story. Look at the plot points of Quincy T. Troupe's life and you will divine a masterpiece of storytelling in the making; a patchwork quilt of the highs and the lows, the ebbs and the flows that are the only constants in life.

We talk about Harlem, where he now resides, two doors down from the iconic actor Danny Glover (*Lethal Weapon* Danny not Childish Gambino Donald) and New York Knicks legend Earl "The Pearl" Monroe, with whom who he wrote a memoir in 2013. We talk about all the fights he had growing up in St Louis, Missouri, where he was a standout basketball and baseball player (just as his father, Quincy Troupe, had been). He received an athletic scholarship to Grambling State University but was kicked out for all those fights. "That's just the way it was," he confides when I ask how come so many. "I didn't like people getting in my face. I was a different person than I am now." He would later go on to play basketball in Europe as his son, Porter Troupe, now does.

We also talk about his mother, a small beautiful woman who was responsible for his towering accomplishment, and about the gentrification of Harlem, the neighborhood where American culture popped globally into 3D with the birth of the Harlem Renaissance. We talk about the state of our democracy and the larger culture. This griot jali is a jazz man. He riffs. Improvises. Talks about tough talk with Nobel Prize winner Derek Walcott. Asks about his old friend Ishmael Reed. Recalls Toni Morrison writing *Tar Baby* in his apartment.

In 2010 Troupe received the American Book Award for Lifetime Literary Achievement. As he took down corners in the culture with *Miles: The Autobiography of Miles Davis*, the memoir *Miles and Me*, *The Pursuit of Happyness*, written with Chris Gardner, and his other books, by his side throughout was an incredible partner, Margaret Troupe, executive director of the Gloster Project and Harlem Arts Project. Quincy comments: "She's a great woman. We've been together for forty years now." *Miles and Me* is soon to become a major motion picture, with Laurence Fishburne playing him in the film, produced by Richard Langley, who also produced *Hurricane* with Denzel Washington.

He has been at work finishing two projects, but I caught up with him on a tour of his past stomping grounds (he is a professor emeritus at UC San Diego), during which he has performed poetry readings in San Diego, Los Angeles, and Riverside, this last at UCR's famed Writers Week.

Patrick A. Howell: Let's start with a big question: Where do you see African American culture now?

Quincy Troupe: The way I look at African American culture — and American culture also, because all of it is intertwined — I look at it as a continuum. Because I go all the way back to the Harlem Renaissance, and then it starts to come forward, and before that even we had Paul Laurence Dunbar. People try to think in blocks, but I try not to think in blocks. It was important to go back to slavery and then go forward to Paul Laurence Dunbar and then come into the Harlem Renaissance and Langston and Countee. Sterling Brown, more so than Countee Cullen or Langston Hughes — he was a huge influence on me — Sterling Brown brought those work songs and blues poems, the true blues. If you saw Sterling Brown, you thought he was a white guy. He taught at Howard. He was a big guy. He went to all those great schools like Harvard. He was privileged but he loved the music and he loved the folklore. He went deep into it — he loved the culture. He was Toni Morrison's teacher.

Sterling Brown was an important mentor to me because he let me come into his house and he accepted me into his life. He loved my work when nobody else would look at it. He said you're going to do it. It's funny because he sounded so country. He was also erudite. He was a great critic, author, teacher. He was brilliant. He was a great poet. He was a great editor. And he was a great teacher. He was my model after I met him. I said, "this guy!"

P.H.: It's interesting. You and your contemporaries of the Black Arts Movement are really architects of the culture, the bridge from the Harlem Renaissance to hip-hop. You put down seeds that blossomed into world culture.

Q.T.: Yes. When I moved out here, I was a terrible kid. I was a great basketball player but I was a terrible kid. I used to like to whip people. That was fun for me, to hit people with bats. I got the scars to prove it. I've been shot, stabbed. Growing up in St Louis was like that. It was violent.

P.H.: What would instigate these fights?

Q.T.: Just anything! If you step on somebody's shoes at a party. You could be with a girl that somebody else wanted, you know. I wasn't in no gang. My family was the most terrifying family in St Louis. You hit a Troupe? Your [expletive] was [expletive]! Cause Troupes would come from everywhere to whoop your [expletive]. I'm serious. [Both laughing]

I just want to tell the truth about my life and how I came to where I am. That's the way I came up.

My mother had books around the house. My mother was Dorothy Smith Marshall — that was her name. Her maiden name was Smith but she married my father who was a great baseball player. My father was the third greatest catcher of all time in the old Negro Leagues. Everybody used to come to my house. She was Dorothy Smith Troupe Brown Marshall — 'cause she had married a musician called

China Brown. That was all her names. She always had books around the house. She was a great beauty — a beautiful woman — and a great reader. People loved her.

Men loved her. I used to tell her, "Mom, come on! You know what you was doing!" She would leave a handprint on my face. She was 5'2". She read everything. She would make me read books. She made me not only read books, she made sure I had a library card to all the libraries in St Louis — the county library, the city library, the local library — and I had to read all the books. They had a prize for the most read books — it was a book with a worm through it.

The people who used to vie for that were myself, Erlene Richardson, and this guy named Michael who went off the rails and got killed. Also, Walter Lipsey who went to jail. Walter was brilliant. I was. And Michael was. Erlene was more brilliant that all of us. She was the top student in the school.

P.H.: What does that mean, book with a worm through it?

Q.T.: The contest was called Book Worms. So, a worm through a little plastic or steel or copper tunnel and the bigger the worm, the better. There was first place, second place, third place. I used to always get second or third. I could never beat Erlene Richardson. Erlene Richardson read more books than all of us. I used to be mad as hell at her. One time she beat me by one book. She was smart!

What I'm getting to is I played basketball and baseball. My father was also the heavyweight boxing champion for Golden Glove, open division, heavyweight boxing champion who knocked out fifty-five straight people. So, he did not play. All he had to do was look at us and show us his hand and everybody's mouth was zipped. He didn't have to say nothing! He whooped me once and I never forgot it, with his bare hand. Seem like I couldn't walk for two days.

P.H.: How old were you?

Q.T.: I was like thirteen or fourteen… I didn't stay with him. I stayed with my mother and China downtown. He had told me to stay and watch the house. I went to play baseball and football. I came back and he was in the house. He was 6'3", weighed 220. He says, "What did I tell you junior?" [silence] "You told me to stay in the house." [silence] "And what did you do?" [laughing] He administered the whooping of my life. That whooping was too much. I didn't never not listen to him no more! [still laughing] And I didn't live with him. But if he told me to do something, I did it.

I was like that though. I could go off the rails. And I was hanging with all them boys.

P.H.: Did he see you at the height of your success?

Q.T.: He saw me when I was getting there.

P.H.: Was he proud of you?

Q.T.: Yes. He and my mother, I used to take her everywhere. But I was running with some bad guys. I was running with some killers. Fred was my good friend, went to Grambling with me. We both got kicked out of Grambling college… together. For beating up people.

P.H.: Why? Why did you get in so many fights?

Q.T.: Somebody just says something stupid. It was always the football players. He was a track star and I was on the basketball and baseball team. I thought the football players were idiots. They would say something smart. I would say you got some head injuries with all that tackling you do with your head. Something had to reduce your brain power. Basketball players? We got a lot of finesse and grace. I used to run with all these people — Fred Holmes — we were all like half-ass gangsters. I got into trouble behind that. I was running with the wrong people. We were watching all those gangster movies and plus there were a lot of bad dudes in St Louis. In order to survive you had to be as terrifying as the next guy or more. I got kicked out of college for beating up a guy... I had a bad temper.

P.H.: Do you still have any of that temper?

Q.T.: No. I'm cool now. *But don't nobody bother me.* I don't try to bother nobody.

P.H.: Why do you love Harlem? Why do you live there now and what are you working on?

Q.T.: I love Harlem. It's beautiful. The culture is there. You got a lot of great restaurants there. It's really integrated now. It's a lot of music. It's a walking city. There's a lot to do. So, we've been working on this Rudy Langlais who was my editor at the *Village Voice*. I like small presses.

I'm working on the screenplay for *Miles and Me*. I'm working on my memoir now which is called *The Accordion Years* and it is two-thirds finished. And then there is this novel, *The Legacy of Charlie Putnam*, which I have been writing for twenty-five years. The novel is basically about his son Langston Putnam. It takes place in St. Louis and Los Angeles.

The memoir is in eleven parts — it starts in 1965 in Los Angeles and it goes back and forth. Hence the name

Accordion, it goes back and forward, it goes back and ends in today.

P.H.: Does it end in harmony?

Q.T.: We'll see. [laughing] I'm happy right now because of my wife and kids.

6/26/19

THE EVANGELISTS

MILES, BEYOND 2000: A FINAL ELEGY (FOR MILES DAVIS)

BY ASKIA TOURÉ

"Jazz is finished. We better get it together!"
— Miles, 1975

Driving through America's neon graffiti,
one remembers Miles' furious quest:
a master disciplined, fiery, determined;
a man — zealous, powerful, elegant— forging
a creative epiphany in depths few "squares"
could imagine. This fierce genius immersed
in the fluidity of grace: a dark, griot mind
exploring depths of Inner Space— and Time
so marginal in his magical paradigm blazing
like a nuclear sun. Miles who created new
Essence and rhythms via Great Black Voices —
orality, beyond puritan morality, unleashing
Apocalypse. A prophet seeking visions, past
Bluesy "style" collapsed beneath the ferocious
Genocide of "Dollarism": Anglo imperialists
scheming to blast our Harlems into myriad
Free Fire Zones among Dantesque Infernos.
So, how would life flourish within this
Nation of Poets, Shouters, Screamers when
the Blue Song fades in Urban Gulags,
and only primitives remain among its echoes?

Who would we be then: what ancient agony
withered, though essential, awaits in bleak
Silence spewed with crack pipes, condoms,
glocks, and the shock of recognition among
nameless, faceless spirits writhing in the dusk?

BLOODIED ORANGE POETRY

ANGELA NARCISO TORRES, ACTIVIST, POET & EDITOR

Angela Narciso Torres by Rowie Torres ©

Angela Narciso Torres is a prize-winning poet whose book of poetry has garnered exceptional reviews from poets, the public and academic communities alike. She is a literary enthusiast, teacher and editor as well — basically, she is a culturalist who moves the needle in the literary and poetic communities nationally and globally. We had the opportunity to meet at a mutual friend's poetry breakfast and I have also been able to listen to her readings and read her book of poetry *Blood Orange*, which was awarded the Willow Books Literature Awards Grand Prize for Poetry. It was an interesting time to catch up with the poet, who is also a recent transplant from Chicago to Los Angeles and one of the senior editors of *RHINO*, a prize-winning Chicago journal. She had just arrived in the Philippines as she took time to read, consider and answer my questions.

Patrick A. Howell: First off, you said something of interest today as it relates to your aesthetic deriving itself from your American and Filipino roots. Can you talk a little bit more about that? How it impacts you, how you view the world and, of course, your work?

Angela Narciso Torres: If I recall correctly, we were discussing about the particular aesthetic "lens" I use when writing poems. Having grown up in Manila then living most of my adult life in the US, automatically there are these two perspectives, not unlike those 3D glasses you wear at the movies — one side red, the other blue, which allows you to see three-dimensionally. So as long as I've been writing poems [in my adult life], I've always seen the world through both Filipina and American lenses — further refined, of course, by everything else that colors and informs who I am: e.g. my being a woman, mother, daughter, my political and religious beliefs, aesthetic sensibilities, etc. It's not like I can turn off one or the other, or prioritize one over the other — and even if I could, the picture would be lopsided, incomplete, not representative of my truth. I like to think that having this multi-dimensional perspective makes for a fuller, more encompassing, and hopefully, more compassionate view of what being human in the world means.

P.H.: You are a senior editor of *RHINO Poetry* out of Chicago — can you talk a little bit more about your work with the prodigious literary journal over here on the left coast?

A.N.T.: I'm one of three senior editors of this independent literary journal which has been running for over forty-five years now. We're a staff of twelve editors with a changing staff of interns, all volunteers. Most of us are working poets representing diverse age groups, ethnicities, sexual orientations, and poetic sensibilities. Our selection process is unique and democratic: each poem gets at least four editor-readers; the highest-rated ones are brought to table and read aloud at our bimonthly meetings, then voted upon. It's a hands-on process, which I believe is what makes our journal incredibly strong: we constantly insist on finding the best poems based not on any one poetic style or school, but looking through various lenses at once, and remaining open to each other's sometimes divergent perspectives. Needless to say, being a "remote" editor (I've since relocated to the west coast after nine years with the journal), I'm a little removed from the editorial process, though I continue to read submissions and participate in choosing prize winners for our various contests. However, I'm about to launch two exciting programs, which we're hoping will expand our presence here on the West coast. One is *RHINO* Reads! West, which will be the left coast chapter of our monthly poetry reading series in Chicago, where we've featured both emerging and acclaimed poets as well as a regular open mic. Secondly, I'm starting *RHINO* Reviews! — a reviews column on our website, rhinopoetry.org.

P.H.: "My Father's Rib," "Ironing Woman," "Waiting for My Father at the University Hospital Lab" and "Things to Tell My Son about the Moon" are all works in your widely celebrated and award-winning collection *Blood Orange*. Family is a powerful trope, metaphor and theme interwoven throughout your work. Can you talk a little more about that?

A.N.T.: It may sound simplistic, but I write the poems I write because they're the themes that matter most to me. In *Blood Orange*, which I consider a poetic memoir of my growing up in the Philippines and my later life in the US as an adult, my poems are often narratives or dramatic lyrics based on lived or felt experiences. I couldn't do otherwise, i.e., couldn't make myself produce willfully disjunctive or opaque poems "just because." Poems to me are a vehicle for feeling about experiences, things, people — and to me, at least in my first book, the most important of these had to do with family. Every single lesson I've learned about love, loss, living and dying, I learned first at home, with the people who know and love me best, so it's natural that my poems would start there. I think that when we write deeply about the undercurrents of what makes us human, we can transcend all kinds of barriers — familial, cultural, ethnic, or otherwise.

P.H.: You are travelling back to the Philippines this holiday season. When you are there, Angela, how does it affect your spirit? Where do you go? What do you see there that is not here?

A.N.T.: I love coming home. Every trip home is food for my writing. A veritable feast. The humidity, the lush green landscape, the tropical foliage, the pollution and traffic, the crowds, the rain, the relentless mosquitoes, the dust, the home-cooked meals, the way every meal is a social event — all of it. But especially the people. And the food. Did I mention the food? Then of course, there's my mother's house, which is where I grew up. I love seeing the objects, the pictures, the furniture, the setting of my childhood and growing up years: the bookcases that housed my favorite stories, a chair I used to read in as a child, the particular turn of a knob or crack in the floor, the mirror before which my mom put on her makeup daily before going to work. When I come home, I just take it all in. It's like being the madeleine soaked in the Proustian cup of tea — everything brings back some memory I didn't know I had, evokes a feeling I haven't felt in years. Every conversation with a friend brings back a piece of me that I otherwise may have lost. It's particularly rich this time because I have my three boys with me and it's Christmas, easily the biggest holiday of the year in the Philippines. The last time we spent Christmas in Manila with my folks was eighteen years ago. Like the poem you referenced, it's like experiencing my home all over again, but through my children's eyes. A rich, rich time indeed.

P.H.: You are a full-time writer? Which do you find more fulfilling, the life of an educator or writer? Why? Are they related? How are they different?

A.N.T.: Teaching and writing require opposite energies; each nourishes me in different ways. In teaching, energy is directed outward. Writing requires going inward, into the self. Being naturally an introvert, I lean more towards the latter — or perhaps I should say I feel more comfortable inhabiting that inner space. This is not to say I don't love teaching; just that the energy it requires from me is tremendous, though every bit worth it — the rewards are immeasurable. There's no way to give any less than 100%

when I'm teaching and I wouldn't have it any other way, yet it also saps me, not just physically but mentally and emotionally as well. In teaching poetry you're really teaching life; you're drawing not just from books and knowledge but from heart and soul as well. Teaching requires so much self-awareness, and this is how writing, which is so much about exploring and knowing the self, is truly the best foundation for the teaching life. Whether I'm teaching older adults or high school students, I'm in awe of how much I learn about poetry from them. I get inspired by the persistence and courage of adult students who have just started writing poetry and are undaunted by the blank page. It thrills me to see young people taking risks, or discovering the magic of a poem—whether centuries old or just published. I'm encouraged by my young students' spontaneity and candor, and by the wisdom older students share from their lived experience. I take this all down to "where all the ladders start—the rag and bone shop of the heart" (Yeats) — and am grateful for the inspiration and creative energy that teaching generates for my own writing.

How long the day seemed, how little
we knew of what our mother hoped
to forget, their cares kept hidden
like coins we buried in the vacant lot
— "Night Jasmine"

P.H.: In "Night Jasmine," "Ironing Woman," "Lucky" and "Sheer," you refer to the wisdom and ways of matrons; specifically women who have immeasurable wealth in the form of old ways or ancestral troves. What is your relationship to these women? Why do their ways configure so prominently in *Blood Orange* and other work?

A.N.T.: I grew up in a matriarchal household where women held sway not just in the family, but also in business, in academia, in medicine (my mother was a physician and head of her department), and other fields. I suppose this is true for Filipino society as a whole — women are often empowered and revered as sources of wisdom and power, all beginning with the grandmother, who is the center and the driving force of the family, but also in the realms of politics, business, art, etc. Since Marcos fell in 1986, we have had two women presidents (Corazon Aquino and Gloria Macapagal Arroyo), which means women have ruled for at least half the time since Marcos's dictatorship was toppled. My poems celebrate this universe where the women in my life have a voice, have agency and power to make change. My mother taught me by example that women have say in a world that may often show us otherwise. At age twenty-six, an immigrant from Manila with two toddlers, she was the only woman *and* person of color in a well-regarded medical residency program at the Jewish Hospital in Brooklyn. She always spoke up for injustice in any situation and taught me to always stand up for what is right. From her I learned that hard as the world might try, it cannot put a good woman down.

12/24/17

THE POWER OF GOOD

MOROWA YEJIDÉ, AUTHOR

Morowa Yejidé. Photo taken by Sarah Fillman of Fillman Foto, 2016

Razor-sharp intellects are oftentimes fenced by a benign and kind presence. They are quiet, thoughtful in their listening, measured and precise in their approach to life. They are gentle and unassuming, but their effect, the outcome of their work, is powerful and long-lasting. Think about it — Barack Obama, the quality of grace, Sunday mornings, an Anita Baker or Sade song, or, the lingering effect of a single fork of pecan pie. Anita Baker doesn't have the volume of work that Nicki Minaj (*no dis fellow Trini*) does, but "Sweet Love" and "Same Ole Love" are already timeless. Barack Obama, certainly kind and decent, will more than likely be noted in history as the transformative figure of the twenty-first century. How the gentle approach often underscores its powerful message is stuff of world history and legend.

That's how Morowa's work, *Time of the Locust*, and presence function. It is thoughtful, slow to answer, but when the syllables and paragraphs form, it might be deafening and overwhelming like a swarm of locusts descending from the heavens. The *Washington Post* has said of Morowa's debut work, *Time of the Locust*, that it "deftly brings together the fantastic and the realistic, and touches on a variety of issues, from politics, race, and murder to disability, domestic tragedy, and myth... [and] spins them with gold and possibility." *Publisher's Weekly* has said of the critically well-received work:

> Beautiful prose conveys the sadness and fractured selves of these characters, who are both strong and fragile. The depth of pain can make for difficult reading, but the rendering of Sephiri's interior life, in particular, is arresting, and the novel is challenging and memorable.

I had the opportunity this week to talk with Morowa about her work, which was longlisted for the 2015 PEN/Robert W. Bingham Prize, and her work as a PEN Faulkner Writer in Nantucket with high school children this past spring.

Patrick A. Howell: What was your inspiration for the *Time of the Locust*? If you had to give a breakdown of percentage inspiration to percentage of journaling, what would be the breakdown? Does that breakdown apply to most of your works or does it vary? What is the percentage of dream, vision, reality and artistic inspiration for your work?

Morowa Yejidé: I didn't have a linear process for creating *Time of the Locust* or anything else I've written. My writing always starts with an image or a concept that can be represented with an image. From there, I develop the "frame" of the characters and the elements that I would like to explore through the characters. Research is a big part of the process. The research is an odyssey. I never know what I'll find. The world and everything in it becomes part of my toolchest. From there, the story takes on a more organic process and then concepts that I originally started with become clearer in my mind. I try to add more layers to make them richer and more vivid.

I hammer at getting as close to the image/concept until I think it is on the page in the way I wanted. I write different parts of a novel at once. It's like painting a big mural in my mind: add darkness here, add light there, shape and mold the character for this, sharpen the angles of the happenings in this part of the story for that. Then I pull back to "assemble" it and begin shaping the final piece. I need that journey through the labyrinth. I need to feel like I'm launching into something to see what I can find. It's the odyssey of writing that attracts me. It's the trip down the rabbit hole that calls to me and I try to go as far as I can. After all of that, I put on my editing hat and go through the story with a ruthless eye.

Trina thinks about allowing them to go on, while everyone is pretending not to be listening. But she pauses in the blackness of stealth, a desire to stun them growing in the crevice of her bra. All these long days she has kept silent. She has learned the weight of custom and restraint, and how words spoken too quickly sink to unknown depths. But couldn't she say something just once? Say it. "I'm an exchange student at Waseda," she quips in Japanese, instantly becoming holy.

— Morowa Yejidé, "Tokyo Chocolate"

P.H.: Let's talk about "Tokyo Chocolate," a story I think gets short shrift because of all the attention *Time of the Locust* has garnered. How did you come to write about homegirl Trina in Nishifunabashi, Japan with the ghost of Mama-san? Do you have a relationship with any of these characters any longer? Will Trina show up in further work?

M.Y.: "Tokyo Chocolate" was inspired by my own experiences as an exchange student going to college for a year in Japan and living with a host family. It was a wonderful and tremendously eye-opening view into different ways of looking at the world, America, and myself. I remember one day, years later, I found the journal I scribbled in during the long train commute from downtown to the Tokyo suburbs. So the little snippets in the story (the snacks, overhearing conversations in Japanese, tea time with Mama-san, all the studying) are a fictionalized account of some of the things I experienced. I really did have teatime every afternoon at four o'clock with my host mother and those were some of the most amazing chats. We talked about everything. Love and hate. War and peace. History and what we thought our place in it was (or should have been). How we felt the future should be. I wanted to capture the uniqueness of such intimate exchanges. I wanted to share the adventures of a young Black girl in Japan and what she learned about human behavior. I still keep in touch with my host parents (both now in their late eighties and still going on vacations). They were tickled to get a copy of *Time of the Locust* even though they can't read anything in English!

I have written many short stories over the years but I continue to be amazed at how far and wide this story has traveled. Even the *Japan Times* gave it a wonderful review when it was included in an anthology there. The story has taken on a life of its own and was recently picked up at Eastern High School in D.C. as part of the *"Time of the Locust/*

Tokyo Chocolate Book Club" for 2017. It's unbelievable in a wonderful way. Who knows where it will go next!

P.H.: You have had no shortage of accolades for your work — I am always struck by the lack of cause/result relationship between recognition and excellence. There *can* be a relationship but it is not explicit. How many mothers and fathers who have labored quietly for years to realize excellence in their children think nothing of reward for themselves? Or, think about Zora Neale Hurston, who could almost be considered a founder of the Harlem Renaissance, not getting her due until sister Alice Walker put in the work on behalf of our ancestor? How do you maintain the balance between humility and confidence essential to writing great work and when it is recognized for its exceptional merit? How much do you push and how much do you allow the opportunity to find you?

M.Y.: Writing and reading are such a subjective process and I accept that I can't control the life my work takes on once it is released. But I know that no matter what happens, I fulfilled a pact with myself in creating the best work that I believed I could create — that I did the characters and what they represented justice in the context of the mythology I envisioned.

I just try to take the good with the bad and be accessible to those who are interested in my writing and never take them for granted. After all, writing is really a dialogue between the person who put the words down and the person who reads and sees those words in his/her mind. How wonderful it is to have that connection when the opportunity arises. What I was seeking with *Time of the Locust* is that great mirror that stories can offer: someone looks into it (and may or may not be comfortable with what he/she sees). It's the glimpse that keeps me going, that gives me the thrill. When someone tells me they feel that thrill with something I wrote, it inspires me to keep writing. I think that this openness has allowed terrific things to walk into my life like the PEN/Faulkner Foundation and its Writers in Schools Program, literary circles and boards in Washington, and some really wonderful people.

It's a big world and I am always in the process of becoming a better me in it. Believing in my abilities while recognizing fortunate developments and positive people when they cross my path are a part of that becoming. And I have the constants of my husband and three sons to encourage, challenge, and anchor me. They've grown with me in this writing thing. They know it's a part of me and because of that it is a part of our family. They wave from the shore when I'm out there doing events or working on a project or feeling weary. They remind me of what matters.

P.H.: What is your favorite television show? Favorite all time movie? Who would you choose, given Oprah or Spielberg power, to direct *Time of the Locust* and who would be ideal in the role of Brenda, Horus and/or Sephiri?

M.Y.: It's hard to pick a favorite television show or movie since books are my thrill. But I do get a kick out re-runs of *The X-Files*, films with "crazy writers" like *Secret Window*, and science fiction classics like *Aliens*.

Even though *Time of the Locust* is steeped in imagery, mysticism, and intensity, I don't really think of my work in a film medium. There are so many tremendous actors out there who could play anything (Jeffrey Wright or Chiwetel Ejiofor as Horus, for example). Brenda was written as a composite of so many women I have known that it's difficult for me to think of her as just one person. Brenda is every woman. To pick from a pool of so many brilliant actresses who could play anyone to any degree would be tough. Sephiri is such an otherworldly boy and I believe that there is a young natural somewhere that is his character come to life. Ava DuVernay films like *I Will Follow* show characters as complex, multidimensional people- which I love. The Hughes Brothers would be tremendous because of their ethereal cinematic vision in such films as *From Hell* and *Book of Eli*. But in the end, I'd have to leave it all to the professionals.

P.H.: What work do you have waiting in the wings?

M.Y.: My adventure with writing continues with a new novel I am completing — a tale of magical realism set in Washington D.C. Every book is different. This one has new labyrinths and I love the odyssey. It's a fantastic deep dive into the mind, what place means, and the hidden currents that drive people. It's another trip down into the rabbit hole and the quest is worth every word.

10/29/16

Morowa Yejidé's *Creatures of Passage* will be published by Akashic Books in 2020.

THE POWER THAT WOKE US

NATE HOWARD, ACTIVIST AND VISIONARY

"Woke as a political term of African-American origin refers to a perceived awareness of issues concerning social justice and racial justice. It is derived from the African-American Vernacular English expression "stay woke," whose grammatical aspect refers to a continuing awareness of these issues."
— Wikipedia

We say that a lot now — *woke*. Not sure when it came into the popular lexicon, but it is here now. Willow and Jaden Smith, *they woke*. Solange Knowles, *she woke too*, with a whole lotta style that is not of this world, not of this zip code. Solange's album, *A Seat at the Table*, that's woke too, especially that joint with Q-Tip, "Borderline (An Ode to Self Care)." That book, *Invisible Man, Got the Whole World Watching: A Young Black Man's Education* by scribe Mychal Denzel Smith, *that's woke too*. Colin Kaepernick taking that knee — *woke!* Zulaikha Patel, the eighteen-year-old South African girl with the wild afro, the one who woke up the world to her power and clenched her fist around a baton pass from Angela Davis — *she way woke too*.

The catch word "woke" is at such a zenith, it is in the TV entertainment/gossip show, *Extra*. It was even in *Time Magazine* and the *New York Times* — that's how you know it's mainstream, that's the certification there, right? Movement BE is woke too. This movement was founded by Nate Howard in 2013. Nate was on the front page of the *LA Times* for sparking a movement against racial profiling after seventy-nine LAPD officers shut down his event at USC where he was attending school as an undergraduate. Movement BE is a non-profit organization that helps the youth tell their story with the motto, "tell your story before they do." It has impacted thousands of students around the world and in urban neighborhoods across the USA.

Nate Howard has been on a tour around the country and world, awakening hundreds of students from Accra, Ghana to Loyola University in New Orleans, to DePauw University in Indiana, to schools in his native San Diego. Nate says being "woke," means "being awakened to ourselves. Being woke is being awakened to who we really are. Tell your own story — don't let anybody except you tell your story. You are conditioned all of your life by society to be "successful." But I have learned to talk about greatness — true greatness that comes from living one's purpose and leaving a legacy for those that come after us. This is *my* purpose. Those that have come before us as Dr Cornel West have challenged these notions of success which are really a prison to keep us away from individual greatness. It's a mental thing, a mental prison and we have to free our spirits right now."

Nate Howard was selected by NBC as one of the top twenty-eight Black leaders, along with Olympian Simone Biles and Golden State Warrior Stephen Curry. He was also featured on the *Today Show* as one of the "Best and Brightest: Game Changers Making History." But, he woke so he doesn't dote on himself:

We have to forget what we are being told about "success." We have to hold onto our ancestors and what they have fought for. When we understand what Langston Hughes and Maya Angelou have done with their work, we will know who we are. Their poetry really changed society. It's how we change the world.

In a trailer for the movie adaptation of the August Wilson play *Fences*, Denzel Washington's character Troy is chided by his son Cory, played by newcomer Jovan Adepo, into answering the question, "Hey Pop, can I ask you a question? How come you ain't never liked me?" Denzel's grizzled character, an eighteen-year veteran of the garbage disposal industry, responds, "Like you? What law is there say that I got to like you?... I ain't got to like you. Now, I done give you everything I got. I give you your life!... Now don't you go through life worrying about whether somebody like you or not. You best be making sure that *they doing right by you.* You understand what I'm saying?" In this brief excerpt, is August Wilson's play dramatization for the purposes of *real woke*.

Materially, "woke" are the Mothers of the Movement of slain Sandra Bland, Eric Garner, Trayvon Martin, Jordan Davis, Mike Brown, Hadiya Pendleton and Dontré Hamilton appearing hand in hand at the 2016 Democratic National Convention, speaking to a generation, galvanizing and saying with their mere presence, "This is how we do it — we do it." We don't dare back down at the specter of seeming inevitable odds, impossible realities. We embrace the struggle. That's Africa. That's the Black equation for survival *and* excellence in America.

For all of us "woke" spirits walking the planet now, they are the architects that made the woke folk, and they are made of pure strength, uncut wisdom. I call them Power Griots, but nothing about them is PG, although I suppose there is guidance involved. Before us Woke Beauties, it was the Power Griots and they laid it down, did all the heavy lifting... no problem. All of us, every single one of us, wholly woke or nodding off into nap, even those of us sleep-walking in a coma, have the Power Griots to thank for our beautiful selves. They are now silver-haired, and the glint has dulled just a tad (but when they see us, their Woke Beauties, who need the sun), are a little less with appearances but no matter, when they stand we see institutions rising, we hear time vanishing. We know what they can do because they did it all for us.

Nate concludes, "Poetry is the voice of the unacknowledged world. The acknowledged world is the whole universe of individuals who continue to be voiceless. We speak from a place of vulnerability, our pain, and beauty. It allows us to say, 'This is who I am', not just who the world says you are or who you are supposed to be. When I was in Ghana, there was this whole idea of language and who we are and have been. Spoken word, poetry, expressing the unexpressed — this is who I am. And it's not entertainment." Yes, yes, yes — as Nate has spoken during his keynotes, "Find your story. Tell your story. Be your story."

It's gritty reality, beautiful magic and awakening — *Woke*. Be who we be — Movement Be.

Yes, that's the power that woke us. From kingdoms, kings, queens and chieftains of the ancient empire Ghana to woke citizens of a new future power world, *woke is awakened to our cosmic possibility and walking in that truth*.

10/17/16

Movement BE is currently in twenty-five schools in the San Diego School District, the Juvenile Halls, and in Los Angeles working with the homeless.

THE GALACTIC RESISTANCE IS REAL

LESLEY-ANN BROWN, ACTIVIST AND TEACHER

I am every breath of great grandmothers laboring for new generations, carrying the dna of every herstorical murmer and dance that I would become. I am the lessons of personal evolutions and revolutions and I am praying that I have more spinning inside of me because we ain't done yet... we came here to BE a life worthy of all the sacrifices, scars, drowned bones, and the very loss of our authentic names.
— Jaki Shelton Green, Poet Laureate of the People, Messenger of the Land

Lesley-Ann Brown is West-Indian Trinidadian — that's already a very telling, well... tell *sign*.

You know who else is from Trinidad, that small boot shaped island in the Caribbean off the coast of Venezuela, right? The little island renowned for its Calypso and Socas and its international Carnival season? That's right — the revolutionaries. Dr Eric Williams, the first Prime Minister of the island, widely considered the "Father of the Nation." C.L.R. James, a tireless Afro-Trinidadian activist, historian and journalist — he wrote books like *The Black Jacobins*, the widely respected book that talks about Toussaint L'Ouverture and the San Domingo Revolution, as well as *State Capitalism and World Revolution* and *Nkrumah and the Ghana Revolution*. There is also Stokely Carmichael a.k.a. Kwame Ture, a great Trinidadian-American who is recognized as the honorary Prime Minister of the Black Panther Party, initially as a leader of the Student Nonviolent

Coordinating Committee and in later years instrumental in the global Pan-African movement.

You know who else comes by way of the West Indies, right? Malcolm X, Louis Farrakhan, Shirley Chisholm, Marcus Garvey, Harry Belafonte, Sidney Poitier, Kamala Harris — it's this type of erudite *breed* of human being that comes out of these small Caribbean islands. As someone who derives one half of his bloodline from Trinidad, I've come to find this — we are the ones who will torch your house, then sit down over a coffee and explain to you afterwards in a very folksy, sanguine, intimate and charismatic manner *exactly how we did it* and why it *had* to be done.

Now, if you *see* Lesley-Ann Brown, you'll see someone who is folksy and booksy like a librarian. Like an English teacher or speech coach, right? But, Jesus H., be careful, for in those eyes, there is something a little *different* — something harnessed over her several decades on the planet. *It is fire*. And I'm not talking about the orange and yellow flames that are on the tip of the fire. I'm talking about that blue core. That inner core of the candle flame that is light *blue and* has a temperature of around 1500°C. That's what we're talking about here — we're talking about this kind of *blue* human. This kind of *ethos*. This kind of revolutionary has a blue sort of knowing.

January 21, 2016, the day after President Donald J. Trump's inauguration, there were historic protests around the globe, possibly one of the largest demonstrations in American history. Nearly 3.3 million took to the streets to decry a nascent president who inversely lost the general election by nearly three million votes. Five thousand of those global protesters were organized by Lesley-Ann Brown and her friends in Copenhagen. At 2:00pm, Copenhageners came together outside the US Embassy in Østerbro in solidarity with the outraged masses across the globe. She also organized the Women's March in

Copenhagen, which was one of 616 sister marches that took place globally alongside the historic Women's March in Washington D.C.

Rebel alliances, lords with an authoritarian penchant and startling command upon unlimited power, global struggles, good versus evil, machinations at once sinister, chaotic and Machiavellian. We've all seen this before, right? This is *Episode IV* in the Civil Rights struggle for humanity, right? Right.

Well, what if George Lucas is not just some all-time great filmmaker? What if he is a clairvoyant and visionary for late twentieth- or early twenty-first-century living? With a government that has boasted the talents of senior cabinet members as Steve Bannon, Jeff Sessions and Ben Carson, you no longer have to wonder if the Galactic Empire and First Order of the *Star Wars* universe are pure fiction. I mean, you can *see* Darth Vader on your television these days, right? Just tune into the nightly news… CNN, MSNBC or FOX will do. Does the Sith Lord really need the black armor, and cape and machine enhanced voice to announce his presence — or does this all feel really "real" in a way that is well, somehow *real?* Think reality TV. Who needs a fantastical space opera when we have reality television world produced for us?

But know this — *the Resistance is real*. And it always has been. In 1215, the Magna Carta was signed in England, providing the concepts of government accountability and protection of individual rights, acknowledging that even a "sovereign" is not above the law. In the eighteenth and nineteenth centuries, there was the French Revolution and the Declaration of the Rights of Man and of the Citizen. In 1902, there was the International Alliance for Suffrage and equal citizenship. The Resistance is part of that continuum.

Star Wars has its Princess Leia. Well, The Resistance has Lesley-Ann Brown, who has been in Copenhagen since 1999. From her self-publishing and entrepreneurial endeavors with Bandit Queen Press to memoir and blogging work with Black Girl on Mars to her work as a contributor with NBC. On a Google search, you will also see the smattering of praise from world travelers, artists, intellectuals and thought leaders — a leader amongst leaders. Those who know — *know* Lesley-Ann Brown.

So, Lesley-Ann Brown leads the Resistance in Copenhagen, Denmark. Below is her account of our current struggle:

I first heard of the Women's March in Washington through a parent of a former student of mine. I was employed by the Copenhagen Municipality to teach a class, every Saturday, of kids who had English as their mother-tongue. There was once a time when there were Mother-tongue programmes throughout Denmark, but despite the many studies that show such pedagogy is key in bilingual/trilingual learning, it was one of the programs that was cut heavily at the beginning of what one could call a neoliberal agenda in Danish politics.

I was thrilled to have gotten the job. I beat a lot of other teachers for the job, my interviewing soon-to-be boss told me. For about four months, I would have a group of varying ages, every Saturday, to work with. I was thrilled.

Until I read the teacher's lesson plan.

I took over the class in January and the teacher, a fellow American, had decided that there was no better time to teach the class about Martin Luther King Jr. as January was the month that his birthday is celebrated. Now, as a Black person reading this, I'm sure you're thinking, "Wow! That's cool!" But to a Black woman who has been teaching in Denmark for over 10 years — I have to say that when it comes to teaching lessons about race and its historical impact to a class of mostly white students, I was weary.

This comes from many years of experience. This comes from having to witness the discomfort and eventual boredom with a subject that unfortunately, many just don't want to relate to. Don't get me wrong: I've taught many a class about the role of race and its historical implications to passionately engaged students. But when it's a mostly white classroom, well, the disconnect is alarming. This disconnect is worsened by the parents' insistence that well, "Those things don't happen in Denmark."

But being the professional that I am, I forged through with the task at hand. Mostly white, varying from ages seven to twelve, we spent a few Saturdays talking about Martin Luther King Jr, the Civil Rights Movement and where we are today. To be fair, the class was interested and it helped matters even more that we ended up reciting Langston Hughes' A Seat at the Table, which the class had to recite in front of the entire school. Although shy, and not prepared for the crowd that showed up that day, my class recited this poem about racial acceptance, somewhere in Copenhagen on a grey day.

Axel was one of the students who was particularly interested in the subject. I'll never forget the day when he asked, "Why is it that all the good people end up getting killed?" Talk about difficult questions and moments in a classroom.

So when Axel's mother reached out to me, I was just happy to be still connected to a parent. And then she told me about the march and how she and some other American women were planning a sister march in Copenhagen.

I said yes because of Axel. I soon learned that that yes was a gift, not only to the others involved, but to myself as well. I've been reading every last criticism of the march: and most of them I can agree with. I understand the cynicism many of us in the Black community have towards the Women's March, and the charges that it was a "white women's march." It didn't help that, less than a week after the march, articles started circulating that the woman who accused Emmett Till of making advances to her had admitted that her accusations were false. Meaning that the young boy who was brutally murdered, and whose murderers got away, including her, had died for no other reason than white supremacy. And now this white supremacy is out and loud and it had been making me quite uncomfortable.

At first, some of the other organizers were shooting for 1 million marchers in Copenhagen. Denmark has a population of 5.7 million. I and a few others focused on attendance: Let's make it about who shows up. Many of us were new to this: although I have organised before, this was definitely taking things to another level. I have organised panels and literary events here in Denmark, and while I usually have pretty healthy turnouts, I didn't think a movement that started in America would translate wholly here, although it should.

As the march's spokesperson, I was charged with talking with the media. One of the most recurring and unoriginal questions was: What does this have to do with women in Denmark? My answer? Everything. Although considered a bastion of gender equality, Denmark in numbers show a completely different story.

In 2017 domestic violence will no longer be a valid reason for a woman to lose her job and she will be protected by her union.

So, flames coming from her eyes, out of her mouth, in her voice, trailing her fingertips. The crisp scent of the air having been cleared in winter. It's all so blue. Blue. Perhaps, you're thinking cold or *cool* but it's the hottest part of the fire, the part that sets our bodies and minds afire on an undeniable quest for justice. A sanguine look upon her beautiful patient face and the erudite posture upon the one who takes roots from the West Indies and Trinidad and Tobago. The leaders for the next continuum of the Civil Rights struggle are not only alert but hard at work. Consciousnesses awaken and the people march, right? Yes, we do. We march for women's self-determination, we march for Muslims, we march for decency, we march for the marginalized, we march for the poor, we march for our children. We have *been* marching and we march *now*.

2/9/17

PLATINUM GOLDEN

TORI "LA" REID, HEALER AND THE GREATEST MEMOIRIST OF HER GENERATION

Photo by Curtis Dowd

"The wound is the place where the light enters you."
— Rumi

In Japan there is an artform known as *Kintsugi* (金継ぎ, "golden joinery"). Also known as *Kintsukuroi* (金繕い,

"golden repair"), it is the art of repairing broken pottery with lacquer that has been dusted or mixed with powdered gold, silver, or platinum. Basically, pain or brokenness is repaired with light and excellence. Broken pottery becomes art. *Kintsugi* is an apt metaphor for the pastel quilt that is *Love Yourself Through It*, the debut work of non-fiction by the Hollywood insider, creative producer and emerging cultural tour de force, Tori "LA" Reid.

Tori and I initially met at Connie Briscoe's beta format of Craft Your Novel, an online writers' craft workshop by the *New York Times* Best Selling author. She left the group, and after I had my first collection of poetry published, I reached out to her. Her marketing and branding assets — photos with the iconic Richard Pryor, a young Senator Obama and with her father, the iconic sitcom auteur Tim Reid — as well as her effortless grace and philosophical panache are hemmed in all her writing like little jewels. Her writing is reminiscent of Alice Walker's *We Are The Ones We Have Been Waiting For* or Amy Tan's *Where the Past Begins,* non-fiction opuses without any of the fuss of pity, just a wholesome pure determination to change and evolve into a poppin' loving light. I recall the wise words from the 1993 Nobel Laureate (and greatest storyteller in a generation) Toni Morrison that the readers in her circle were precious commodities with whom she spared no expense. As much as I can, I have tried to emulate this mantra with my own coterie of writers, editors and poets.

Love Yourself Through It promises to be a brash harbinger of a new culture beyond the old tropes of the feminist movement. *Love Yourself Through It* touches base on the thirty-year-old college rape at a historically Black college and university and the self-sabotage, self-care, tribulation and eventual ascension of the human spirit. It also deals with the illusion of the Hollywood myth from a second-generation insider; being at the center of that solstice of artificial manmade light of that industrial complex. It makes light of dense work.

Love Yourself Through It is a coming-of-age masterpiece of a reiki master by means other than gemstones and actual light. She has converted those conventional elements into her mind and soul, exemplifying those themes in her work — healing, clarity, inviting the light into dark corners, love, grace, beauty, using rare minerals as gold and platinum to cover over the wounds — the work is a wonder. It is spiritual *Kintsugi*.

Oh, and before we dive into the interview, *Reiki* is also Japanese. It is made of two words — the first *Rei*, meaning "God's Wisdom or the Higher Power"; the second *Ki*, which is the "life force energy." Reiki is "spiritually guided life force energy." *Kintsugi* is crafted by *Reiki* masters. And *Love Yourself Through It* is a masterful debut by Tori "LA" Reid.

Patrick A. Howell: In two recent appearances — the Pasadena Literary Festival panel discussion (Black Memoirists in Los Angeles) and on the pilot for your podcast, *Simply, Tori* — you said something about "dream catchers." Specifically, you mentioned that you come from a family of "dream catchers." Talk about what that means to you and your family. What is the difference between a dreamer and a dream catcher?

Tori "LA" Reid: My family dreams big. But more importantly, we take the necessary steps to bring our dreams to fruition. That's the difference between a dreamer and a dream catcher.

A dreamer can dream endlessly but never fulfill their aspirations and desires. The key is to venture beyond any limits to catch the dream. And that's what we do. For example, my father built the second Black-owned, full-service movie studio. Ever. The first was the great pioneer Oscar Micheaux exactly one hundred years ago. We believe in hard work, and take the necessary steps to accomplish the dream, whether it's taking risks, sacrificing time or money, seeking wisdom and direction, or using available resources. I come from a family of warriors. We go for it, no matter what. And to me, one succeeds when he or she fulfills their dream.

Catching dreams is everything.

P.H.: You've been working on your memoir for just about a decade. Speaking with literary agents in NYC, Atlanta and across the nation, you seem to be on the cusp of a breakthrough in the literary world. What is the secret to literary success according to the Tori "LA" Reid bible?

T.L.A.R.: For me, the secret to literary success begins with having a well-written and effective book proposal. Now this may take weeks, maybe even months, to write and rewrite, and perfect, but once you do, you've struck gold. It took many months for me to reach the gold. But, if only the process ended there. You're just getting started. The next secret is developing solid genuine relationships. For this, you really must not focus on getting the book deal, but really paying attention to the person on the other end of the email or phone. This is tricky because of course you're in sales mode. Your only priority is to convince someone that you have the next best thing for bookshelves around the world. But I found during the pitch, there actually was a spirit listening and maybe even hoping that you blow their mind. And so, you do your best, but you also get to know the person you're dealing with.

Persistence is key. And yes, we've read it and been told how important it is. But it's not the most comfortable thing to do, and it's certainly not the easiest. My writing partner had to hold my hand through this, and I resisted for a few months. But once you begin seeing the positive results by doing so, you won't look back and will move full speed ahead in persistence. It can feel like an arduous process. Rejection never feels pleasant, and my patience was tested a time or two. But what fueled the process was reminding myself why I wanted to write my book in the first place. For me, it was to write something that I needed during a time in my life that I also believed would help other women to know that, they too, are "enough" no matter what. Something comforting, candid, and truthful at the core. And you will have to remember your reason to keep you going. Trust me, it works.

P.H.: You recently began work on your podcast, *Simply, Tori*. Also, you have also founded a new storytelling company "Victory & Noble." Can you talk a little about each venture and how it plays into your increasing national identity as a writer and purveyor of culture?

T.L.A.R.: I think of *Simply, Tori* as a deep dive conversational podcast of all the things I love and am challenged with, and ultimately what it means to become your ultimate self. From relationships to staying in your light to sexual assault to the art of becoming unstuck, I explore all these topics with vibrancy and love. These open-minded talks are with people who inspire me, those who I love, and there are some celebrities throughout as well.

I'm very excited about Victory & Noble and the brilliant team that I'll be working alongside. The reason we call it a storytelling company as opposed to a traditional production company is because the emphasis will always be on the story itself. We are storytellers manifesting the new and ancient stories for the brilliant new age. We'll focus on book-to-film adaptations, which is a wonderful way to reintroduce books to the masses, as well as some original content.

Having been in the film and television development and production world for as long as I can remember, I have an eye for original, stirring content and a love for filmmaking. I'll play a major role as CEO in co-managing the creative aspects of literary works and developing and producing film and television projects.

P.H.: Why do you love writing? How long have you been writing and what do you love most about it?

T.L.A.R.: Writing has always been my air. I express myself better on the page. I love writing because it affords me the opportunity to express my dreams, my fears, my thoughts and my journey. My hopeful belief is that women understand that they are capable, significant, powerful and ultimately, worthy.

I love the self-discovery that happens during the writing process. For example, during a UCLA writing course, my insightful instructor asked the question, "What is the wound that drives your life?" She explained when one discovers the answer, all the questions and doubts would disappear and what was left was your driving force. Writing the answer to that question became a defining moment.

Writing began as therapy for me in adulthood, and as a child, it was my favorite way to let my imagination run free. When I should have been on some doctor's couch, I would open my journal, and it would listen. Comfort. Support whatever was on my mind and challenge me to do better. Be better. And through writing, I'm able to do just that.

P.H.: What was your first publication? How old were you? What was the title of the book? What was the book about?

T.L.A.R.: Ah, yes, my first "publication" or story I told on the page was called, "Tori and the Bubble Factory." I was nine years old when I wrote and illustrated what I thought then could be a bestseller. Insert laughter here. It was about a little girl who stumbled into a bubble factory and because she was so sweet, she could live there with her mother. I still have it, as well as the several that followed. My writing improved the more I wrote, and the stories became more interesting and original.

6/25/19

Love Yourself Though It is the debut non-fiction by the Hollywood producer and scion of a Hollywood family. She's got next.

GHAZAL COSMOPOLITAN

SHADAB ZEEST HASHMI, LITERARY ACTIVIST AND POET

The ghazal fuses the old with the new, the friend with the stranger — reflecting, refracting, and constantly reminding us that America too is a convergence of sorts, a cultivation of diversity — at least the promise of it... The ghazal fuses the old with the new, the friend with the stranger — reflecting, refracting, and constantly reminding us that America too is a convergence of sorts, a cultivation of diversity — at least the promise of it.
— Shadab Zeest Hashmi, *Ghazal Cosmopolitan*

Hip-hop is not the first and only form to use words by which the world sways. How we forget the different melodies, rhythms and times.

There is a space... a place in the world where pure poetry, serious poetry, will sift light from dark, steep reality thick with dreams and visions and form new consciousnesses. There is a place in this existence where the utterance of words with certain intention, composition and musicality will shift reality, change being; places where the mendacity of life is lifted and words reveal all of the beauty that is the balance to our unbearable pain. There is a place where poems are part of dreams, reality and every utterance in between; places where the wealthy bathe in poetry and words are currency; and, yes, places where poems are better, more powerful, than any movie ever produced. Somalia is one such place. I remember my friend and poet Ladan Osman speaking to the wonders of a land where serious poetry is central to life, and not marginalized as within Western cultures. In fact, most of the Arabic world is that way.

Pakistan is another such place. There are all sorts of poems and poetry forms — it's like Universities of poetry in Pakistan. There is Urdu written in the calligraphy style of the Perso-Arabic script. There is Nazm poetry and it is wild, except where philosophy is concerned and written in rhymed verse. Then there are Hamd (poetic pieces in praise of God), Naat... and Ghazals.

Poetry is of course a universal art, but is it possible for a particular poetic form to be not only universally (or largely) adaptable but also act as a vessel for the mercurial shifts that define the cosmopolitan?
— Shadab Zeest Hashmi

"Ghazal" is a word in Arabic that translated literally means "talking to women." However, both men and women sing and recite ghazals. Ghazals were famous in the eighteenth and nineteenth centuries. The purpose of a ghazal is to make a point in two lines and each "Sher" (as the two-line couplet is referred to in Persian) is considered a complete poem in and of itself. Minimally, a ghazal is composed of five couplets of shers, typically no more than fifteen. This ancient form of poetry originated in Arabia and traveled to the Middle East and India. Ghazals can be set to music but are oftentimes read as poetry. According to Poetry Foundation, a ghazal was "Originally an Arabic verse form dealing with loss and romantic love, medieval Persian poets embraced the ghazal, eventually making it their own. Consisting of syntactically and grammatically complete couplets, the form also has an intricate rhyme scheme. Each couplet ends on the same word or phrase (the *radif*), and is preceded by the couplet's rhyming word (the *qafia*, which appears twice in the first couplet)."

With sections titled "Silk Road Sherbert," "Have I Taken Language as a Loan" and "Ghazal, Sufism, and the Birth of a Language," Shadab's book of poetry *Ghazal Cosmopolitan* is a transportation to a different time, place and space in the world, one where beauty and pain are given equal billing. *Ghazal Cosmopolitan* is its own magic, or as its publisher Richard Krawiec has noted:

> What is brilliant about this book is that it works equally well as a collection of superb ghazals, a scholarly analysis of the history and form, and a riveting memoir. When has anyone ever done that with a poetic form?

I had the opportunity to join Shadab Zeest Hashmi for a five-part book event for *Ghazal Cosmopolitan* that included a book-signing, an hour-long program of Urdu Mushaira-style poetry reading, and live music performed by world-renowned poets and musician friends. There was also high tea and dessert. However, the Ghazals were the main thing. Some of them were read by poets, other sung by world-class musicians. Below is one by Shadab:

> Your August birth, my taking oath as an American, were only weeks apart. The most I can remember is your rocking to a dull ache before we were apart.
>
> Our hill was plush, the whole place soaked up the scent of raisin pulao. On the last day of July the umbilical cord was cut, yet still we were barely apart.
>
> I had sworn to bear arms for this country. A cat prowled between the young apple tree and dry lobelia; camouflaged, I couldn't tell her parts apart.
>
> I acted mother first when I frantically covered you, half-dreaming you were the tender bird of prey and a feline form was the country of which I was a part.

Bear arms? Kill like a predator? In other dreams I bore you through the cold months, through snow in Julian, rain in Sedona. Not for a single minute were we apart.
— Ghazal for the Ninth Month

A ghazal is magical space, a spirit from within words, a place where the stars gather on the ground that is earth, spirits leave their bodies, finely attuned to the frequencies of love, hope and sharing as harmonies played by world-renowned sitar and harmonium players. A ghazal is a place where poetry connects to the heavens aided only by waterfalls and candle lit fires.

Imagine ghazal artists gathered for the enjoyment of a small intimate group for an evening. Imagine a sitar player with a wild black mane and a sharp black mustache that is particular to another era. Imagine on that stage, another master playing a Harmonium, a small organ, and singing a hymnal in which his voice leaves his body and becomes a soul in air. Imagine a space where the lights dim around a garden and waterfalls, and a gentle spirit of remembering, knowing and love crowds a space under the stars, where mist falls upon little boys who recite their ghazals as almost a coming of age. Around this soft, undulating light people are lying and sitting on Persian carpets and pillows. Littered everywhere are pearl and crimson rose petals. There are ceramic bowls with pools of fire flames. Imagine this because ghazals are real. A ghazal is majesty. Ghazal is the sound of community;

Ghazal is a new American sound from the ancient.

REAL TALK AFRICA

ESTHER ARMAH, INTERNATIONAL RADIO PHENOM AND PLAYWRIGHT

Esther Armah was born in London to Kwesi Armah, the Ghanaian ambassador to the United Kingdom and a Ghanaian politician. She's seen some things. The 1966 military coup in Ghana was one of them. Her father was on a diplomatic mission to Vietnam. Her mother was nearly murdered and the family spent two years under house arrest before being allowed to return to England.

Back in London, Esther Armah hosted *Talking Africa*, a current affairs program, then became a reporter for BBC Radio and BBC World Service. In New York City she hosted her radio show *Wakeup Call* Mondays through Thursdays until August 2013. She was also a regular guest panelist on the MSNBC weekend shows *Up with Chris Hayes*, *All in with Chris Hayes*, *The Melissa Harris-Perry Show*, *Newsnation with Tamron Hall*, and *Weekends with Alex Witt*. She has written for *Ebony*, *Gawker*, *Salon*, and others.

When we talk, it is early afternoon my time and early evening her time. It's dark where she is in Accra, Ghana. She tells me the sun has just gone down and does so quickly. Her countenance is lit and filled with energy as if she had just woken up, had a tea and is in the early part of her day.

Esther Armah: My show airs here in Ghana, in London and across the US in Arizona, Iowa, New Jersey, New York, Mississippi, Georgia, North Carolina, Ohio,

South Carolina — so it's a blend of Black women's voices talking across borders and into communities that might never meet or know or hear us and our lens on the world. There has always been back and forth movement between the Diaspora and the Motherland. I definitely feel more people are coming back to Ghana, or seeking to see if they can work, contribute, build, create somewhere in Africa. And I think it is both spiritual and practical. I always say now I breathe racial-violence free air, and that is a sweet, sweet feeling, living thing.

Patrick A. Howell: Over a year ago, you left your home in New York City to live in Accra. Why?

E.A.: Several reasons. I have always wanted to live and bring my journalism to Accra. And I am a daughter of the Diaspora, connected to London, New York and Ghana — I want my work to reflect that. There were also personal reasons — one was my mother was turning eighty. I had been in New York for eight years and not gone back to Accra once. When I lived in London, I would travel back to Ghana every year. Plus, my emotional health — the work I do is called "emotional justice."

I use media to create space to hold tough conversations about the legacies of untreated trauma that connect us as global Black people and manifest in how we move through the world. That is also global work for me, connecting it by living it matters to me. You said my home in New York City — I consider New York a creative home where I have chosen family and a precious creative community. I am Ghanaian as well as Black British — my sister moved here, my mother lives here, so Accra is home too. I love that I breathe racial violence free air here. My body changes because of that single reality.

Of course, Accra is complex and comfortable; welcoming and alienating; full of promise and frustration equally — it is a home for me. My body and spirit and heart feel good. Home is a conversation for me — it is no longer purely geographical. I travelled to Chicago where my fourth play was being performed by ETA Creative Arts. I landed and Chicago felt like home, I had the same feeling when I traveled to Nairobi in Kenya. I did not feel that way when I went to South Africa. So, home is belonging, creative community, unexpected room to breathe.

P.H.: Do you think Pan-African literature, filmmaking, sculpture, painting, intellectualism... Black artistic expression is at a renaissance? Or, is the culture currently cast?

E.A.: Culture is never cast. Its beauty and its challenge is that it is constantly evolving. Nina Simone reminded us an artist's job is to reflect the times in which they live. The election of No. 45 provoked a profound need for connection as a White House sang a song of marginalizing the marginalized; erasing voices, creating fresh economies of violence and claiming this toxic mix would somehow make America great again. Connection between oppressed peoples and people reimagining resistance and seeking examples of organized resistance have emerged, continue to build and grow. That is powerful, and it is the part that lifts my spirit and reminds me resistance is something African peoples have done with their culture, dance, art, literature, film. This time is a particular conversation that is still being crafted.

Pan-African art is imagining a future even as it confronts the present and takes on the political in creative, imaginative and profound ways. In Accra, I am watching a creative community emerge that mixes feminism with

Pan-Africanism and technology and fashion and art and intellectuals and media. I see Ghanaian men begin to confront toxic masculinity and engage with vulnerability in ways that are antithetical to Ghana's particular brand of masculinity that mirrors the global reality of toxic masculinity. I am witness to how the Diaspora find their way and make a path to this space geographically and then construct creative homes. We are watching brilliant Ghanaian women create stories of stigmatized issues using the digital world as a connection point to wider worlds. Art is such a crucial part of our resistance. It has been historically. It is right now, in profound, unspoken and maybe unspeakable ways.

P.H.: You have been on radio for a while now – who are some of your favorite interviews?

E.A.: Radio is my first love in media.

I write, I do radio and I have been on television and been a producer for documentary television. For me radio is the twenty-first-century drum. I am born of an Ashanti woman, raised in the villages of Ghana, so the drum holds a particular power for me. There is something magical about the voice, not just the words spoken but the emotions a voice — unmatched by visuals — can convey. And the silence speaks languages when it comes to radio. I have always loved radio's intimacy, and the relationships it creates. I listen to local radio everywhere I have ever travelled, whether I understand the language or not.

Here in Ghana, morning radio is a beast. Millions and millions of Ghanaians listen to it. It carries particular power. It is male dominated. I am a commentator on Ghana's Starr FM, a national radio station. I have a twice weekly slot on their morning talk show called *Morning Starr*. I also host my show called *The Spin*. It airs globally in

Ghana, London and across the US. It is a global production team of Starr FM radio in Ghana, NPR in Washington DC, the African American Public Radio Consortium — the New York-based distributor and a Los Angeles-based editor. When it comes to favorites, I have so many. In New York, I hosted a morning talk show called *Wake Up Call* on Pacifica Radio's WBAI. From there, I loved my interviews with Oscar-nominated filmmaker Ava DuVernay. I also created a segment called *Art in the Apple* to engage and celebrate the extraordinary conscious art community. I loved so many of the interviews and discussions held through that segment.

For *The Spin*, I created a global discussion series on consent called #theCONSENTconvo. It was a public conversation campaign on consent. One of my favorites was an exchange between Nana Akosua Hanson — a Ghanaian woman and Beverley Nambozo — a Ugandan woman. They spoke of their personal journeys to consent, the betrayal of what it meant to be a virgin, a good girl, and how that shaped their experience of sex. It was a revealing series that I did in partnership with *Ebony and Essence*. I interviewed Marissa Alexander, an African American mother from Florida who fired a warning shot at her abusive husband and then got convicted and sentenced to twenty years. I was part of a national activist campaign to raise awareness about her case — and then after she was released from prison, I interviewed her on *The Spin*. One of the most painful things she said was that in order to survive prison she had to forget she had a daughter. She had to erase her daughter from her mind, body and soul in order to survive incarceration. To hear her say that stopped me. Then it made me think of enslaved African women and what they went through with children sold away, pulled from their arms and so often never seen again.

The Spin has a rostrum of amazing women of color from the worlds of academia, art, activism, journalism — I love this show. It is challenging, the production is complex, it pulls from all the different parts of my journalism experience — and I love it. It is something I created, it is something I fight to maintain — and it means so much to me. It is one of the things I am most proud of in my long journey of global media.

P.H.: What is Ghana's response to the election of Donald J. Trump?

E.A.: In Ghana, I was stunned by the amount of support Trump had among different generations of men. They spoke of his business smarts, they loved what they called his tell it like it is approach and they saw him as Alpha, powerful — the kind of men they wanted to be. In Ghana, we have something called the 'Oga' — the Oga is the head of a family, village, organization — he is Top Dog, Alpha, his word is to be obeyed, his orders are to be followed.

No. 45 reminds me of the African strongmen that have led different parts of this Continent through its turbulent years from colonial freedom to colonial legacy. Their support of him, their enthusiasm for him has been shocking. It has disgusted me. And then there have been other groups. They, like me, are appalled — as millions of Americans are — by his election, his 140-character madness and his narcissistic brand of fake news, alternative facts leadership. Frankly, though Ghana has more to fear from her economic relationship with China than from America's current political shenanigans.

Ghana claimed former President Barack Obama and former First Lady Michelle Obama. My mother's church created a special Prayer Circle for him — and this group of elders, of Ghanaian women, gathered, donned beautiful African attire and prayed for President Obama who they described as "our son." They were loved — not necessarily for their politics, but for the part of them that claimed this Continent and created a precious unbreakable connection. President Obama came to Ghana and spoke of building strong institutions. Ghana is a nation that combines contradictions of individual excellence, governmental assistance and fractured institutions. When it came to the Obamas, it was a Ghanaian kind of love. We all decided this was a man who had no time for Naija Jollof and clearly only ate Ghana Jollof.

5/4/17

Esther Armah is now Executive Director of The Armah Institute of Emotional Justice (AEIJ).

THE VERTIKAL LIFE — WHO DEFINES WHO WE ARE?

CELESTE DUCKWORTH, PUBLISHER, ENTREPRENEUR AND AUTHOR

Some of the earliest conversations I had about this idea of the Global International African Arts Movement outside of those with Marvin L. Mills were with Celeste, who would share stories about her upbringing and how the founders of the Black Arts Movement would pass through her home growing up — like Maya Angelou and Amiri Baraka. She painted a vision of how these folks who are now legends were just real ones trying to elevate the culture, elevate all of us and bring us closer to our whole purpose. To be frank, Celeste was in a period of mourning over the loss of her friend, confidant and former fiancé Norman Anderson. Our conversations were healing ones about a common vision, a love of literature and the poetry of when we come together. It was a conversation about the people coming together.

Patrick A. Howell: Celeste, since 2016 you and I have been working together on podcasts as part of the Global International African Arts Movement. I have known you to be diligent, faithful and prudent in carrying out your vision for the Vertikal Media family, which you have been executing since 2010. You have now been acquired by Voxnest, the largest podcast monetization platform on the market. Where do you get the inspiration to keep growing the inspiration for the Vertikal vision? What does that mean, Vertikal?

Celeste Duckworth: The word Vertikal was created by Norman A. Anderson when he first founded Vertikal as the name of a skate team he sponsored at a nearby park in Atlanta. He would go to the park daily and watch the kids on their skateboards and decided to form a team that could compete with other teams across the US. He even had team t-shirts made that he had in twenty-seven stores on the East Coast. His message to the boys was "Live True, Live Free," always moving up with a no-nonsense life, and their parents and his friends felt it was so uplifting that he should start a magazine as a way to spread positive messages and *Vertikal Magazine* was born. We both had the same passion when it comes to helping people and he admired my creativity being the first magazine to publish four of my poems.

We had a lot of dreams about how we would grow the magazine and help others in the process. God has breathed a lot of ideas and inspiration into this vision in the way of creating departments that could support Vertikal! Like our Digital Marketing Collaborations and Publishing Section of Vertikal Media Group. Making sure everything aligned to form a worldwide media and communications company. Today we have four digital marketing collaborators and five affiliate magazines in the UK and Canada.

Although Vertikal is 80% virtual we run it exactly like a brick-and-mortar office with departments, protocols, strategic meetings and looking as far as we can into the future. I am inspired by my Father in heaven, my family and friends, the people we want to inspire and enhance their knowledge. We want to change the narrative of the media worldwide. There is no place else to go but up.

P.H.: I know that you grew Vertikal from the love of your life and you now extend that legacy of love to your children and grandchildren as a legacy of community, conversations that move the human family forward and promoting the culture of books, poetry and reading. Vertikal Life's mission is to "uplift, educate and inspire social change in our local neighborhood for the betterment of our global community." Where do you go from here?

C.D.: 2019 is a year of intention and growth. So it is time to set up the scholarships, the workshops, and teen camps that we have been writing protocol for over the last few years. *Vertikal Life Magazine* gets closer to being the *Life Magazine* of the world, while having more inspirational and empowering programs through Vertikal Radio. Starting our social enterprise and taking our first creative venture that is a real retreat for the writer and refreshing of thought! We want to make more connections with individuals from other countries to create sustainable bridges within other countries where we can help each other grow from mutual collaborations and co-ops.

Our programs such as *Women on the Rise* where we wanted to feature women who were pursuing their passions after leaving corporate America, or maybe a stay at home mom with a great idea for other moms. Many women such as Tara Richter, Micki Esposito, Laura Bulluck, and *Star Trek*'s Marina Sirtis have told their stories of following their dreams after tough family situations that were truly inspiring for us to hear. *The Reading Room* was for my mom who passed away after a long illness. There were many nights my mom was up and couldn't sleep and I thought about how she loved to listen to our weekly radio programs and we enjoyed talking about them after they were over. *The Reading Room* was designed to help give people a chance to experience the imagination-based entertainment of America's Radio Days with online book readings which are set to music.

We are hoping to expand with more authors donating their books and a few wonderful readers to read those books. Then we have Vertikal Media Group — we saw a need to help small businesses create their digital presence online. So we developed a small consulting section where we develop websites, mobile apps, tools for marketing and promotion to help them become more efficient and sustainable. This year we will introduce our own Vertikal Life Mobile App that will include easy access to our programs. One project we hope to announce at the end of the year is SouthCentral. Shop, a way for small businesses in small communities to have digital marketing services at an affordable price.

P.H.: Most know you as the visionary who does the big ticket items with Vertikal but you also do quite a bit of the day-to-day work like production, training and the following-up on strategic partnerships. The marketing pieces you create — visuals for the podcasts — are always positively charged and carry energy for the new-new. Where did you learn your skills as a graphic design artist?

C.D.: Growing up, I painted acrylics on canvas and some mixed media, posters. Everything on my walls when I had my first apartment I had painted. Or it was mixed media. I think creatives have a variety of talents they are partial to. I could sing, play the guitar, and when I found my voice, write. My sense of colors comes from my mom's love for travel: we would go down to Mexico or Oregon to pick berries in the summer or Arizona to visit my aunt. Every trip was a history lesson and the colors of the ocean and the forests were very colorful and never the same. So most of the graphics I did previously was mostly skill and talent and then I took some graphic editing classes when I went to college but I still trust my intuitive energy to make color choices and what the design should be, so it all flows according to my energy aligning with my source of strength in art.

P.H.: What individual writing projects are you currently working on? How do they feed into your greater vision?

C.D: Oh my! LOL!
   Lucy – editing
   The Thirteenth Dimension — novel
   "The Truth of Cultural Appropriation" — essay
   "The Clearing" — short story
   "Embracing Identity"
   "Where the Red Leaves Fall" — short story
   "Pygmalion" — re-visited poem
   The Focus
   Letters to my Children — thoughts, prayers, praise
   Promises of God – every child's handbook

All my writing started in speculative fiction. I love what-if conversations. They are my call to action to the reader to look deeper. There are a lot of things in real life with science, biology, and genetics we can't answer. But a lot of my writing has to do with the Legacy and the knowledge I share about how to overcome life.

But I also like rebuking false history and teaching truth. Like I believe Vertikal can change the narrative of news and information. I believe my writing can do the same thing. I'm not just a Black female writer I am a writer.

P.H.: Why Arizona? Why not Atlanta where your family is or San Diego where you grew up in Southern California?

CD.: Family resides in your heart and really should not be a factor when deciding where you live. I've followed that inner voice from California to Virginia, to Ireland to Arizona.

Many miss out on opportunities within their own life and even in pursuing their passion by making emotional decisions. Not saying if you want to live around family not to do it but I am saying you need to spread your wings, broaden your horizon. I look at Abraham and how God said take your family, which included his wife and people of his household and who worked for him, and go to a new place. His family was in his heart and he had roads to pave.

Growing up in Los Angeles gave me my love of wanting to know who people are, their likes, dislikes, and dreams. That mixture of cultures and grit mixed with dreams and history with just enough mysticism was attractive to me. Riding my bike down hills as fast as I could. Going down to Santa Monica beach and body surfing every day in the summer brought a different freedom to me.

Atlanta was never in the running. I didn't get to meet my family there until I was an adult and started being interested in my family history. There were a lot of questions I felt in my soul about who I was that kept coming to the surface. Why I liked certain foods or didn't like. We were more connected to our family that had migrated from Atlanta to Ohio so we really did have a sense of Atlanta.

Arizona was my childhood safe haven. Many of our childhood hardships happened when our parents were working hard or going through relationship issues in their adult world. We were sent to stay with my Aunt Joan and Uncle Bern. Uncle Bern was a Dean and well-respected educator and AME Pastor and Aunt Joan was a speech pathologist and English Composition and African American Literature professor, a published author, poet, award-winning playwright and deaconess.

The landscape alone in some places is spiritual, with the smell of desert sage after rain. They were memories I used when I needed peace and to keep me calm. It's not my real home but it's one place that I connect with.

6/15/2017

IS THERE A WAR IN AMERICA?

WORLD TRAVELLER AND FREE SPIRIT MARVIN L. MILLS II, CO-FOUNDER OF THE GLOBAL INTERNATIONAL AFRICAN ARTS MOVEMENT

I hope and pray for the unity of the people
hands clasped initial glance reveals
I may have the world in my hands
but this, man is just a man,
but didn't God put power in my hands?
a Black man from a land where my ancestors backs and hands
have been deconstructed into the soil and the oceans and the USA
mansions and wall streets and territorial expansions and
the sand.
— Marvin L. Mills II, *Black Man Eyes: The Collective — Is There a War in America?*

I have known Marvin L. Mills II for nearly ten years now, since he was a standout student at Loyola Marymount and a prodigy of social commentator and professor Dr Michael Datcher. He found me on LinkedIn and we bonded over a love of words, arts and all things African. Together we co-founded the Global International African Arts Movement (or the Global I Aam). He has honed his craft as a writer, refined and tested his beliefs with world travels, enlarged his expanse. He has reimagined himself, stronger. He has increased his expanse, polished his powers. In the coming months, he will release his new album *Black Man Eyes: Pasttime*. At the time of writing, he has lived, worked and traveled in seventeen countries, from South Korea to

Ethiopia, from Ghana to Vietnam. Herein, a kaleidoscope view into the world that is Marvin L. Mills II.

Patrick A. Howell: Talk a little bit about *Black Man Eyes: The Collective*. Volume 1 came out last year. That joint was subtitled, "Is There a War in America?," very apropos and visionary given that it predated the current divisions and schisms within the American soul. It did well on the underground scene with academics, hip-hop heads, bloggers — kind of like those old school hip-hop mixtapes. Talk a little about what you were trying to accomplish with the cult classic. Can you talk about the reception to that work?

Marvin Mills: The goal was to collect together these diverse, Black male perspectives I was coming across as I connected with other brothas around the world, perspective I felt needed to be heard and published as authentically as possible. I don't think the in-depth, wrestling and intimate Black male perspective is heard enough. The collection was downloaded both in the USA and abroad, probably natural considering the contributors. It also made some feel uneasy, and that's cool, too.

I think there's a fight for the soul and the identity of a country, and both sides understand that much more clearly now, and both sides understand that much more clearly than, I think, any time since the Civil War.
— Michael Voris, right-wing commentator

War is when two sides don't agree with each other's ideologies
War is when the line has been crossed and there's no room for apologies
War is tanks, artillery and soldiers on the front line

*So, is it war to put a Black man in the back of a van and break his
damn spine?*
War is airplanes unless it's a drone in the hood
War is army fatigue unless you protest for good
The police, only officers I know are my sis and my pastor
*I thought the police couldn't touch me when I first obtained my
masters*
Police, police our cities supposedly to stop all of the bad
*A young man went to the store for iced tea and skittles, now
someone's dad is hella sad, hell... I'd be mad*
— L.A. Durrah, "War, Police, Black Man," *Black Man Eyes: The
Collective — Is There a War in America?*

P.H.: Your website is another brand in your MLM
conglomerate. The website's subtitle is: "From LA to Spain,
from Seoul to Ghana, the music and writings of Marvin Lee
explore self and world. Hip-hop inspired, jazz infused and
globally cultivated. Get the perspective. It's pasttime." First
of all, congratulations on your global and inner travel. You
are a wealthy man. That's a lot of tracks on the spiritual,
professional and emotional planes — congratulations
brother. What do you have coming down the pipeline for
2017?

SeoulFi, December, 2014

M.M.: I'm finally coming out of my creative shell. I've got a music project entitled *Black Man Eyes: Pasttime* that will be available via my website March 4, which is actually my birthday. Everyone can go there right now and sign up to be one of the first to get access to the full project download when it drops. Folks can also listen to a couple tracks from the project over on Soundcloud.

Pasttime offers insight into my journey as a man seeking truth and knowledge of self while exploring around the world, and I'm excited to share it with people. A couple other things in the works that I won't share just yet.

What I can say is that my mission is to help people pursue and realize a global and abundant life, no matter the setbacks or circumstances.

Our fathers fought bravely. But do you know the biggest weapon unleashed by the enemy against them? It was not the Maxim gun. It was division among them. Why? Because a people united in faith are stronger than the bomb.
— Kenyan writer Ngũgĩ wa Thiong'o

P.H.: Your travels to Africa, including Ethiopia, Ghana and South Africa, coincided with Henry Louis "Skip" Gates forthcoming National Geographic series *Africa's Great Civilizations*. You two met there, right? Both on trips of discovery of self and larger discovery and exploration for one's peoples? Talk a little about that meeting and what it meant.

M.M.: It was great meeting big brotha Skip over in Lalibela, Ethiopia. Often times when watching discovery or travel shows the destinations can seem so far away but exploring the rock hewn churches of Lalibela and meeting Skip Gates was like my ten-year-old self sitting on a couch at home in Los Angeles, watching one of Skip's shows and suddenly being sucked into the TV screen right where he is. It was cool. He is cool.

I see meeting Skip Gates as an omen in line with those young Santiago came across in *The Alchemist*, like a whisper in my ear or a signpost that said "keep goin."

P.H.: Finally, Marvin, can you talk a little about the Global International African Arts Movement or Global I Aam?

M.M.: Back in 2012, you and I, Patrick, we were discussing what we saw happening online and around the world — this emergence of melanated artists, intellects, travelers, painters, singers, musicians, entrepreneurs and more — and that these individual examples of African excellence existed but that it wasn't as clearly evident because everything was so spread out, and that is how Global I Aam was born, out of our interest in there being some curation of what we were seeing.

Global I Aam is that spirit in us folk of Afrikan descent that *we* manifest as we create, travel, endeavor, struggle, endure, provide, resist and imbue the world with our being.

P.H.: Thanks Marvin for your time and insights. They don't come cheap nor easy. They come with a singular dedication and agape for one's people — a deep abiding passion greater than any current divisions in our community. Your spirit comes by way of the ancestors and numerous mentors who have seen the light shine bright in your entrepreneurial aspirational soul. Keep me updated on your work and continued milestones — I want to make sure your work, love and hallmarks reach the broadest possible audience. Maaaan, it's not even Kwanzaa but I'll say it anyhow – Ujoma! Sankofa! Hotep!

3/10/17

FUTURE. LOVE. PARADISE.

NANA AND ESSIE BREW HAMMOND, SISTERS, ENTREPRENEURS AND FASHIONISTAS

But if only you could see them
You would know from their faces
There were kings and queens
Followed by princes and princesses
There were future power people
From the loved to the loveless
Shining a light 'cause they wanted it seen.
— Seal, "Future Love Paradise"

Anyone who knows me, knows I have been humming those bars for over two decades now like some kind of a savant... we're talking Dustin Hoffman in *Rain Man*, something real special savant. I'll be in San Francisco International Airport and just start whistling it (yes, it sounds good, perfectly sweet, vibrating at those higher frequencies). Or, sitting with other parents at the swim club, watching my son, SharkHeart, prepare for the Junior Olympics, I'll have at it. Hell, I could be doing the dishes after SuperBowl Sunday and just start humming the bars in anticipation of Monday. It's religion, a hymnal. It is a philosophical query and sedative. Released in 1991 by Nigerian-British pop superstar Seal, its themes are afro-futuristic, new age and, if you ask me, biblical. It is about a new generation doing special work on the planet and opening new ways of being and doing business. I guess that is the long "smart" explanation for the fact that song just feels so good. It is aspirational and all sorts of wonderful like a bowl of mangoes, kiwis, strawberries and pineapple drizzled with honey and sprinkled with cinnamon magic dust.

You can tell the intro part of the melody is sampled from the Marvin Gaye's "Inner City Blues," which is genius because Marvin's song, while filled with melody magic, is about things other than Future Love Paradise, like hustling hard to survive. Marvin Gaye's "Inner City Blues" is about the struggle — Marvin sings in the opening bars, "Money, we make it/For we see it you take it/Oh, make you wanna holler" — and the struggle is real. And this is cool because the struggle that is rapped about in Marvin Gaye's anthem is the rejoinder decades later for "Future Love Paradise" by one Seal Henry Olusegun Olumide Adeola Samuel.

And the fact that these two songs are decades apart means they are part of the African oral tradition — that is how we tell our stories and make them last century after century, millennium after millennium. It is part of the call and response mechanism that is part of that tradition. It is magic — *that Black magic*. It's the African system of politics and self-love at work, in real time.

Recently I saw some holiday Instagram posts by Essie and her sister Nana Brew Hammond, and it instantaneously recalled "Future Love Paradise" to mind. In 2017, they are living the song's lyrics out loud in the stunning primary colors of reality.

In fact, the holiday on which the photos were taken took place during a period of time in which Ghana elected a new president. About the election, Johnnie Carson, former US assistant secretary of state for Africa, said: "This is about the most professionally run electoral process that I have seen in Africa in the last twenty years."

But that's politics. What I'm talking about is what these songs sing about — our collective, universal *humanity.*

Patrick A. Howell: I saw a December tweet from Ghana's president-elect Nana Akufo-Addo with the caption, "Thank you Ghana. #ChangeHasCome." It's interesting as that seems a direct quote from a 2008 president-elect Barack Obama. In personal, cultural, visionary and social terms, what sort of change has come to Ghana, if any?

Nana Brew-Hammond: Ghana has definitely changed in the last twenty-seven years that I've been paying attention, but I don't think one man, woman, or politician can take credit for it. It's true that the 2016 election marked the first time in Ghana's history that an incumbent was democratically denied a second term in office, but this is one of many changes in the country that have been accruing over time.

When I came to secondary school in Ghana in 1990, it was under the military dictatorship of Flight Lieutenant Jerry John Rawlings, and I remember family members warning me not to discuss politics or political leadership with anyone. That real fear of retribution for openly speaking out against the government slowly gave way to an outspoken free press and citizenry when Rawlings transitioned from dictator to democratically elected president in 1992.

Ghana was also far less developed in terms of infrastructure when I first came to school here. The old colonial neighborhoods in the capital, Accra, were built up for the most part, while shanties, buildings under construction, and large tracts of dirt road, bush, and swamp dominated the landscape. There were no street names. There were fewer hospitals and university options.

Today, some neighborhoods are unrecognizable for all the development. Many more roads are paved, you can't see the shanties behind the homes and shops that have risen around them, and the streets were recently named or renamed. Hospitals and universities have sprung up as well, giving citizens more options for these services and access to specialized service.

Now, the economy needs to catch up so all Ghanaians can afford to participate in the development and enjoy quality housing, healthcare, and education, as well as reliable access to clean drinking water and electricity.

P.H.: Nana, in our last conversation you noted an impassioned exchange between author Taiye Selasi, Awam Amkpa and Wole Soyinka of Pan-African, intergenerational relations. Having crossed over from 2016 to 2017, in Ghana, during this interesting period in world history, you are a witness to the African Diaspora as it is, not as we wish it to be. Not as we hope it to be. But as it is and can be. What do you see? Please give personal, familial observations. I don't want us to be political — I want to be literary and visionary.

Specifically, you noted:

I loved when Selasi asked Professor Soyinka and Amkpa [shared] their thoughts on why their generation can be dismissive of African-Americans as "second-hand" Africans. Professor Soyinka noted, in part, that the relationship between African, American, and Caribbean Blacks, has been bumpy for a long time, going back to the 1950s, '60s and '70s. He recounted that, until Ghana won independence, many American Blacks did not want to be associated with Africa and their African identity. He also noted that in London, Africans felt like "princes" and looked down on Caribbeans as "the labor."

N.B-H.: There is a sense among Ghanaians that Ghanaians born or living in other countries are not authentically Ghanaian, and, therefore, they treat us like foreigners. For example, we tend to be given the foreigner rate for certain goods and services or otherwise taken advantage of for not being familiar with certain cultural mores. It is hard to quibble in good conscience over a few Ghana Cedis when one US dollar is currently worth more than four GHS, one Euro a little more than that, and one British pound is equivalent to over five GHS, especially since goods and services in Ghana tend to be much cheaper than what they would be in America or Europe, but it hurts to be seen and treated as a stranger, and reinforces separation and division.

Conversely, among many Ghanaian diasporans, there is a sense that we know better than those born and raised in Ghana or poor Ghanaians because of our education abroad and access to foreign goods, services, experiences, and opportunities. This attitude also contributes to an Us vs Them mentality and calcifies divisions.

I think as Ghanaian diasporans visit more regularly or move to Ghana, which I've seen happen in increasing numbers in recent years, and there are more instances of everyday connections between Ghanaians of all stripes, some of this tension will naturally abate. If Ghana's government concurrently spurs economic growth to erode the disparity of purchasing power, and puts regulations in place to control selective price gouging, that will help too.

P.H.: Essie, I have not had the opportunity to "meet you" yet but feel I know you through your sister and social media. Your family is wonderful. There seems to be strong emphasis on education, success and family with your mother, father, brother and sister. You are an accomplished teacher and Nana has been known to flourish with the pen and paper. Also, both of you seem to be, well... fashion divas. Tell me a little more about the society of sorority that exists between you and Nana. Specifically, it seems like you two have fun, grow and learn from one another?

Essie Brew-Hammond: As big sister to Nana and our brother, I am committed to keeping our tripod secure. It's about loving each other unconditionally, supporting our growth, and motivating one another to do better and be our best. For us, that means taking time to develop our shared interests.

Nana and I have always loved fashion so we enjoy coming up with designs and getting clothes made by Ghanaian tailors and seamstresses. I, in particular, have always been drawn to the modeling aspect of the industry because it challenged the idea that there was only definition of beauty and showed the power women are capable of.

I grew up in the age of Naomi Campbell and her fellow supermodels. They were these young women changing the culture and commanding top dollar for it, with no apologies. Even more inspiring, they were flipping the superficial to do impactful things. Naomi reportedly donated to South Africa's African National Congress in support of Nelson Mandela, and later stood with Mandela to raise money for his Children's Fund. Meanwhile, Christy Turlington was using her platform to advocate for global maternal health.

As a teacher, when my scholars tell me I look like a model and ask why I'm in the classroom with them, I'm quick to let them know it's important to me to be a model teacher and help them become the model citizens I know they can and will be if they are equipped with a good education.

2/29/17

SO, WHAT IF GOD IS A BLACK MAN AND WHAT IF THE MOVEMENT IS A SPIRITUAL ACT, A SACROSANCT OBLIGATION OF AFRICAN SOULS?

DARNELL L. MOORE, ACTIVIST AND AUTHOR

Change will not come if we wait for some other person or some other time. We are the ones we've been waiting for. We are the change that we seek."
— Attributed to poet June Jordan before Barack Obama's historic 2008 campaign

I've come to "know" brother Darnell L. Moore through his media presence and his social media — the videos, articles by him and about him on MSNBC and in the *Guardian*, *Ebony*, the *Root and the Advocate,* his postings on Facebook and Twitter and Instagram. And it is interesting — he keeps bringing to my mind the Nation of Islam. And it's not that I am a nation member. And he is a devout Christian, who for a period attended seminary school and has been a visiting scholar at Yale's Divinity School. Perhaps it is Darnell's dark skin, or that beard. But those are superficial observations when compared to the essence of his erudite unapologetic *Blackness.* Yes, yes, yes — that negritude.

Africa comports herself within his svelte frame. A razor-sharp intellect exudes itself from his eyes, which at times come off as onyx in photos. Yes, there is the warrior within him. So, I guess, I sense an African Warrior King. Perhaps, it is the sartorial splendor in which he cloaks himself — a lot of blacks and grays to offset his mahogany skin and salt-and-pepper beard. All of the wools. Also, there is a kindness, the grace and presence of a gentleman. He is a man *outside* time and there is no doubt where his allegiances lie.

There is something *defiant* and *militant* in his presence. Something combative to those who are not with him. Something embracing. The ultimate protector of those to whom he has assigned himself. I guess you might say he is a prince or an angel man or something like that.

Now, hear this: revolution has never been strictly about war. So, I'm not suggesting violence. Matter of fact, revolution or change may be absent any sort of violent conflict. *But there is always a battle to be won or lost. What is going on in America now is every bit as spiritual as any battle in the field.* The struggle can be about elevating the battle to the highest possible frequency ("when they go low, we go high"). What I seem to sense from brother Darnell L. Moore is the majestic characteristic of *courage*. And that is where the spirit of the warrior comes from — that intangible quality that defines a generation of Civil Rights warriors and is now characteristic of the generation which has *already* emerged from within our midst — if you will.

It was a cool ride communicating, sharing and exploring with Darnell who was gracious, inspiring and fearless in his answers including... is God a Black man?

Patrick A. Howell: Darnell, you have been doing a lot of work with our youth. What do you see with the generation that has grown up with a "Black president" in the White House? Their promise and potential, their obstacles as well?

Darnell L. Moore: Black youth who have come of age under President Obama have an extraordinary optic through which they can view the world. Those of us who grew up before Obama's tenure had reason to dream about the possibility of a Black person being elected to the nation's highest office. Some, like James Baldwin, were a bit more circumspect of the prospect. But younger generations lived through the manifestation of some of those dreams. The paradox at the center of this manifestation is the stark difference between the symbolic representation of a first Black president and the material realities of the violence that still impacted Black people despite having a brown skinned biracial seemingly progressive man in office. Trayvon Martin was killed by George Zimmerman, who walked free after shooting him, under the nation's first Black POTUS. And so many Black people continued to die at the hands of police, many of whom did so with impunity, during the same time sparking a fiery social movement that sought to name and dismantle anti-Black systemic forms of state and structural violence impeding Black wellbeing and ending Black lives. This paradox ate away much of the hope that Obama's ascent may have engendered.

P.H.: Darnell, you spend a lot of time in the community, doing the hard work and projecting that work out to global communities. I might be talking about the macro of your work in our communities but I am specifically referring to your work on the Mic series, the Movement. This is Black History Month (wow, they give us, the creators, a whole month) — but in this spirit, one produced from by our ancestors, in the spirit of "the revolution will not be televised," what's the situation in Africa America?

D.L.M.: The series offered a glimpse into the lived realities of Black people across the US. It exposed how the differences in region, socio-economic status, gender and other markers of difference shape the lives of Black people. For example, the lives of Black people who live in the rural south are similar to and different from the lives of Black people who live in the northeast part of the country. Those types of differences demand our attention. I was also interested in highlighting the people who daily combat the social issues so many of us complain or talk about. What I hope viewers gained was a sense that so many Black and brown people across the country are at work bettering their communities with and without fanfare.

P.H.: Is there any element of your spirit, mind and body that channels ancestor James Baldwin? Maya Angelou? If so, what is the transmission?

D.L.M.: That's an interesting question to consider. I don't know if I channel Baldwin or Angelou, but I know I've been shaped by their works and the animating presence of their spirits in the world. I do recall calling upon June Jordan for wisdom when traveling through Palestine. I wrote the first rough draft of a collective statement the group I traveled with later edited and adopted as its official statement on the occupation. The clarity, power, courage, and love that was present when writing those words on a small bus in the West Bank is owed to June Jordan. So much of my strength is owed to my ancestors.

P.H.: Given that this is "Black History Month" give the most influential activists that inform, motivate and inspire your current work. Living and ancestors are apropos — as long as they inform your spirit.

D.L.M.: There are so many activists, artists and intellectuals who inspire me, but I count Cheryl Clark, M. Jacqui Alexander, James Credle, the late Essex Hemphill and Joseph Beam, Charles Stephens, Robin Kelley, Monica Dennis, dream hampton, Thenjiwe McHarris, Monifa and Lumumba Bandele, and Baldwin as people and spirits who make up a congregation of inspiration. I watch and learn from their examples.

P.H.: Do you listen to Prince? His music just came out on Spotify, Apple etc. What is his best album? Which songs do you listen to on repeat?

D.L.M.: I love Prince. I was so in love with him as a kid. *Around the World in a Day* was my all-time favorite. I lost myself while listening to that album.

P.H.: Did you participate in what was the first Resistance march on January 20th? It was called a Women's March but it was an opportunity for the anti-Trump forces to come together and organize. Can you see into 2019/2020 and where the Resistance will go? Is it Black Lives Matter or Occupy Wall Street by other means? Or, is this something altogether different?

D.L.M.: I didn't participate in the Women's March but I did party with some amazing women who did. In the near future, I foresee the forging of more coalitions. I sense solidarity will be a practice many will need to perfect and not just theorize.

P.H.: In your work and social media presence, family seems to factor into a big part of who you are. How does that sense of family carry over into your work?

D.L.M.: My family means the world to me. It is through their example and relationships I've come to understand the true meaning of radical love. If I preach a thing in public but refuse to offer those dearest to me the thing I preach, I fail. And if my family can't get free, I never will... and I should not talk about freedom if my family is not part of my vision for liberation, if I can't help to create the conditions for their survival, wellbeing and happiness. All I know and all I am, my family — in Camden, NJ — made possible.

P.H.: Do you believe God is a Black man?

D.L.M.: I believe God is best conceived as non-gendered. The God concept I imagine and prefer is one that escapes notions of gender that we create. God is gender non-conforming. A god that is shaped by patriarchy, whose being is deeply steeped in sexist and misogynist ideas, can't be imagined as a source of freedom. For me, I prefer not to render God as a Black man. While I believe that god favors the plight of Black people under the conditions of anti-Blackness, I strive toward a God concept that is incarnate, lived through the lives of those who exist on the underside of power and Empire. Maybe "God" is best understood as a feminine spirit, as queer. What if God is the collective spirit of all those things we despise under white racist capitalist heteropatriarchy? I want to imagine God uninhibited by such trivial human-made forms of identification.

2/24/17

IF I WERE AN AMERICAN

RICHARD PAA KOFI BOTCHWEY, AUTHOR

So the emails weren't classified at the time and the new emails have nothing to do with Hillary, but we should lock her up. Meanwhile, a man of little experience or knowledge, who is a self-admitted sexual predator, a self-admitted tax evader, who ran a fraudulent university, who wants to befriend our enemies and alienate our allies, and who insults everyone he pleases might run the most powerful country on the planet. Am I in some new Wonderland — or am I dreaming and can't wake up?
— Author Gillian Royes, on Facebook

When I asked international author Richard Paa Kofi Botchwey to respond to the above quote, he said:

I've tried taking my eyes off the life and engagements of Donald Trump ever since he landed himself on the American political scene. Quite shocking to see him still in the race, and with thousands of Americans rooting for him to become the president of America. Few days ago I saw a video of him in which he was pressing the private parts of two half naked white women on the streets. I was disappointed. I felt we are not giving honor to our women. My worry is, what sort of leader and role model is he? He doesn't motivate me one bit. He's been given too much attention. Rather shocking to see how the press keeps pushing him. For me, he's not someone I'd like to have as a president. Clearly, should he become president, more women are going to be raped; very likely the private parts of our women are going to be played with just as he played with the private parts of the women in the video. African Americans are going to suffer under his regime. Because I can tell he's bigoted. He is willing to win so he can punish his enemies. And the reality is, anyone regardless of your color can be his enemy. And that's clear that he's his own enemy. I do not hate him as a person. But I personally think he's not ready to become a president. A nation isn't ruled by a double-minded person. America has come too far to backslide. He is not near Barack Obama. And there is something Americans ought to realize. Donald Trump is giving us countless reasons why Barack Obama will forever be exceptional and a favorite of many Americans.

With his forthcoming and third novel *If I Were An American,* Richard provides Americans with an interesting opportunity to see ourselves through the lens of the world. While we are in the thick of a political storm, he is on the dry lands of Accra, Ghana with a clear-eyed periscope, offering a clean perspective of a bloody election battle that, perhaps, should not be as spiritually disruptive as it is.

Richard Paa Kofi Botchwey is an internationally published Ghanaian writer, essayist, poet, author, photojournalist, and a social entrepreneur. His first book, *The Tale of an Orphan: A Lesson to Learn*, has transcended borders. He has travelled across Europe and Africa, inspiring thousands of people with his amazing story. In his tours abroad, he has appeared on the *Pauline Long Show* (Sky) and Trinity Broadcasting Network in the United Kingdom, as well as several television and radio shows in Ghana, and online publications and newspapers. The Urban Books, Authors and Writers of America ranked the book among their Top 100 Books of 2013.

Richard Botchwey is a generational thought leader and incredible socially-oriented business mind who believes that "even in ashes, there is hope." In October 2015, he was nominated for a Black Entertainment Fashion Film Television & Arts Award in the Best Author category in the United Kingdom, and is the 2015 winner of the Africa Youth Award for Literacy Excellence.

His forthcoming book, *If I Were An American*, offers further insights into the unique period of time we are currently inhabiting. The following excerpt, in which Adjoa India, a twenty-year-old woman from the Cape Coast, reflects on the election of America's 44th president, Barack Hussein Obama, was specially granted by Richard for the purposes of this article:

When I heard in 2009 that Senator Barack Obama had won the American election and was the first Black president of the United States of America, I thought he was that child they said I was going to give birth to. That night I couldn't sleep. I couldn't sit either. I felt like kiting over the neighborhood like an owl. I stood up in front of the TV with my hands resting on my breast. On and on I hopped, danced, and sang: You'll win when you believe by Whitney Houston. What I felt was bigger than happiness. Can't be compared to feelings. And I'm not sure I have a word for what it was. If you know of any word after happiness, I don't mean synonym, then that's it. Papa was watching Barack Obama on the screen like how men watch a woman especially when they can see her nipples or booty through her see-through dress. I felt like a spinach leaf dipped in boiling water but now swimming in a cool pool. Again and again I kept asking myself, "Is this actually happening? Is my son now the president of America?" I just couldn't believe it. My soul was stupefied. I called Barack to come for me, so I could go with him to the White House. I don't know what happened, Barry hasn't returned any of my calls ever since. Maybe now that he's ex-president of America, he'll... I don't know. I'm just saying something though I don't believe it's too late. Barack, Bara, Barack...how many times have I, Momma called you? What's keeping you from responding?

Ha! Seems I'm going insane? Nah, this howling isn't a sign of a girl-going-insane. The brains are functioning perfectly. It's just that those clairvoyants were even telling me my boobs were going to enlarge naturally in a few days. Look how my chest is flat like the chopping board in your kitchen. Look how my back is flat like iPhone 7 plus. I was told my booty will be pure in sight. They said Donald Trump likes pumpkins like me, and I was hoping to meet up with him pretty soon. D.T. is now a big-time politician. Ladies are so wild about him. I feel akin to greenly trump-ed apple left on the New York to Princeton train rails. Who knows what would become of me should a train pass on me? Those twenty-first-century clairvoyants were just rubbing lemons in my eyes every day, every year. And really could not tell why I could not stop them.

11/2/16

AMERICAN FILM MAKER

MOBOLAJI OLAMBIWONNU, DOCUMENTARY FILMMAKER, FATHER AND TEACHER

War seems to be all around us these days. Earlier this week, coverage of Iraq's offensive on the Isis stronghold of Mosul was all over the news. Russia and Syria made headlines for pausing their bombardment of Aleppo. In the United States, there is the undeclared war on Black bodies (I would call that domestic terrorism by means of systemic discrimination, but that's just me #BlackLivesMatter.) Then, there is our national political discourse on presidential politics, about which Carl von Clausewitz, the Prussian general, wisely surmised, "War is the continuation of politics by other means." So it can be stated, conversely, "politics is the theater and marketing of war by alternative measures."

So it's nice to get some news about an offensive being waged on behalf of hope, love and beauty with a project called just that — Hope, Love, Beauty. *Ferguson Rises* is the first in a series of films to be produced by the Hope, Love and Beauty Project. As I was doing research for this article, I couldn't help but feel proud of my friend Mobolaji Olambiwonnu, who is the project's director and producer. I've known Mobolaji for nearly five years now. My wife and I met him when he was launching his clothing brand, African Cowboy. Since then he has gotten married and is father to a beautiful boy.

Without hesitation, Mobolaji acknowledges, the impact his son has had on his work. "He is the inspiration for this film because without having a child I wouldn't have thought so much about the impact a future without police violence could have on our youth and even police themselves. With a child, I always think about what world we are going to be living in. I wouldn't be thinking about this movie in the same way if it weren't for him."

Mobolaji Olambiwonnu is the recipient of several awards, including the prestigious Directors Guild of America Student Filmmaker Award for his MFA thesis *The Visit*, which he made while attending the American Film Institute. He is also the CEO for Dreamseeker Media and has won two Hermes Awards for six commercials he directed for the Los Angeles Metro's new $1.8 billion dollar line to LAX airport. Mobolaji's reasons for the project seem personal and deeply rooted in the greater good, all at once and without an iota of seeming self-serving.

As an investment banker, I was curious about the film's financing and how a project like this gets made when agendas in Hollywood seem to be set by a cabal of Donald Trump and Tea Party sycophants with political and social agendas. I was impressed to see the same level of creativity exhibited around producing this film as is involved in the visioning for the film. To date, the film has been funded with a crowdfunding campaign and private angel investors. Specifically, I asked him if he needed more funding for the project.

Mobolaji said, "We have to definitely look at the possibility of raising more money. We hadn't thought about it because we brought on rapper J. Cole as an executive producer. We have raised about $400,000. Some of it came from my personal funds, and other investors. We want to raise another $300,000 and we haven't really talked about who we're going to go to next."

The 250-year-old American quest for social justice and realizing the tenants of the Dream that created the

Barack Obama presidency, are never far from the quest for financial freedom promised in the 1865's "4 Acres and a Mule." As a matter of fact, they are one and the same. The vision for the new America and one in which the spirit of Dr. Martin Luther King's vision are wholly realized, seems to have possessed Mobolaji more completely than he seems to realize, "The goal is to produce inspiring films and events that bring hope, healing, dignity and investment to communities in need across the globe," said Mobolaji in an interview with his hometown's *Pasadena Weekly*. "We're trying to bring another layer to the current conversation to help facilitate that dialogue in a way that's a bit more constructive for everybody involved."

What's the price for a Black man life?
I check the toe tag, not one zero in sight
I turn the TV on, not one hero in sight
Unless he dribble or he fiddles with mics
Look out the window cause tonight the city lit up with lights
Cameras and action
— J. Cole, "January 28th (2014 Forest Hills Drive)"

Tanayi Seabrook is a producer of *Ferguson Rises* and one of Mobolaji's and Ferguson's most passionate fans. Tanayi has performed multiple roles in the filmmaking process over the past fifteen years. Her journey in documentary filmmaking began as an associate producer of the critically acclaimed PBS/WGBH civil rights documentary series *This Far By Faith*. Tanayi then worked on the Blackside documentary called *I'll Make Me A World: A Century of African American Art and Artists*.

Tanayi speaks movingly of the journey Mobolaji and she have taken to create *Ferguson Rises*. "Mobolaji and I have worked together for four years. This project is going into its third year. We started doing smaller pieces for *Los Angeles*

Metro. I've always been drawn to Mobolaji and his work, his ethos has always been very human. When he talked to me about just the seed for Hope Love and Beauty, we began looking at ways to re-frame tragedy, something filmmakers do all the time with storytelling. Where do we find hope? What do we find beautiful? The answers to these questions are what connect us all as human beings regardless of our ethnic background, religion or socio-economic status.

"I have my own personal journey which has been really about how people think that what makes them different, makes them distinct. But when we acknowledge another person's humanity that's what makes us all one. When we think about what they love and realize that it is probably not that much different than what we love, we realize that conversations about these common threads are missing in today's national conversation.

"Both Mobolaji and I went through conflict resolution training through the city of Los Angeles. It is a program that trains people to be mediators. One of the principles in the program is training people to find commonalities and from there you can broach conversations that are more difficult."

When I asked Tanayi what was the motivating force for her involvement with the film, she said, "I felt that this was part of my life's work as well. We can get real righteous about what is right in the world but until we can have conversation one on one with one another, I think that having a broader conversation on a societal level is unrealistic. It is about changing attitudes and then practices will change, changing practices. The law should apply to everyone the same. I have two Black children and I don't want their encounters to be different than their white friends."

I asked Tanayi about how the project began and she enthusiastically responded, "We began the project in Watts because we wanted to start Hope, Love and Beauty by re-framing this historically Black community that has been portrayed as crime ridden, poor and hopeless... so that people could see that these are valuable people already. But in the middle of this project, Ferguson happened. It was with the non-indictment of officer Darren Wilson that Mobolaji knew he had to go there. That's how *Ferguson Rises* was born. There were so many elements in play for him. We went to Ferguson and went to work. I feel that *Ferguson Rises* is the next conversation in conjunction with Black Lives Matter. What we discovered in Ferguson was that the people on the other side of the protest weren't bad people."

"I think with the film we get to show that Ferguson has been framed wrong. Ferguson is a microcosm of the entire United States. I feel like this conversation that *Ferguson Rises* and the Hope, Love and Beauty Project present offers solutions around issues of police brutality, the criminal justice system and the prison industrial complex. If we don't realize our shared humanity, then we have nowhere to go — the conversations with our neighbors, in our cities and in the nation will continue to be what they are now and we can do better than this. I feel we need to look at problems from the paradigm of hope, love and beauty."

Ferguson Rises seems to be gaining traction and will be part of the larger conversation that will begin the healing and finding common ground that is required for the nation to come together.

"*Ferguson Rises* is my best and most sincere offering toward that goal. It is the story of a small town that suffered a powerful loss and became the flash point for a modern day civil rights movement. It features interviews with some of the most interesting and inspiring people we met on our many visits. Their voices form a conversation that gives us a variety of perspectives. They show us how they have transformed their own struggle and adversity into action, healing and empowerment. They teach us that even in times of tragedy and hopelessness, there still can be — and must be — room for hope, love and beauty. It is our hope that this film will provide much-needed healing around the global issues that were brought to light in Ferguson."

I asked Mobolaji, how is Mike Brown's family doing? "Mike Brown Sr and Calvina Brown are doing fine. I think they are still struggling but they are focusing that energy and doing a lot of work with the Chosen for Change foundation and specifically their work with fathers who have lost their sons to police violence. So I think that work has brought a lot of healing and fulfillment. They are both running the foundation, working on it day to day. I am grateful for their example of leadership and continued work in the community. It inspires and motivates me in my work."

Finally, I had to ask Mobolaji, "Do you think this story can change this world?" He answered with the authority of ancestors and the confidence of a warrior griot coming into his own, "I am definitely a proponent for the belief that story telling can change the world. It's been used to get us into war numerous times. It can be used to get us out of discord. It is probably the most important tool that we have at our disposal."

I'm grateful for the conversation that *Ferguson Rises* brings to a nation in search of answers. As a recovering investment banker, I will bring my skills to bear in this conversation. There are any number of good citizens and now is the time to bring our good works and love, hope and beauty to bear. Congratulations to the Hope, Love and Beauty team for seeing the future and seizing it. We're following your lead.

10/26/16

PALACE GATES

CHLOE MARTINEZ, POET AND PROFESSOR

Writing is a solo endeavor. However, it is also about camaraderie, sharing, and support. In fact, if you look at any acknowledgments page, you will find thanks being given to a host of editors, poets, writers, spouses, fans, and readers. Every writer is ensconced within a community, local or far-flung, of writers. It's like an order of Buddhist monks, or, maybe more appropriately, writers are an order of spiritual blades of grass — singular, ripe, and green, harnessing creative energy, but growing in bunches. That metaphor brings me to Dr Chloe Martinez, someone I liken to Dr Indiana Jones (calling her the "Poet Professor") because of her PhD in Religious Studies and her work on medieval India. But she is also organic to the most essential atom of a community — family — as a doting mother and amazing partner-wife.

I first met Martinez through a mutual friend, the poet Shadab Zeest Hashmi, who has hosted a number of amazing poetry events at her home. At the launch party for Hashmi's newest book, *Ghazal Cosmopolitan*, I had the opportunity to sit next to Ms. Martinez, who was giving a lot of wonderful attention to her two beautiful daughters. When we met at another reading, we made a plan to help one another reach the finish line in our current projects. The interaction has been efficient and productive, and it is illustrative of how the community of writers can work. Writing is not only solitary — it is also about the matter of our humanity, forming communities and connecting them to other worlds and higher effects.

Patrick A. Howell: Chloe, you were born in New Bedford, Massachusetts — a working-class fishing town about an hour south of Boston. Yet your work is inspired by, and you write of, ancient civilizations and literary traditions like Hindi and Sanskrit. Explain the connection between these worlds. How did Dr Chloe Martinez come to be?

Chloe Martinez: When I was growing up in my small town, I mostly wanted to be somewhere else more exciting. My parents had grown up in New York City and had gone to art school at the Cooper Union in Lower Manhattan, and New Bedford seemed to me so dull in comparison. I went to New York as soon as I could, to Barnard College, and by my sophomore year I became interested in South Asian religions. I started learning Hindi-Urdu and Sanskrit, spent half of my junior year abroad in India, and went on to get a PhD in Religious Studies. These days when I return to my hometown, I see it with different eyes. New Bedford has a fascinating history, from being a wealthy whaling town (see *Moby Dick*) to serving as a stop on the Underground Railroad (Frederick Douglass escaped to New Bedford and lived there for some time) to being the gritty, more economically depressed fishing town it is today. Because of fishing it's also always been a diverse place, with large Portuguese and Cape Verdean populations, Norwegian and Lebanese communities, and more recently, South American immigrants. And nowadays those fishing boats and old mill buildings look beautiful to me in ways they didn't when I was younger. History, diversity, and beauty in unexpected places — what drew me to India and what has always drawn me to poetry was right under my nose.

P.H.: You're working on publishing your first collection of poetry, *Palace Gate*, which I assume is a reference to portals to ancient cultures. I have had an opportunity to view your work — splendid, magical, wonderful, and whimsical — as we made our submissions to the National Poetry Series. Your work can, at times, be whimsical and at other times, profound. Do you think this collection is more from the Chloe Martinez of New Bedford, MA, or from the professor-poet who has dived into religious studies with all of her intellectual gifts?

C.M.: You are too kind! I hope it's all of those things. I think that being a scholar pushes me to think in new ways about what poetry can do — how a poem, like any other work of art, can make arguments about ethics or politics or religion, and can ultimately challenge and expand our worldviews. I write poems about things I come across as a scholar; some of the poems in this collection came out of experiences I had while doing research in India, while others were inspired by the research itself. The poem "Babur at Agra" was inspired by the Baburnama, the autobiography of the first Mughal emperor. He is known for his conquest of South Asia, but the story is so different from his perspective — it's one of exile and loss. So I think poetry can complicate the narrative just as good scholarship can. At the same time, when I write poems I get to play with language in ways a scholar can't; the potential for silliness, paradox, and experimentation, which I see as my poetic inheritance from Rumi or Kabir as well as from Kenneth Koch or Heather McHugh, is one of the reasons I write poetry.

P.H.: I have had the opportunity to work with you as we support one another in our literary endeavors. Your forthcoming *Palace Gate* is divinely ordered and balanced — from the ancient to the modern; the familiar to exotic;

traditional to experimental; profound to whimsical. What do you see as the unifying themes in your work? These are all seeming opposites but many ancient sources cite the marriage of opposites as a place of commonalities. Also, I love your title poem "Palace Gate." Its use of color, how it takes the reader and submerges us in an ancient world with the most prosaic of references, ("Red, the Toyota hatchback," "barking dogs") to the most simple lesson of the piece. Can you talk about that work?

C.M.: I've been so glad to have your encouragement and company in revising and submitting my book manuscript. Many of these poems have been with me for many years now, sort of changing and growing as I tote them along from place to place. Perhaps for that reason, the book has taken form as a series of thematic sections, rather than a single narrative. *Palace Gate*, both the collection and the title poem, refers to a particular place, a real palace gate in Rajasthan, but also points at questions of access and vision that seem to recur in my poems. How do we see better, whether we're looking at the past or the present, at ourselves or the people we love? How do we move through different kinds of spaces, and how does our passage through those spaces change us? What do we carry with us as we move around in the world? And what do we leave or give up to get through those gates? When I wrote the poem, "Palace Gate," I was trying to find a way to write about an accident I'd had in India as a college student, in which I was pretty badly injured. When it happened I was traveling alone (which was a dumb thing to do, as an 18-year-old woman in a foreign country) and so I had to figure out on my own how to get myself care, how to get myself to safety, and I did. It was very frightening, and also of course it now seems emblematic of all the growing up I was doing at that time. "Palace Gate" came to me, years later, as a poem about how we interpret the world and navigate it really on the fly. In moments of crisis we have the most haphazard assortment of resources with which to improvise — whatever is at hand, whoever we can call on for help, and, it turns out, the daffodils and Toyotas that have formed us.

P.H.: All of your "erasures" ("Buried Cities," "Manoeuver," "How," "The Moon," and "Out of the Fog") are experimental in form. How do you know where to put the page and line breaks?

C.M.: When I was doing my MFA at Warren Wilson College, Mary Ruefle was on the faculty and I read her amazing book of erasure poems, *Little White Shadow*. At some time or other when I was stuck in my writing, I was playing around on Wave Books' awesome erasure website. It felt like a way to turn my brain off temporarily and see what happened, to let new kinds of weirdness into my poetic language. I kept the words roughly in their original places on the page, so the line breaks aren't really mine — they come from the source texts. I tried to use erasure as a sort of formal constraint, like a sonnet, a restriction that actually frees you to do something new.

P.H.: Your 2010 poem "Apollo" was nominated for the Pushcart Prize. In seven stanzas, you express the body of what could have been written in a dissertation. Which do you prefer? Academic work or poetry? Why?

C.M.: I love both academic work and poetry. They feed each other and also feel like different kinds of discipline. Lots of my favorite poets had other kinds of careers alongside poetry: W.C. Williams was a doctor, Stevens an insurance exec, Larkin a university librarian, and Frank O'Hara a curator at the Museum of Modern Art. Robert Hayden worked in academia for much of his career. So I'm hoping it will be fruitful for me too, to keep both kinds of work going.

P.H.: In addition to being a poet and professor, you are a family person— a doting parent and partner. How do you balance all of these professions when they require so much? I guess it reminds me a little of the Rumi poem: "Your task is not to seek for love, but merely to seek and find all the barriers within yourself that you have built against it."

C.M.: That's a lovely Rumi quote. I have no idea how I balance all these things that I am trying to do — mostly it feels like I'm not balancing them at all!

5/17/18

#BEINGATOURMANAGERISLIKE

TINA FARRIS, TOUR MANAGER

Photo by @iamsuede

Open up Spotify. Go! Whatever then... Pandora... Tidal. Do, it real quick. *Quick, quick, quick.*

OK, now go into that hip-hop zone, fade real allegro unto that frequency — the *good* hip-hop, not the junk — and you will run into Tina Farris. See her? You may not know it when you are on iTunes or SoundCloud, but her footprints are there — large footprints. She's there on the Roots' tracks. By Allah, I swear she's there. Her spirit is there on the Lauryn Hill tracks too and all of the soul D'Angelo — the one about "Until It's Done":

> In a world where we all circle the fiery sun
> With a need for love

What have we become?
Tragedy flows unbound and there's no place to run
Till it's done
Questions that call to us, we all reflect upon
Where do we belong? Where do we come from?
Questions that call to us, we all reflect upon
Till it's done
Till it's done

Then, there she is again with Ty Dolla Sign. Wow, guess I forgot to mention will.i.am and Mary Mary. She has also worked with Lil' Wayne, Fergie, the Black Eyed Peas, Nicki Minaj, Queen Latifah, Jill Scott, Maxwell, and Mayer Hawthorne. Neo Soul: *the new soul, the new soul, new soul.* Tina Farris is the new power soul, building structures around that solid brown vibration, giving stage directions to the stars. Her company is Tina Farris Tours: "Tour managers, tour assistants and personal assistants designed to exceed the expectation of the most discriminating high profile client."

Now that you are getting the picture, seeing the show, vibrating at a higher frequency, I'll clue you in — if these constellation acts are like royalty, then she is the power behind the throne. She is the vastness of the cosmos, contrasting her grind with the glaring lights of super stardom. She is the one making it do what it do. In political metaphor, like Valerie Jarrett or David Axelrod are to Barack Obama. Or in Hollywood metaphor, think Shonda Rhimes to Kerry Washington or Viola Davis. Tina Farris the one who make it do what it do. And she ain't playing. And it ain't no joke. And yeah she's real, as real as a woman will get. But her work is pure *magic*. It's the sort of elixir you roll a whole lifetime joint into, then just walk the planet as pretty as can be. effervescent. *She's nice, iridescent.* Dig it? No?

OK, I'll lay it on thicker.

Tina Farris has hit the road with the Black Eyed Peas, taking them through fifteen countries, 76 cities and 99 sold out shows before 1.3 million attendees, grossing more than $86 million dollars along the way. No. This ain't Pam Grier in a pantsuit in some contemporary Ava DuVernay redux of Foxy Brown or Coffy. This is the *real* world with a very real Tina Farris. She's the one who helped manifest the ghost D'Angelo during his comeback tour in the United States and Europe. Damn — now he's ghost again. So apropos that spirit D'Angelo come and go. But I'm serious — she's The Woman, the Lady with a Plan, the Super Nova taken human form. She is a galaxy contained in the form of a woman. She's moving at the speed of light, literally hopping planes and travelling at the higher frequencies. Well, I reached up high and caught that spirit on its way to NYC.

This is how that exchange went — it was fast, it was real — it was hard... and cold, filled with a hot nucleus of joy. The phone picks up to the raucous percussion of Black woman laugh, winding into a silent kind of "Yo, whattup dude."

Patrick A. Howell: You've lived an amazing life, Tina — from the small town of Sacramento to travelling the world, working the world and impacting the culture with an unique imprint. You've had the opportunity to work with, have fun with and develop relationships with who I like to call the 1%. A matter of fact, you are one of the 1%ers – the creatives who infuse our planet with spirit, energy and love in so many forms. You provide the boogie in the step, the hop in our hips, the stars in our eyes. You really have a unique vantage point into all the trappings of what can make a successful lifestyle. You're not Oprah. Or Rihanna.

Or Beyoncé. You are Tina Farris. For young kids that are just getting started, what advice can you impart about following your own path?

Tina Farris: Thank you. I tell young people to fill up their "tool belt." What I mean by that is life is long. You have to position yourself to be in the room. You get to be in these rooms by having certain tools. My first tool was music. My family is musical. Grandfather was a Motown producer, both uncles are bass and guitar players. I played upright bass from 4th grade through high school. So I created an "ear" for basslines. Next tool was education. I started at UCLA and was in a room of diverse people who introduced me to other genres of music. Mainly east coast hip-hop. I'm a west coast baby so this was new. The homie introduced me to the Roots, who happened to visit the school, who I happened to be in the front row for, who I happened to meet, who I decided to follow around the world, who I befriended, who I then became the tour manager. Along the way I got a masters degree and taught high school. All of those tools helped me become a great tour manager.

P.H.: As a people and a culture, we have just come out of a really interesting period — having elected and been presided over by our first "Black president," and in a current "Black Lives Matter" moment, we are now in a very different era with a very different vibe. How do you see the culture responding to the change in global temperature?

T.F.: There will be division as usual. But this is also a great moment for activation. No longer resting in the "we made it zone," the culture will respond to the work that remains for us to do. It also is a shout out to the rest of the folks who were hanging onto the culture. Either you with us or you against us.

P.H.: In "If My Homie Calls.," Tupac famously rapped "It ain't what I expected it's hectic it's sleazy." Is that the music industry? What is your guiding philosophy? What is your perspective of the recording industry after putting in work?

T.F.: It's not for the faint of heart. It's not fair. Lots of dues. It will be crooked. You will be let down. It's like any other industry. What are you going to do to stand out? If you don't stand out you are subject to be on a long road to the above. There are no shortcuts.

P.H.: This is a tough one because you are an industry insider but what are your top 5 all time albums?

T.F.: Hmmmm. *Hotter than July*, *Prince* (self-titled album), *Things Fall Apart*, *Ego Death*, *Baduizm*, *Southern Playalistic Cadillac Music*, *Who is Jill Scott?*, *808s & Heartbreaks*, I dunno. This is hard and hella political. Lol.

P.H.: What's the deal with you and Jeff Goldblum? I've seen some hints on your social media world (Twitter and Facebook) of a serious crush. I see him and I get some serious... shudders. Start thinking about that joint from when we were kids — *The Fly*.

T.F.: I was super adolescent when *The Fly* came out. He showed his ass. I think that was like porn to me. Kinda shaped my quirky, tall Sephardic-esque stream of attraction. Immigration in Dubai's airport? Dude...

P.H.: How was your visit to the White House?

T.F.: There were two visits to the White House. One was the BET farewell to the president. And the other one was a get down party. The president didn't have a tie on and I bumped into him on accident. The president was dabbing with Chance and Janelle Monae. It was just a house party or like being at your uncle's cookout.

2/24/17

RESISTANCE BY POETRY POWER

WILLIAM ALLEGREZZA, AMERICAN POET AND PUBLISHER OF MORIA BOOKS AND LOCOFO CHAPBOOKS

Photo by Keira Allegrezza

Like many disciplines, poetry is an art form which requires patience, fortitude, solace and bravery. American history has been annotated by publishing houses, poets and heroes... patriotic provocateurs who did the unimaginable with flair and zest when no one else was watching, when it was needed or when nobody else dared. American literature, poetry and drama is written by brave hearts who looked their time squarely in the eye, challenging America to be better. At times these men and women are outcasts; at others, heroes; and at others still, villains.

William Blake wrote "America, a Prophecy" in 1793, seventeen years after America's independence. There is Joni Mitchell, Nobel Prize-winner Bob Dylan, and Allen Ginsberg, whose "Howl" immortalizes the Fifties ("Follow your inner moonlight; don't hide the madness"). In this century and in the twentieth, will history argue that artists such as Saul Williams, N.W.A., Eminem, Tupac Shakur and Kendrick Lamar were not only wordsmiths but vanguards who outlined a new age — new possibilities — with their belligerent diatribes? But even before any of that, there was Phillis Wheatley (the first published African American female poet, born in West Africa) and Henry Wadsworth Longfellow (an American poet and educator whose works include "Paul Revere's Ride"), along with a host of other revolutionaries annotating American history with lines like Ralph Waldo Emerson's:

> Not gold but only men can make
> A people great and strong;
> Men who for truth and honor's sake
> Stand fast and suffer long.

The nineteenth century was, of course, a time of identity for a world power coming into its own. America was not a world power. The center of the world was Europe. World Wars I and II had not yet been fought, America was still an agricultural society built on the pillars of slave trade and "free labor" and the United Nations did not exist. In the nineteenth century, America was exploring westward to the gold rush and would fight the Civil War, a conflict so central to the American soul it is still being battled in Charlottesville and in twenty-first-century American elections.

It appears that the twenty-first century is also a place of questioning and identity formation, battles and ongoing conflicts centuries old. Walt Whitman is one of the poets who William Allegrezza, publisher of Locofo Chaps, lists as one of his favorites. Walt Whitman, like William Allegrezza, was one part outdoors man, one part poet, another teacher, and yet another musician. Who knows, maybe this William Allegrezza character is Walt Whitman, in parts, reincarnated?

William Allegrezza's (or "Bill" to fellow poets and friends) Lofoco Chaps has sent hundreds of chapbooks from poets around the world, including *In These Days of Rage, Liberal Elite Media Rag, SAD!* and *Defying Trumplandia: Pithy Peminist Poetry* by the postal bagful to #45 at 1600 Pennsylvania Avenue in Washington, D.C. (Their website also sells hard copies for $5 a piece.)

I took a little time to speak with Bill about his brave and timely project, as well as his passion for poetry for the people.

Patrick A. Howell: When did you begin writing/reading poetry, Bill?

William Allegrezza: I have been writing poetry in some form since I was a teenager and reading widely since college. My focus in college and graduate school was poetry, and I have followed that focus ever since by starting presses, readings series, teaching, and writing.

P.H.: Why did you and Moria Books start Locofo Chapbooks (Also, what is a Locofo)? Where did you get the idea? How hard was it to implement once conceived? Were there any real obstacles?

W.A.: I was angry when Trump was elected and knew that I must have some creative outlet to focus that anger, and I also heard from many other poets that they were in the same place. I started writing some political pieces and thought about the focus on the first one hundred days of a presidency. Moria Books was already up and running, so I thought it would be easy to have poets do a chapbook response, but since political poetry is not the focus of Moria Books, I thought it would be best to work it out under an imprint. My original idea was to have one hundred poets do one hundred chapbooks as a response to the first one hundred days, and I was not sure that I would get enough poets to join me.

P.H.: How many books have you published since beginning your quest? Which book(s) stand out in your memory? Why? How many folks have visited the site? How many books have been published?

W.A.: We have published 120, and I have twelve more ready to go to print. There are so many excellent chapbooks that I don't want to focus on any one. I did like the several anthologies that came from the project though, because the poets were great and are from poets who do not get enough space in the poetry scene. As of November, there have been over 180,000 individual visits to the Locofo website and over 400,000 page views.

The poets provided ideas for the project after it got started. For example, I individually mailed the chapbooks to the White House, and one poet suggested taking photos of the process. A poet also suggested having the poets write reviews of other chapbooks in the project to build steam, and for the many readings outside Chicago where I am based, the poets put them together. Locofo is a reference to the Locofoco political movement, a small political splinter group from the Democratic party in the 1900s that was originally meant to light a match for a new movement. Several major American poets were part of that political movement.

P.H.: Is there a tipping point? What/when/where is the stopping point for Locofo Chaps?

W.A.: I thought it was originally the one hundred chapbooks, but as the project has continued, I am not sure when it will stop. I have long thought that American poets need to be more specifically political, so perhaps the project will morph in that direction after this year.

P.H.: Why do you write, Bill?

W.A.: If you were to ask what poetry does, I could spout out a list, or if you were to ask why people write poetry, I could throw out a plethora of reasons, but when you ask why I write, then it turns personal. I specifically left my name out of the Locofo Chaps project. I presented my own protest work elsewhere and let the 140 or so poets who are part of the project speak for me. When I was younger, I had a list of reasons of why I wrote, but now I just want to write.

So why do I write? I feel compelled to do so. I would like to leave the answer there, but I hear the question, what compels the urge? Is my muse political, social, religious, personal, or psychological? None and all. In a poem from fifteen years ago, I wrote, "To write/is to engage with an agenda." I still believe that, yet I'm content, pushing the words on the page and watching the interplay of sound and form without so much focus on content. I want my poetry to touch the personal without my own personal and without really needing to be personal. I want to write poems that are a view from the mountain but also the whisper of two conspirators in religion, love, friendship, whatever with words that are charged but daily. I want to repeat Whitman, "Do I contradict myself? Very well, I contradict myself," but I know that my multitudes have shifted since his period.

11/30/17

THE SEERS

BLOODSONG

BY TONY MEDINA

Didn't I tell you
That the heart
Is a mouth
On paper
That the paper
Is a flame
Split into lips
Pursed like an arrow
And that arrow
Bleeds into the drum
Of one's tongue
Trapped in memory's ear
Didn't I tell you
It is hard
For the wound
To forget
The migrating blood
Forced out
By exile
Or eviction
That one man's journey
Is another man's
Fast removal
From the face
Of the earth
That some travel
In the hulls

Of slave ships
While others
Hug the bottom
Of rafts
Swallowing
Oceans
Of mud

BLACK PANTHERS IN THE FIFTH DIMENSION

MALIK AND KAREN SENEFERU, BAY AREA ARTISTS AND ACTIVISTS

Photo by Tarika Lewis

The Black artist… is desperately needed to change the images his people identify with, by asserting Black feeling, Black mind, Black

judgment... Art, Religion, and Politics are impressive vectors of a culture. Art describes culture. Black artists must have an image of what the Black sensibility is in this land. Religion elevates a culture. The Black Man must aspire to Blackness. God is man idealized. The Black Man must idealize himself as Black. And realize and aspire to that... The Black man must seek a Black politics, and ordering of the world that is beneficial to his culture, to his interiorization and judgment of the world. This is strength. And we are hordes.
— Amiri Baraka, co-founder of the Black Arts Movement (1965-1975)

If you're in the greater Bay Area (Oakland, San Francisco and Berkeley) and have not been influenced or directly impacted by Malik and Karen Seneferu, you must be living under a rock. Under a rock like Ted Kaczynski, the Unabomber, type of situation. Their work and influence is ubiquitous. "Remain Creative," "The Black Woman is God," "Passages," "Young Gods in Training," "Blood Lines," "Black Love Matters" and "Blue Tree Inc." are all concepts, art shows and exhibitions that the couple have introduced into the lexicon, the fabric of the cities that brought us Tupac Amaru Shakur, the Black Panthers, Eldridge Cleaver, Stokely Carmichael, Huey P. Newton and Angela Davis at the height of their powers. Those powers were then solidified with the election and terms of representatives Barbara Lee, Ron Dellums and now Kamala Harris. While Malik and Karen inform the struggle with their fearless advocacy and activism, their work and exhibits have appeared in the California African American Art Museum, the Skirball Cultural Center, New York City's Schomburg Center and the Smithsonian. They are culture and counter-culture united in a representation of spirituality, Black love and effervescent sunshine and blue skies.

Afrikan history is world history. World history is human history. And the Black Woman Is God. These are proven facts. Repeatedly great Afrikan scholars have spent their lives at varying points in the continuum of our Afrikan world history proving them.
— Malaika H. Kambon, 2013, *The San Francisco Bay View*

Surrounded by San Francisco, Oakland and Berkeley, Richmond is a Bay Area city that gets short shrift. Over the past twenty-five years, Malik Seneferu has thrived as a self-taught mixed media artist, draughtsman, photographer, muralist, sculptor, poet and illustrator, and has manifested over one thousand pieces, including paintings, murals and mixed media projects. He is also a teacher at Parker Elementary Middle School and Redwood Heights. His wife, Karen Seneferu, is also a self-taught artist who proudly recognizes her husband as an inspiration and her first teacher. She received her BA in English from the University of California at Berkeley, her MA in English at CSU, Eastbay, and teaches art at Berkeley City College.

Notwithstanding the memories of slavery, and in the face of poverty, ignorance, terrorism, and subjugation still deeply woven into their lives, the embittered past of Blacks was taken onto a much higher plane of intellectual and artistic consideration during the Renaissance.
— Clement Alexander Price, *Encyclopedia of the Harlem Renaissance*

Their work features elements of what is known as magic realism but could also be termed as "Cosmic Realism". Magic realism is defined as: "an artistic genre in which realistic narrative and naturalistic technique are combined with surreal elements of dream or fantasy." "Cosmic Realism" is a movement which shifts perception and reality from the "ordinary" everyday lives and mainstream media projections to a more fundamental energy and spirit coursing through our lives. It recognizes the great I Am that we all are. Cosmic Realism is definitely not religious, but rather spiritual. Cosmic Realism does not deny the connection of emotion to another more profound reality. It does not deny the effects of electromagnetic media, as television but it is not tethered to them either. Cosmic Realism, on balance, is committed to organic, holistic living.

In their social work, performance art and art work, Karen and Malik seem to have mastered a medium that marries political activism with community service, Afrofuturism, Afropunk, art shows, a brand of event consciousness, and a whole lot of spirit. I am not sure there has ever been an artistic movement to encompass the tonality of their unique brand of cosmic sentiment, social activism and artistic vision.

Certainly, the wood, stone, bronze, or clay sculptures of griot Elizabeth Catlett were formed if not informed by those fires of political protest, picket lines and arrests throughout her seventy-year career. And then there is ancestor Jacob Lawrence, the painter and creative giant who marked his stay on the planet with more than sixty-five years and two hundred museum collections of paintings, visual stories and illustrations. And, I cannot leave this paragraph without mentioning the immortal Charles White, an illustrator, whose work has depicted the African American history, our socio-economic struggles and human relationships. These earlier painters are all precedents for and influences on Karen and Malik's works.

Karen and Malik Seneferu's contribution to the painting and the visual arts are an extension of and homage to the generation of visual griots who came before, imagining and implementing the new here-and-now reality with their work. As with the griots and ancestors before Malik and

Karen, metaphor and visual medium are simply ways to create the future.

As Karen stated in an interview for this piece, "'Cosmic Realism' has arisen from the community organically. It is part of each Black body's organic spirituality. It has always been here but now it is pronounced. It has been in the Black African churches in our hymnals, religious practices, evangelizing from the pulpit, choir singing and dancing. But cosmic realism is not religion. Black people have always brought these mystical, and some would say, magical elements together but the aggregation and pronouncement of that spirit is more apparent than ever in American global culture. It can be part and parcel of the struggle but it exists independent to the resistance to systemic discrimination and white colonization. It is rooted in African ideology, cultural practices and cosmology."

Indeed, Malik and Karen's exhibition *Black Woman is God/Black Love Matters* has had nearly five art events in 2015, drawing 2,500 attendees and over 10,000 views on social media.

Photo by Osaze Seneferu

A subdued people, found their own voice and their identity in an outpour of hope, courage and newfound confidence. Many great poets, writers, musicians and artists emerged, to redefine the African American way of thought. Some beautiful quotes from this fiery period of renaissance and the men and women who drove it, are presented in this Buzzle article. Take a look...
— Zora Neale Hurston

I asked Karen if their movement for expression is not informed by the Black Arts Movement. She says, "It is definitely impacted by Black art history. We live in the time of Marvin X and the work he did with the Black Arts Movement. We have had access to members and the Black Arts District here in Oakland. The geographical area we are in has a spirit embedded that comes from the Black revolutionary spirit of the people. People like Emory Douglas, Tarika Lewis and Elaine Brown, the latter two being the first women to join the Black Panther Movement, are living, breathing memories of the institutions before we came onto the scene. The spirit of the people they were and are is still here. If you have an understanding of the purpose of art which is to affirm culture and dominance over all other cultures, then you understand the revolutionary work of these individuals. You understand that the Black artist in and of themselves, by their very nature, walking history.

"Everything that we have done is birthed out of the love that Karen and I have for one another and the spiritual events that took place in our coming together." In fact, the Black Woman is God exhibit was literally pre-dated by the Black Love Matters exhibit in 2015.

When I asked Malik what his inspiration was for his life's work, he said: "I grew up in Bayview Hunters Point, San Francisco. I was born in 1971, in a time that the Black Panther Party was being taken out. It was like I came into the world the night before hip-hop came into being. Before I knew the word 'hip-hop', I was dancing to break beats. Most of the people I knew were in-the-closet artists. A lot of these artists I was able to bring them out of the closet and onto the surface.

"Seeing how crack cocaine in the late Seventies into the Eighties wiped out the men I knew and communities I lived in, I already had a clue that there was a plan to attack our very existence, so I wanted to do artwork that reflected that reality. My first body of work, called 'The Raw' and started in 1990 and ended in 2001, reflected my experiences in the Eighties and Nineties. My audience was a war-torn community of poverty, addicts and pushers. They would question me about the meaning behind my work and when I started doing exhibits in the Projects my career was born. I remember I was a part of an Anne Frank exhibit and was on the cover of the *Marin Herald*, when I was twenty-three years of age. My first experience of traveling outside of the US was going to Haiti with JoeSam, who was my fatherly mentor at that time. It is these experiences which helped to birth my mantra, 'Remain Creative'. I saw my own peers make money and I started to develop my artwork so I could make a living for the family I have today."

Their Black Love Matters movement is not the first but second time he and his wife have worked together. They also worked on "What is Buried is not Lost: Relics, Shrines and Sacred Objects" with Anyka Barber's Betti Ono Gallery in 2012. In 2015, Malik had a show co-founded with the Impact HUB in Oakland and curated by Ashara Ekundayo. "At that exhibit, the whole place was packed. A lot of people had never seen a Black couple exhibiting together in the Bay Area. I still wonder if it was the first of its kind. So when my wife stepped out this year with 'The Black Woman Is God,' it was like a tsunami. I am grateful that when me and my wife work in this spirit, we are well received."

Karen agrees with Malik, "The concerns that people have for the community can't happen without love. Black Lives Matter... that doesn't happen without *Black Love Matters*."

Karen notes, "I think that Malik and I are at a place where we are fortunate to look back on history at the artists and the political leaders and the cultural icons who shaped Black identity in ways that certainly galvanized the spirit and integrated that ethos into the work, in such a way, that we connect to the community as teachers as well. I think we are very fortunate in that sense. From our vantage point, teaching and leading is how we express ourselves and we shape spaces that we are curating as artists and activists. It is a responsibility we take seriously.

"The climate into which 'The Black Woman Is God' emerged is one where the Black body has been clearly devalued and annihilated. The system seeks to exterminate the Black body through technology. People are desensitized to Black lives as human when they see it repetitively destroyed. So by the time the Black Woman is God exhibit came, people wanted a space where they could mourn so they could release the energy of "no way out" toward a solution that could happen though the spirit. It is a resistance against the system of the tyranny that attacks and has attacked the Black body for well over 350 years in America."

12/30/16

THE POET WHO PAINTS, THE BUSINESS THAT GIVES

DANNY SIMMONS, ABSTRACT EXPRESSIONIST AND PHILANTHROPIST

Photo by Todd Agostini

The first thing I had to do when I talked to Danny Simmons was ask him about that painting that is his cover photo on Facebook. To me, it looked like horses racing at the Saratoga tracks. Don't ask me how that popped into my head, it just did. Maybe it has something to do with the Del Mar track season opening this weekend down where I live. I see the thrusts of violent competitive motion, the primary color silks of the jockeys and the Black silk tails of horses. All of this on the background of a green race track. But I guess that's the point of neo-African abstract painting —

to invite connotations and associations where the viewer may be an artist by interpretation.

According to Danny, when I ask him about his process, he says in a congenial manner colored as much by an infectious cool as gregarious humanity, "I think more about a large idea. Painting is akin to traditional aboriginal art insofar as it is connected to spirit. The work that they did in those cultures were connected to spirits. If I do it properly, I become a conduit and create a communication between the spirit, the reader and myself. It's a medium, a meditation." Danny's spirit is contagious — he creates aesthetic just by flowing with his being.

When I asked him about his process for arriving at the piece above and its contents, he said: "I bought a Galaxy Note phone and started making some digital drawings and putting things together that were in my head and then had those vectorized so that I couldn't lose their content on the computer." Vectorized, so you know, is taking that image from electronic to solid form on matted paper or canvas.

Finally, the explanation for that crazy piece with the green background: "It is small parts of everything that make us who we are. It's sort of a DNA code. There are a lot of little separate pieces that make up a whole." The means by which an abstract expressionist piece is created was made famous by Jackson Pollock. The painter allows paint to drip onto the canvas while rhythmically dancing above the piece. The art form originated in New York City in the 1940s, so it might have caught Danny. Some other famous abstract expressionists are Robert De Niro Sr and Willem de Kooning. Personally, I had the opportunity to tour Dick Marconi's studio in San Juan Capistrano with my son in 2014.

Personally, I get a sense of acute intellectual energy in addition to spiritual and emotional vibes, so I asked Danny

Simmons about the effect of books on his work. Along with his brother, Russell Simmons, he is one of the architects behind Def Poetry Jam. He is also the accomplished author of *Three Days As the Crow Flies* (Atria Books, 2003) and three volumes of poetry, *I Dreamed My People Were Calling But Couldn't Find My Ways Home*, *Deep In Your Best Reflection* and *The Brown Beatnik Tomes*. Danny is a self-confessed bibliophile: "There are a couple areas of literature that have really influenced my creation around art and writing. First there are the works by Ishmael Reed. He is an abstract writer — he just is — particularly in his earlier work, like *The Freelance Pallbearers* and *Mumbo Jumbo*. It's like with Allen Ginsberg and the free-form writing in "Howl." The poetics and politics unroll from those works.

"The next thing would be existential books where man finds the meaning of himself within himself versus the outside world. Not so much that there isn't any god, because I'm not down with that — but that you will connect with him by connecting from within yourself. There's the tradition created by French artists and writers in the 1940s, such as Jean-Paul Sartre with his play *No Exit*, which was about a young intellectual torn between theory and the dichotomy of racism in America. Then there is *The Stranger* by Albert Camus or *Waiting for Godot* by Samuel Becket or *Being and Nothingness* by Nietzsche — all of these works play a huge part in the creation of my work, the space in my brain from which I create. Those are books that I have read and re-read. They deal with the sanctity and sovereignty of the individual human being, individual existence, freedom and choice."

Danny Simmons is the son of Daniel Simmons, Sr, a Black history professor who also wrote poetry, and Evelyn Simmons, a teacher who painted as a hobby. It seems all of the brothers, including the Rev. Run and Russell Simmons, are also infected with a funky love for their people, a contagious love of capitalist pursuits (read: hip-hop industry creating high-frequency hustle) and just plain silly creation. But Danny is the one who followed almost verbatim the pursuits of his parents as painter and poet.

He acknowledges, "When Russell came along moms had to take care of me and Russell. I am four years older so those first four years I was going to museums, finger painting and playing with colors. All of us, though, got my father's gift of gab. I remember former mayor David Dinkins once said of our dad, 'Your father used to sit across from the library and would freeform on poetry with a bunch of women surrounding him.' My father was a very vocal person about not only civil rights but the human condition. He was a funny man, a very brave man. Everything he did, he shared with his kids. There was so much encouragement that came from my father and mother. And you definitely see that in myself and brothers.

"They raised us to make sure that we had each other's back through life. We were very close all three of us and that was because of what my mother put into us. Do what you want to do — don't worry about it because we got you. When Russell was starting off in hip-hop, I gave him a loan from my college loan he got me later on and we just go back and forth like that."

Danny is the Chairman of Rush Philanthropic Arts Foundation (1995 to present), which provides disadvantaged urban youth with access to arts education. Danny also founded the Rush Arts Gallery and converted his loft in Brooklyn into the Corridor Gallery. The galleries provide exhibition opportunities to early- and mid-career artists who do not have commercial representation through galleries or private dealers. That is also a staple of the Simmons' repertoire, *building and giving*.

"Russel and Joey were more businessmen than anything else with how well they promoted themselves. I just knew that we had the opportunity to leverage their celebrity for the good of the community and I knew I could do this because I was their big brother. It was something we all had to do because of who daddy was and the Civil Rights struggle he and mommy represented — that whole era. We moved forward and we worked within the community. It was a family affair from the beginning. It just had to do with helping artists get their work out there and have that opportunity."

Finally, I asked him about the growing Global I Aam or Global International African Arts Movement. "I don't think this is anything new. I think it's becoming more recognized. I think we as a people have been doing what we've been doing for a long time. But Black people have been doing within this niche and promoting from within our community as far back as the Harlem Renaissance. Both Max and Malaika Adero helped me with *Three Days Of The Crow Flies*. Malaika believed in and published the project. Max gave me the opportunity to read from the book.

"I think within our community, the creators that are within our community all sort of intersect. We need each other to get all this dope stuff done. I can't do it all by myself."

12/30/16

THE DISTINCT CASE OF THE INTERNATIONAL RUNWAY MODEL AND HER MBA

SARA ISHAG, FINANCIER AND INTERNATIONAL MODEL

We have a powerful potential in our youth, and we must have the courage to change old ideas and practices so that we may direct their power toward good ends.
— Renowned educator Mary McLeod Bethune

You know Iman? Iman Mohamed Abdulmajid, the one with the multi-million-dollar ethnic cosmetics and philanthropic work? The one who was married to Eighties icon David Bowie? Fashion model Sara Ishag says of the iconic African, "Iman is just an inspiring model to look up to. She came from Somalia, East Africa, and is one of the first, if not the first, to make it from that part of the world."

The funny thing with Sara is she is a vice president, premier relationship manager at HSBC Wealth Management, dealing with highly accredited investors and building a profitable portfolio. Alan Stone, CEO of Wall Street Research says proudly of the prodigy, "Sara Ishag formerly of Wall Street Research and Southern California Investment Forum is an incredibly talented young woman with a great career ahead in banking and finance now with HSBC. She is a big business development and aid to top level financiers and CEOs." And, I haven't begun to speak about her USC MBA. I guess you could say she is a brilliant financier... I mean runway fashion model. I mean, mogul prodigy. Distinct, right?

The Sudanese-American model was born in Kuwait and raised in Los Angeles, California. She has been featured in several national and international magazines such as *Essence, Elle, Vogue, Sheen,* and *Most Fashion Magazine.* I asked her how she got her start. She answered in the no-nonsense manner that characterizes her voice and underscores her cosmopolitan beauty, "I started modeling at a young age and I had to learn through trial and error. I have been fortunate to have people that have inspired and helped me — agents, managers and other people I collaborated with — designers and photographers.

"I got my first break when I was approached to do a national magazine when I was sixteen years old — at the mall in the South Bay Gallery in Redondo Mall. The magazine was *Ebony.*"

She has worked with international designers and world-renowned photographers, booking national ad campaigns for successful cosmetic brands such as L'Oréal-owned Mizani. Last year alone, she was in Los Angeles, New York, SF, Dubai and Canada. She has already booked her trip to Sweden for a show in 2017. "I've participated in some of the biggest fashion weeks! Aside from being born in Kuwait and being from Sudan, I've lived in Qatar, London and Malaysia and did quite a bit of traveling all over. I've also been published in magazines in the UK and Japan."

However, as was noted previously, Sara Ishag's penchant for excellence is even more pronounced in her pursuit of higher education. She is currently in the second year of her MBA at the University of Southern California Marshall School of Business. Sara concedes her pedigree, "It has always been an overall goal. I am a firm believer in education. I always knew I would go back and pursue my education no matter what I was doing. My father is one of my biggest inspirations and he always taught me to have a high work ethic and that knowledge is the one thing that can never be taken away from you." Both of Sara's parents are engineers. Her brothers are as well.

Fellow USC film student Aaron Ashby says of the second year MBA student, "The cool thing about Sara is she has the business side and creative side going on at the same time." Sara is described by her peers as someone with strong character. Sara graduated with honors from the University of California as the top 10% of her business class.

Sara is also scheduled to launch her online jewelry brand "annakqua" in February of 2017. She will be collaborating with the very same mentors she has had throughout her modeling and finance career to build a strong brand. It seems to me, however, the emphasis is, as Benjamin Franklin noted on education, where "An investment in knowledge pays the best interest."

1/8/17

CUBA, AMERICA, BLACK FINE LINES, MAGIC MIND AND THE REAL

JULES ARTHUR, AFRICAN CLASSICIST PAINTER AND SCULPTOR

Jules Arthur's work is artful *at an atomic level*, meaning it is nuclear — looks classic and understated but is prolific in the culture at large and in the private collections of our culture's thought leaders, indisputable movers and shakers. It is seemingly demure in presentation but explosive in its impact. It is on this earth but cosmic in its vision and reach.

His work is displayed in the collections of Senator Cory Booker, Jay-Z, Van Jones, Marc Lamont Hill, Henry Louis Gates, Kate Hudson and Pras Michel of the Fugees. You realize upon review of Jules Arthur that *it is everywhere.*

You realize upon further contemplation of his process, that it always has been and always will be. It is *ubiquitous.* His work has been the subject of over a dozen exhibitions since 2001. It is on movie posters, US senators' offices and is displayed at the Schomburg Cultural Center for Research in Black Culture and Hutchins Center for African & African American Research at Harvard University. As described, Jules Arthur's work is *chévere* — slang in Cuba, Puerto Rico, the Dominican Republic, Venezuela and Colombia for cool, awesome or terrific. His commitment to the African aesthetic is towering — *he is a vessel through which ancestral energies are expressed and manifested.*

For years now, through a process well documented, Jules has worked with paint, thread, cowrie shells, wooden frames, glue, artifacts, intellect, stencils, gold paint, spiritual alchemy and artifacts to re-create the energy of past worlds in the present. You *see* the eternal rhythms of poetry and the West African djembe — rope-tuned skin-covered goblet drum — in his work. It is the eternal African rhythm in color, on a canvas. The intentions of his spirit are clear with subject matter, and their effect upon patrons. *African accomplishment is magnificent and to be revered. That work must not only be preserved but tower in the present day and in future worlds to come.*

While formally trained with a BFA from NYC's School of Visual Arts (graduating with honors), he was also trained by the masters. He was mentored by our Harlem Renaissance's Robert Blackburn (MacArthur Fellow) while attending the Robert Blackburn Printmaking Workshop. So, he is committed to the aesthetic of excellence that is organic to our culture too. So, when President Obama announced a reversal of decades-old policy, opening American borders to Cuba, it was inevitable that Jules Arthur would make his way back. That's how that Spirit Force works. It is magic contoured with the real. It is mystery walking in daylight. It is the impossible realized. Afro-Cuban culture has been a subject of Jules Arthur's work, with pieces like "Havana's Finest" or "Azucar De La Habana."

This interview deals with not only Jules Arthur's trip to Cuba, but also the spirit of the fighter in his work, Muhammad Ali, the righteous spirit of the fighter in President Barack H. Obama, the African Renaissance that was 2016 and the process by which his work comes to life.

Jules Arthur, Havana's Finest | oil on wood panel, constructed wooden box frame, fabric, leather, 23k gold leaf lettering, brass hardware, cigars from Cuba, mixed media | 41 x 60 x 4 inches | 2016

Patrick A. Howell: What was the purpose of your recent trip to Cuba? What were you looking for?

Jules Arthur: My general consensus is that the majority of people in life dream of setting out into the world and visit their favorite destinations around the world. Traveling in itself is such a crucial educational wonderment that all should be blessed with.

As Cuba was my number one destination, I just went on the journey of my dreams. Cuba represents my thirst for historical crossroads that had huge impacts on world history when people set out for new lands. To answer the question "what was I looking for?", Cuba excites every nerve I possess about diving deep into rich roots and culture. There is a notion that states artists have a duty to speak about his or her times. A duty that states a need to creatively address the issues that grip the era in which they live in. There is a part of me that fully understands the merits in that thinking.

But I feel there is a greater duty to honor what naturally evolves in the artist's spirit. Not to steer it so much but to let the creative spirit gracefully guide the artist to unpredictable creative depths. My artist spirit vigorously keeps my creative mind contemplating the wonders of past history.

You'll find the body of my work exploring the vast riches that have historically evolved and taken place throughout the world. I prefer to juxtapose history's unique moments and convey them in a sense that challenges the status quo or give reason to ask more questions. My work simultaneously gives honor and respect to unsung and celebrated individuals who have made an important mark. And there is no richer place than Cuba with its beautiful turbulent past that reaches back as far as the days when the Taino and Arawakan people ruled the Greater Antilles. As Spanish Conquistadors set out for riches in these lands, I went to Cuba in search of riches in the form of historical crossroads where Native peoples, Africans and Spanish cultures collided in unprecedented events.

P.H.: Is Cuba magic?

J.A.: Cuba is the definition of a magical place in the world. It is magical in the sense that it is a historical epicenter that gave birth and rise to so many new special and powerful ways of living that have lasted through the centuries and into our current day. There is an African tradition that practices the act of intentionally breaking things apart to only reform them in arrangements that provoke greater thought and impact than its original form. Objects and materials like plates, glass, dolls, fabric, dishes, metals, wood etc are broken apart for artistic, spiritual and utilitarian reasons. *They are reconfigured to come back in greater strength and to have a more powerful purpose as a new object, tool or expression.* Through the African Holocaust (the African Slave trade), Cuba is comprised of so many shattered rich West African cultures that gave birth to new forms only imaginable in Cuba.

Through the testament and iron-clad will to live, African people and African traditions shape shifted and survived the brutal atrocities of being stripped of identity and dignity. Through this baptism of fire the African spirit gave rise to new powerful forms in these new lands. These cultures and practices prevailed and influence today's societies across the world. Cuba and neighboring islands that experienced the same baptism gave birth to an explosion of new and powerful artistry, food, fashion, musicality and spirituality.

When you think of jazz, hip-hop, fashion and certain forms of food you must consider its origins that were forged in the bloody fires of the African Antilles. New Orleans is, for all intents and purposes, the birthplace of jazz that echoed out across the world. But it was Cuba, New Orleans's big sister, that gave jazz its heartbeat in African rhythm and syncopation. It was Cuba's legendary merchant ports that supplied the Antilles (Caribbean Nations) and American shores with the latest in fashion trends, foods, spices, textiles, musical expressions and commodities. Cuba is the jewel and the largest of the Caribbean islands; many have fought and died to control this important gateway to the Americas. Spain would rise to the top as a European Empire from its riches derived from its immense cash lucrative plantation crops of sugarcane. Sugar was king and the world demanded it. Cuba was that titan of industry and an epicenter where it supplied a staggering 1/3 of the world's demand for sugar.

My natural affinity to dive deep into this rich lineage fuels my creativity in such a profound way. Cuba becomes this magical place where these combinations of historical accolades, transgressions, baptisms and metamorphosis give my work and creative soul validity. When I walked the streets of Havana or the colonial town of Trinidad de Cuba my observation of the cities is as if the places simply froze in time. Because of the controversial embargo, overt modern elements did not get a chance to come in and gobble up the gorgeous architectural structures that you see throughout the cities today. For an artist like me who finds a number of things distasteful in modernity, Cuba offers a treasure trove of absolutely stunning layers that peel back and expose surfaces of endless color, texture and design. Havana is a city, or, permit me to say, a palette that inspires every artistic sensibility in me. I look forward to my next journey back to this magical realm. May it always be available and may my return be sooner than later.

P.H.: From what you understand, how is the culture in Cuba transforming with the Obama/Castro doctrine in effect?

J.A.: My descriptions speak from a purely artistic view. It is very easy to romanticize Cuba's gorgeous backdrop and its more than hospitable demeanor. Crime in Cuba is 1/10 the issue it is in the US. They have no guns proliferating throughout the streets. They do not tolerate illiteracy so everyone and I mean everyone receives the best education Cuba provides. I witnessed them having the same amount of freedom of speech as we do. Everyone receives healthcare and no matter your race, creed, gender or religion you are cared for without putting yourself in hock. It is far from a utopia and I would never describe it as that. But it becomes easy to fall in love with many aspects of Cuba.

I bring these things up first because visiting the city and being with its beautiful people you can easily forget that Cuba is an "enemy" of my homeland the US. The history between Cuba and the US is so rife with turbulence from the positions of the higher ups and leaders, it makes my standing on Cuban soil surreal when I really think about it. "I am standing on enemy territory. What does that mean?" I am very familiar with the details of history and what happened during the Cuban Revolution and the atrocities that occurred so I don't dare belittle the experiences of those who lived through it.

In traveling to Cuba, I knew I wanted to have purpose driven conversations with Cubans about the embargo and social and political issues between our two nations. I wanted to focus on the perspective of the people from the heartland and not rely so heavily on the two governments' ideology. In having incredibly in depth conversations with a number of Cubans about Cuba's history and social political atmosphere there and with the US, I walk away with respect for an extremely complex web of thoughts that differ from young and old.

I heard varying stances that emotionally speak about Cuba's position and tumultuous history. Without regurgitating documented history, my biggest takeaway is that they are proud and have an immense love for their country. They want to cultivate and preserve Cuban identity.

You need not ask them if the embargo should be lifted. You will hear a resounding, "It should have been done years ago." But they will not trade lifting the embargo at the expense of losing their identity and control. Currently, it's the Cuban people not governments that are suffering from this tightening noose and lack of ability to share the world as others do. They are not looking for a handout and wouldn't accept it if you gave it to them. What the people are enthusiastically looking forward to is an equal partnership with the US on trade and goods. But they won't tolerate America stepping in and controlling their markets or dictating policy over their proprietorship. They saw America's presence in Cuba around the turn of the century until 1959 as a period of industrial boom but also a period of great despair. Similar to the Spanish plantations owner's system of reaping all the benefits of the sugar industry only to send all the cultivated wealth back to Spain.

Azucar De La Havana/ oil on wood panel, gold leaf lettering, brass hardware, vintage shears, mixed media/ 39 x 56 x 4 inches/ 2016/ Visit Artsy Page for Chevere

When America occupied the island, they took over Cuban industry in such a grotesque way it warped the balance of the island. The typical greed of living off the wealth of its resources, taking the money back to the US and barely leaving anything for Cubans kicked into high gear. Cuba became a destination for Americans so they totally rebuke capitalism. The consensus about getting in bed with communist Russia was a major mistake. And accepting Russia's weaponry was the ultimate mistake. So they rebuke communism. They are proud to call themselves socialist but look for a new system that represents a hybrid of fairness and equality. They want a strong Cuban identity and the right to form equal partnerships with the world without someone sneaking in the back door and looting them.

When asked where are we from, we were met with joy. "AMERICA YES! It is a pleasure and honor to have you here. Please enjoy my country." I can't tell you how many times I heard this. Across the board they like Obama. He was not perfect but they are warm towards him. Cubans are looking forward to the changes that Obama was ushering in. Trump has mentioned he will roll back the momentum Obama has gained in relationships with Cuba. So they are puzzled, sad and worried to an extent about lost opportunities. After experiencing this beautiful country I mirror these exact feelings.

3/10/17

WOMEN ALL OVER THE UNIVERSAL WORLD

CHRYSTALLE MAHOP, TELEVISION PERSONALITY AND PRODUCER

Photo by Didier Teurquetil

WAOUW is the door that every woman in the world can step through when beauty and grace are combined with initiative and

entrepreneurship. Every year candidates are chosen by a jury composed of professionals from fashion, entertainment, culture, media and entrepreneurship.
— M-Miss Mahop

Ubiznews is a Paris-based international entertainment channel dedicated to around-the-clock information and entertainment. Perhaps it is a cross between MTV News and Comedy Central's news desk. It's dope and in the mix of the contemporary urban Paris and Pan-African emerging market scenes. Its viewership is wide, diverse, driven by millennials and numbered in the tens of millions with listeners and viewers in the United Kingdom and Africa. Every day, program shorts around themes of news, entertainment and business are broadcast via a telebroadcast and online channels for laptops and PDAs. Ubiz was founded by Amobé Mévégué, a twenty-year veteran audio-visual producer who has worked on many media channels, including Rfi, Cfi, Mcm Africa, TV5, France O, and France24.

Amobé's engagement with personality M-Miss Mahop (producer and entrepreneur Chrystalle Mahop) led to the successful program *Woman All Over the Universal World (WAOUW)*. Together, they have created leading programming popular throughout France, the United Kingdom and Africa.

M-Miss Mahop began her career working as a one-woman production studio as founder of "30Prod," a private audio visual company focusing on fashion shows, movie releases, weddings, birthdays, baptisms and Bat Mitzvahs. I had the opportunity to catch up with M-Miss Mahop and talk about UBiznews, *Women All Over the Universal World*, her favorite interviews, the recent passing of Papa Wemba, and her future plans.

Her interview was animated by a spirit of determination, grace, beauty and a voice that is a part of the present and future of Africa.

Patrick A. Howell: Tell me a little bit about *Women All Over the Universal World (WAOUW)*? What are some of the best interviews you have enjoyed? Would you say you are a storyteller in the tradition of *Jelimuso* or *Jalimuso* dating back to the thirteenth-century West African Empire of Mali?

M-Miss Mahop: I started hosting *WAOUW* two years ago. It has since become one of our flagship programs. The purpose of *WAOUW* (pronounced WOW! and don't forget the exclamation point!) is that it is a program that aims to introduce exceptional women to the world. We broadcast our channel in the United Kingdom and Africa, primarily in French-speaking countries like Chad, Ivory Coast, Côte d'Ivoire and Mali. We are looking to expand into Montreal and Quebec, Haiti and Martinique.

WAOUW is the door that women can step through when beauty and grace are combined with initiative and entrepreneurship. The show is done in connection with the WAOUW contest of the same name. Every year, six candidates are chosen by a jury composed of professionals from fashion, entertainment, culture, media and entrepreneurship.

The concept of *WAOUW* focuses on the spotlighting of the women of the world, which are exemplified in all fields by the quality of excellence. Its aim is to promote the encounters between personalities and the most prominent actors in the world of political and economic life, cultural and social.

Some of the interviews I have enjoyed the best were the ones with Christine Kelly, the first journalist Black woman who presented news on a national French channel. I admire her career. I also enjoyed interviewing Flora Coquerel, Miss France 2014. She's simply a beautiful person inside and out.

I will finish by noting a woman I respect and love so much because of her courage. That woman would be Corine Tonye, who was the winner of the WAOUW 2015. She is creating a bone marrow donation registry in Africa.

I don't know if I can be compared to a *Jelimuso* of the Empire of Mali of the thirteenth century, they were very special with the way they caught people's attention. All I can tell you is that I'm close to people and I like being in connection with the audience as simple as possible.

P.H.: Talk about your travels this past year to Martinique and Ivory Coast. Overall, you have travelled throughout the Pan-African world. What are the commonalities you note? Where do you wish to travel next? Who would be your ideal interview and why?

M.M.M.: I traveled to Martinique in January 2015 with the Ubiznews staff. We went there to make an infomercial of the island, and more precisely of the Hotel Bambou located in Trois Ilets, a French commune. I really enjoyed this trip, because we had so much fun and enjoyed cool activities such as helicopter, buggy, jet ski, and some immersions such as the visit to the Savannah slaves place. That was a particular moment where we learned more about slavery.

Prior to 2015, I visited and lived in several African destinations, such as Cameroon, Chad, Gabon, Senegal, Equatorial Guinea, Niger, Congo, Ivory Coast. I really enjoyed being in Ivory Coast. In my opinion, I think it's a good combination between several cultures... the warmth of the west African, outspokenness of central Africa and the developed side of the western countries.

For the future, I would like to discover Ethiopia. It is a destination that fascinates me because of the world history and culture. The person I would like to interview next, without any hesitation is Michelle Obama. She fascinates me and she is a role model for me and women all over the world with all of her incredible accomplishments.

P.H.: M-Miss Mahop you have had an opportunity to speak with icons of the African pop scene, including Youssou N'Dour and Papa Wemba before he passed away earlier this year.

M.M.M.: Ubiznews offers me many opportunities in my life and allowed me to realize some of my dreams... I had the chance to meet icons such as Youssou N'dour who came to our office in Paris, and with whom we have a partnership between his channel and ours. I also had the opportunity to meet Papa Wemba; I loved him so much. He was simple, generous and very talented. We planned to make a *WAOUW* show for his anniversary... but it never happened, in fact, he passed in Ivory Coast during his concert at the FEMUA festival. I was one of the last people to interview him before he passed. I still cannot believe it happened. It seems unreal.

P.H.: So, what are all of your roles on the station? How did you get to where you are and achieve all of your success?

M.M.M.: I'm in charge of the communication department at Ubiznews TV, an international channel based in France for seven years now. On the editorial charter of Ubiznews, 50% is dedicated to Africa, to the Caribbean and its diaspora and 50% for the rest of the world. 60% of what we do deals with the news and 40 % deals with entertainment.

WAOUW is a concept I came up with years ago with Amobé, the founder and the director of Ubiznews. He has been a mentor to me. He accompanied and encouraged me to accomplish my dreams and they have come through. It was through this process that the concept *WAOUW* came to life. And that life takes form in several forms — first a TV show that I present daily and then a competition which highlights women's initiatives and opens doors. I want women to have the same opportunity I have had to realize my dreams. So, the show works with women who are uniquely beautiful, graceful and filled with determination and accomplishments.

P.H.: Please talk about any special projects you are currently involved in — forthcoming shows, interviews, travel.

M.M.M.: The Ubiz-*WAOUW* family has many projects for 2017, but the nearest is making the election WAOUW international. Regarding my next trip, I'm planning to go to Niger on December for the FIMA festival founded by Alphadi, one of the greatest African stylists.

2/9/17

ICONIC PHOTOGRAPHER OPENS OUR WORLD THROUGH THE LENS OF HIS I

CHESTER HIGGINS JR, PHOTOGRAPHER AND AUTHOR

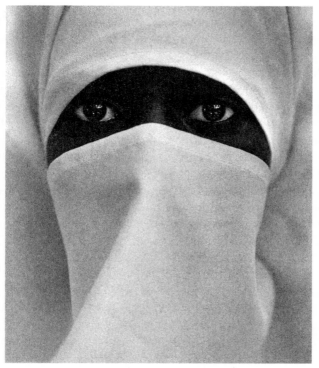

© Chester Higgins Archive

Whenever there is injustice, there will be resistance.
— Chester Higgins Jr

The Eye of Horus is an ancient Egyptian symbol of protection, royal power, and good health. It is the symbol that Chester Higgins, Jr has chosen as a symbol for his website. The spirit permeates a lifetime of work from an iconic photographer who has interpreted generations of Americans and Africans for nearly fifty decades.

The power of his eye to interpret the spirit is singular in American photography and history. That power is ancient and it is transformative. It is the northern light falling upon an age in American history, announcing the new epoch which was, in fact, the ancient one. The significance of this power within each of our persons is not lost upon Chester:

> The eye is the most sacred thing and the eye reveals the soul. Part of my approach when I am looking at eyes is I see myself as a diver into a pool into the soul and the spirit so that you get layers and layers, textures and textures of the person, the moment, the place.
>
> Spirituality is about finding ones place and peace within the awesomeness of Nature. Spirituality embraces the oneness of life, "the us." Spirituality is all about seeing yourself in the continuum of reality while materialism is about stepping outside of "the we" and anchoring yourself into the vortex of one.

Chester Higgins Jr's presence is one filled with grace though pronounced with clarity and knowing. He seems as perched from a tree of life looking upon and surveying the landscape. His assertions are not so much sounds as knowings elegantly stated. When asked if he uses Samsung or iPhone for his work these days, Chester answers, "It doesn't matter what I have in my hand. The piece of equipment can only do what my eye tells it to do." He adds an exclamation to his passion: "The moment when the photo is taken is when my heart smiles. And that is when I make the picture."

I asked him after nearly fifty years working to realize the beauty of a vision, what is he doing these days? His voice is filled with love, a sweet quality of curiosity, wisdom, and kindness in equal parts:

> [My wife and I] do Tai Chi to stay in shape. A lot of my work has been in villages. If I am walking on even terrain and walking from stone to stone, it requires a certain strength. I started doing yoga to create balance and strength. There have been a few times when it has saved my life.

He has transformed himself into an instrument for his labor of love.

> My wife and I have been doing a study on ancient, sacred studies about divinity, an African invention that began on the Blue Nile in Ethiopia moved into Nubia. The belief in a sky god is an African invention. Once in Egypt, it was bifurcated into religion. That has become Christianity, Islam, and Judaism. The Nile has been the corridor of spiritual thinking. The short of it is to keep peoples' attention focused on the Blue Nile.

I ask the question which is natural at this stage of his craft — that of an unquestionable master. I ask if he has been the eye of Horus for his people. I am thinking of a story relayed in *Echo of the Spirit*, an autobiographical book he has written with his wife. There is a story in the opening chapter, called "Chosen by the Spirit," in which he talks of being "awakened" by a spirit in 1955 as a small nine-year-old boy:

After a moment, its eyes opened — light brown eyes that looked at me with an intensity I had never known before. It began to walk very slowly toward me with those outstretched hands. The room rattled with crackling energy. Who was this being coming toward me? Could it be an alien? But my spirit reassured me it was safe.

I wonder if that spirit might have been Horus. Spirits do not know time or limits in the energy spectrums from visions to so-called reality, it is all a singular experience of living. "That's a good question. I never thought of it that way," he says, ever thoughtfully. "Everything vibrates between certainty and doubt. I had a friend who did a sculpture of me as Mercury (the Roman god). That was his way of dealing with what I do with my work. I guess I see myself as the Horus sailing through the celestial ways. You see the eye of Horus sailing off the sailboat. You have the solar part and the moon part of the eye of Horus. Mine is the moon eye riding on the celestial sailboat."

Along with Gordon Parks and Howard Bingham, Chester Higgins Jr's work has captured the quintessential American photograph and created a new perspective on African souls in our current epoch. Their work has created a new paradigm for how the world sees us but more importantly how we see ourselves.

He took his first trip to Ethiopia in 1973. He followed the news that African heads of state were gathering for an Organization of African Unity in Addis Ababa. He met and photographed emperor Haile Selassie and other leaders at the historic meeting. Inspired by a calm sense of self he found among the Ethiopian people, he returned the following year to see other parts of the country.

I continue to ask my questions as Chester engages.

Patrick A. Howell: This is an unfair question because the nature of your work reflects a spirit that is generous and unassuming. Further, you have lived a life of dreams. But what has been your most memorable trip and why?

Chester Higgins Jr: In *Echo of the Spirit*, I talk about my first trip to Ethiopia and seeing Emperor Haile Selassie. That trip remains the most memorable and is the reason why I have returned to Ethiopia annually for twenty years. I enjoy experiencing the four most important traits of my people, which is our decency, dignity, virtuous character and our love for faith.

Emperor Haile Selassie at Africa Hall. Addis Ababa,
Ethiopia. 1973 © Chester Higgins Archive

Amiri Baraka and Maya Angelou at the Schomburg Center. © Chester Higgins Archive

It has taken me decades to get closer to the people and the culture. I know I'm an outsider. As I learn more, I dive deeper in this water. I feel like our society is not as well grounded. We get our reference points from artificiality. Most of us are far removed from a sense of being connected to nature.

P.H.: Some of your work is iconic. You made your way from a town in Alabama to NYC in the 1960s at the height of the Civil Rights movement and amidst significant shifts in American and world history. In fact, it can be argued that many trappings of our NOW moment come from that period in history. You have taken iconic photos of Haile Selassie, Muhammad Ali, Maya Angelou, Gloria Steinem, Alvin Ailey, Rosa Parks, Amiri Baraka, Nelson Mandela, all great personalities who have defined a generation. We are at another moment with many of those trappings. Civil Rights: Black Lives Matter. New Age: Hippie Movement.

Dr. Martin Luther King: Barack Obama (a realization of a vision). Donald Trump: Richard Nixon. Unending wars. Mass Protests: The Resistance. Do you think American society has evolved? Do we go lower or higher from here?

C.H.: Whenever there is injustice, there will be resistance. The human being has an innate sense of worthiness and rebels against any outside force that seeks to diminish their worthiness. Until no person of African descent is unfairly targeted because of their color, the fight against oppression must continue.

P.H.: Since the 1970s, you have spent a great deal of time in Egypt and Ethiopia, at one point travelling to Ethiopia once a year, every year. Those are our first civilizations where original man, our first Christianity comes from and the only nation never occupied (Ethiopia) still stands. Is "the spirit" stronger there? Is there an inverse relationship between spirituality of the world and American materialism? What is your attraction to that part of the world?

C.H.: From what we have learned from stone etchings in Egypt, the earliest scriptures from the tomb of Unas around 2500 BCE, the world of divinity is a metaphysical concept born out of the sacred dreams of ancient African people along the Blue Nile River. In our modern times, these earliest scriptures of spirituality formed the basis of Abrahamic faiths and these teachings have been embraced by believers in half the world.

P.H.: Your love of the diaspora and her people burns bright from your work, like an African sun. It could be stated that has been your life's work. What are some of the common characteristics of Black people around the world?

C.H.: Spirituality is about finding one's place and peace within the awesomeness of Nature. Spirituality embraces the oneness of life, "the us". Materialism is to embrace things outside of yourself, trying to shoe horn things of Nature into personal walls of ownership. Spirituality is all about seeing yourself in the continuum of reality while materialism is about stepping outside of "the we" and anchoring yourself into the vortex of one.

My attraction to Africa is because I want to discover the fullness of myself, which means for me to seek out the many dimensions of my people and history. With the camera, I have sought to discover exactly who I am and where do I belong.

Through his work, Chester Higgins Jr embraces the quality of African spirits, that of African possibility and limitless human possibility. He learned an important lesson from his beloved uncle as a young man: "It's important to make a mark on life unless you die undeclared." He has kept charge of the keep given by his elders and entrusted by ancestors.

It is no wonder or perhaps it is with that wonder that Chester Higgins Jr has become the Eye of Horus in the modern age, showing us a view of ourselves by ourselves outside the Hollywood Industrial complex that seeks to distort, obfuscate and minimize.

Wisdom can be a welcome companion of old age. Those who find Wisdom become the beacons for the rest of us. We are attracted by their peacefulness and the vast reservoir of understanding they have acquired through years of living. As enigmatic as it seems, Wisdom is clearly recognizable. We see it, we feel it, and we want to be part of it.
— *Echo of the Spirit*

Finally, after a pleasant conversation, like two souls sitting on the moon and gazing into the stars, I ask Chester if he had a home in any of the African cities he has traveled; where would he build that castle? He speaks without skipping a beat, "I would have a home in Senegal off the coast because my ancestors are from there going back four generations. I always felt the pull from Senegal. When I had my African ancestry done, it is 100% mandingo from those tribes. If it was in the East, I would take the Blue Nile in Ethiopia. But I always tell everyone if you are going to Africa for the first time, go to Ghana. The people are very religious and warm and loud."

Well, I'll say it now loudly our Eye of Horus, your vision shines brilliantly through generations who see the truth from antiquity. We are awakened to that reality. Hotep.

Amen.

I am the child who traverseth the road of Yesterday. I am Today for untold nations and peoples. I am the One who protected you for millions of years.
— *The Sacred Book of Coming Forth*, Kemet, quoted in the epilogue of *Echo of the Spirit*

SPIRITS OF JOY, BIRDS, TREES AND BUTTERFLIES IN THE MARCH OF MARCHES

LAUREN BACCUS, FREE SPIRIT, MURALIST AND EDUCATOR

Carnival is about telling and retelling our histories but it is also a space for very current social commentary. It is a tool that parades as a pure fun, but that's the illusion. It's accessible and it's participatory, and it is art.
— Lauren Baccus

Carnival is an annual national festival hosted in Trinidad and Tobago, before Ash Wednesday. The event is world renowned for participant's costumes and festive celebrations. Calypso music and steel pans have traditionally ruled the festival, with its origins in celebrating the hardships West and Central Africans endured while enslaved. Lauren Baccus is a painter who spent time growing up between Trinidad and Jamaica. I had the opportunity to talk about the ultimate art experience — calypso!

Patrick A. Howell: Lauren, it looks like you had an amazing trip in Trinidad's Carnival this year. How does the carnival in Trinidad and Tobago differ from St. Lucia's? Give our readers an overview of how you came to Carnival, with whom and where you stayed.

Lauren Baccus: I grew up in Jamaica and moved to Trinidad when I was 10. After about a decade in New York, I moved to St Croix, USVI where I now live. All of these places have some form of carnival and while each are pretty distinct, they all provide an incredible outlet for celebration, release, storytelling, connection... Coming back to Trinidad this year though was especially significant because, for the first time, I was part of the design team for Lost Tribe.

I had just come off of creating my first puppet for St Croix Carnival, or Crucian Christmas Festival, which is smaller and much more of a spectator sport. That presentation, entitled "The Land Belongs to the Land," was a large papier-mâché and cloth egret, and a direct response to these ideas we have about ownership of the earth. The process of creating the piece was especially significant for me as this year marks the 100th anniversary of the transfer of the Virgin Islands from Danish to American rule. I wanted to talk about the legacy of buying and selling an entire territory and its people but from a much larger perspective. Because St Croix is a smaller affair, it's much easier to participate and create freely. The piece did create conversation, but not around the original theme. Still, I felt absolutely grateful for the dialogue that came out of that.

In contrast, The Lost Tribe is an organized collective. Your design voice has to reflect and blend with not just the other designers, but the aesthetic that they represent, a bridge between traditional mas (masquerade) and contemporary design. Being part of the team was three years in the making but it was perfect timing. The entire trip happened very much like that, a little haphazard, lots of last minute planning, but ultimately everything worked out.

P.H.: So you marched under the "Lost Tribe" banner, how was that?

L.B.: This was Lost Tribe's second presentation and it is already considered a large band. Its success is such a testimony to an element of mas that many people felt was missing, or at least was quickly disappearing amongst the ornate "bead and feather" costumes. There might be divided camps on this but I'm actually a fan of those costumes. There's no reason to believe they cannot coexist with, and even inform design that is more heavily influenced by storytelling and traditional masquerade. Lost Tribe manages to balance the two elements, glamor and artistry, really beautifully. I have enormous respect for the creatives of Lost Tribe and Creative Director Valmiki Maharaj and Co-Creative Director Anya Ayoung Chee. I've been waiting for this kind of mas!

The design that ended up as "Arieto" had originally been submitted for Lost Tribe's parent band, Tribe, by my design partner Jeri-Lee Alexander and myself. In retrospect, it absolutely belonged to the Lost Tribe, even though the band had yet to be created. There was some tweaking to the design, but again, that's part of that process of collaboration.

P.H.: As an artist, were you inspired by Carnival? Will you be creating work from your experience?

L.B.: Carnival IS art!

My first memories of Trinidad were of carnival. The creatives that I have always been most drawn to are, among other things, mas makers and puppeteers. My Caribbean history is told through carnival so how can it NOT be a formative part of who I am and the work I produce? Carnival is about telling and retelling our histories but it is also a space for very current social commentary. It is a tool that parades as a pure fun, but that's the illusion. It's accessible and it's participatory, and it's art.

My dream has always been to design for carnival and I'm lucky enough to have access to two. They present very different opportunities to create and for as long as I can, I'll continue to do so.

P.H.: Who was Carnival King and Queen this year?

L.B.: I'm actually not sure who won but I do have a family member who was the queen with the band K2K and came fifth!

P.H.: I heard one of the soca melodies making the rounds this year was by seventy-six-year-old music legend Calypso Rose and titled matter-of-factly "Leave Me Alone." Was there a road march to that tune? What were the big socas?

L.B.: "Leave Me Alone" is not just a good song, it is a direct response to this idea that a woman participating in carnival is essentially inviting harassment. The song is a strong feminist stand and a celebration of this time where women can possess their own bodies and their own sexuality whether in song or dance or just an opportunity to play dress up. Women have been singing empowering songs for years, but right now, there's a groundswell of activism happening in Trinidad around street harassment, victim blaming, body-shaming, and violence towards women. There's a certain brand of persistent misogyny in the Caribbean that has created the necessity for songs like this and the work of activists and artists around these issues.

Organizations like "Say Something" founded by activists Attillah Springer and Angelique V. Nixon are calling for gender-sensitivity training and improved data collection on the part of the government. Other artists are collaborating through organizations like Together WI, creating really effective campaigns around "Leave Me Alone." All of this further increases the visibility of these issues and those willing to speak on it. That this song could capture this movement is the kind of thing that exemplifies the power of carnival. Were there other big socas, absolutely, but this is the one that I hope we'll keep talking about.

P.H.: Tell me most amazing experiences you had at carnival this year?

L.B.: First, of course, was seeing a couple hundred people in a design that I had worked on cross the Savannah stage. That was the pinnacle! It is something that has been a dream for so long and it was finally realized. There's not a lot more I can say about it! As a participant, though, I've got to say that the Lost Tribe experience on the whole was incredibly easy and professional. For all my lack of planning, it definitely was the smoothest part of the trip.

A close second would be Jouvert, the early morning baptism by paint! The "opening day" of carnival and the official first tramp through town. I'm mixing up my carnival language here as "tramp" is more a Crucian word for walking with a band. We played with 3 Canal and were accompanied by the Laventille Rhythm Section. Unlike the blaring trucks with canned music and DJs, this was earthy and raw; iron and drums for the darkness.

Most of my favorite things happen in those darkened hours between 3am and 7am. As one friend put it, that's when the conjuring happens. Carnival is a conjuring in truth, so it makes sense that those hours would seem especially magical. The reenactment of the Canboulay riots also happen at that time and are another favorite memory from the time. Carnival, post emancipation, became an important opportunity for social commentary and even open defiance. Traditions like the stick fighting, canboulay ("cannes brulees" the burning of cane), chantwells and kaiso evolved throughout this transition. For the British authorities, this felt very much like a threat to public order and those forces clashed with the revelers in a series of riots. These are the events that are recreated every year as a reminder of how hard won this celebration actually is. Definitely one of my top three experiences.

P.H.: It is a bit of interesting history on Carnival where calypso music was developed in Trinidad in the seventeenth century from the West African Kaiso and canboulay music brought by African slaves imported to that Caribbean island to work on sugar plantations. As calypso developed, the role of the griot became known as a chantuelle and eventually, calypsonian. As a Caribbean, is there a sense of tradition and history to the TnT Carnival experience?

L.B.: Absolutely but ultimately, that belongs to the participant. In truth, there's history and tradition in all things. The key is looking for those signs; can you even see the past in the present? Musicians and mas makers are still pulling from traditional influences, whether we recognize it or not. We are participating WITHIN history, whether we acknowledge it or not. Carnival in 2017 may be an evolution, but exists just as much within the historical context as 100 years prior. It's still a part of the story.

P.H.: Is there a spiritual dimension to Carnival in Trinidad and Tobago?

L.B.: The kind of spirituality that resonates with me personally are those teachings which embrace our duality, our light and our darkness. The celebration of carnival is also about that which is light and that which is dark, together. The history of carnival is lightness within darkness and vice versa. There's no way to go through carnival, experience the music, bear witness to all of that color and glory and not feel akin to something spiritual.

The process for me is a clearing and a celebration but also refocusing. It's a process that happens both communally and as an intensely personal experience. Yes, there are moments of complete abandon, but those are temporary states. One can chase that euphoric freedom, just as as one can chase enlightenment but that removes you from the present, a lesson which carnival teaches.. Even the greatest case of tabanca, that sadness that inevitably accompanies the end of carnival, is a lesson.

Everything is temporary!

3/12/17

IN HER OWN IMAGE — MOLDING THE FUTURE FROM THE PAST

VINNIE BAGWELL, SCULPTOR AND ENTREPRENEUR

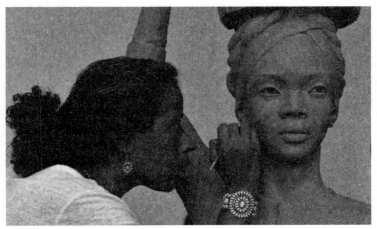

Photo by Jonathan Lewis

Vinnie Bagwell is an encyclopedia of experiences, creative expressions, stories, emotional and psychological gifts. *She is magic.* Yes, Vinnie is a master at what she does. So, all of this is another way to say that she is a griot. Vinnie Bagwell is a seer but she is a doer too. She is a visionary with her feet firmly planted in commerce. She is a self-taught artist who began sculpting in 1993. In her sixth month of painting, renowned Italian artist Bruno Lucchesi told her, "We need to see better. Vision is not what we see. Vision is what you know." So, that is the work, translating the visions in one's mind to this place and time. That's what Vinnie does. Who is to say where the strength of that vision comes from. The past? A glorious future? A place where imagination is real? A place where beauty reigns supreme. A place with no limitations.

Vinnie is singularly dedicated to Black art as a global expression, an expression of our collective humanity. Her art is unapologetic in representing the struggle as beauty. She uses her art to plow humanity and express an aesthetic that includes values like harmony, love of beauty and grace. When she was receiving her education at Morgan State University they told her she had to do what she does and do it at a high level — pursue excellence. She has done that work, the work of a virtuoso.

Then she tells me about a mentor, Harold Esannason, a West Indian Caribbean, who told her, "'Baggs you don't want to work in corporate America.' He taught me how to be a free wheeler. How to do it on my own. And that's hard. Most people want structure. They want a 9-5. When I met Harold he was doing the Black International Leisure. He was also a graphic designer. I mentored under him for five years. 'Baggs you need to work for yourself. Don't be afraid.' He would challenge me to come up with ideas to create my own work."

She created her first piece and there has been no looking back since then.

Patrick A. Howell: How did you begin sculpting and how did it become the work of a lifetime?

Vinnie Bagwell: I was born an artist; in other words, I am God "gifted," "untutored." I could draw very well at an early age, and tried painting in my senior year in high school. Many years later, when I realized I was "blocked," I tried sculpting to "prime the well," and discovered yet another gift. Sculpting came so swiftly and amazingly, I tell people, "God snapped his fingers to change my destiny." Artists are the stewards of civilization, and art is of great value to any people. It's a record of growth and development from generation to generation. Art defines who we are as people and provides an account of our history for the next generation. If our people did not have anything to which we could look back, the wisdom and acts of our forefathers would be forgotten; the experience of a generation would be lost to the succeeding ones. It's an honor to be an artist. I feel highly favored by God.

P.H.: Vinnie, it's "Black History Month," a singular month for the work you have taken to define a whole lifetime's worth of work. Why do you focus on Frederick Douglass, Ella Fitzgerald, our dancers, our women, our men and their sons, our ancestors? Why do you select these particular subjects and their thematic constructs for your amazing work? What informs and inspires your work?

V.B.: When I began sculpting in 1993, there were few examples of African Americans as "people" in public art, and even fewer Black sculptors doing the work. The road for the serious Black artist — one who would produce "racial" art — is most certainly rocky, and the mountain is high. A minor artist with no money goes as hungry as a genius. However, there comes a point in your life when you realize your place in the link to the past and the future, and I realized: No one will do this for us, so I faithfully portray the innermost thoughts and feelings of people of color, with all the fire and romance which lay dormant in our history.

I believe that people, such as myself, are not only choosing art, we are choosing the life of the artist. Art offers us a different way of living, and happiness is achieved through fidelity to a worthy purpose. Celebrating history, today, we can see ourselves in each other's stories and think about how far we have come as a country, and how much further we need to go to erase racism and discrimination from our society. Frederick Douglass asked, "The real question is whether American justice, American liberty, American civil rights, American law, and American Christianity can be made to include all American citizens." Progress is accomplished by people who do things. You don't make progress standing on the sidelines, spectating. You make progress by implementing ideas. Life obliges one to work and dare if one really wants to live, so, artists make art. Every action we take, everything we do, is either a victory or defeat in the struggle to become what we want to be. Better human beings.

You may not have noticed but there is a distinct difference between what I create for myself versus what I create in response to Calls for Artists for public art. "The First Lady of Jazz Ella Fitzgerald" was a commission that I proposed to the City of Yonkers because, in 1993, they only had public art depicting dead presidents and war heroes, nothing about minorities or women. Ella is a beloved, international music icon. She grew up in Yonkers. The commission was to be an acknowledgement of one of the City's most renowned residents, an inspiring woman of color who grew up in what is now a blighted neighborhood.

"Frederick Douglass Circle" was originally designed in response to a Call for Art for the northwest corner of New York City's Central Park in 2003. In 2007, I submitted the concept in response to Hofstra's Call for Art that represents "the history, achievements, and aspirations of people of color" because I felt that if I had to choose any one person in all of history to speak for me, it would be the passionate and eloquent orator Frederick Douglass. Again, my approach to public art is somewhat prescribed. I'm not sure I would've made these works if I didn't make public art. Work I make for myself is designed to be more ethereal. My simple desire is to depict the beauty of Black people as people.

P.H.: In 1992, you co-authored a book with Harold Esannason, *A Study of African American Life in Yonkers from the Turn of the Century*. The city of Yonkers seems to take an "up-front-and-center" seat in your work. What is it about Yonkers? Also, talk a little about your work with Mr Esannason and the project.

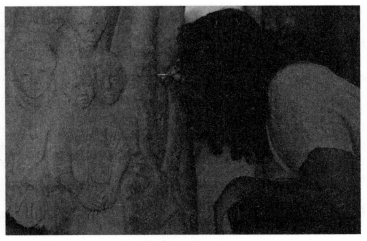

Photo by Jonathan Lewis

V.B.: I was born in Yonkers. My family moved to the town of Greenburgh, further north in Westchester County, New York, when I was ten. There, mentors began guiding me in eighth grade. My first mentor was Toni Abramson (Matthews), my high-school English Chair. She stressed the importance of learning how to articulate my thoughts on paper, how to write well. Dr George Carter, the Psychology Chairman at Morgan State University, helped me navigate college. After college, I met Harold Esannason, a freelance graphic designer and entrepreneur. As my third mentor, he taught me how to think "outside the box"; how to create work for myself rather than work for others, and how to apply my knowledge, skills, and abilities to enhance my community.

In the past, race discrimination, instead of being solely a barrier, was often the glue that held our communities together in tightly-knit survival units. We were held together by kinship, place of origin, and shared region and custom. The segregated communities gave our families a sense of purpose and identity and a strong sense of unified values. *A Study of African American Life in Yonkers From the Turn of the Century* was a labor of love: the book was written about the people, in the words of the people, by one of the people from the community. It was funded by a Federal Community-Development Block Grant from the Department of Housing and Urban Development (HUD) to serve a low-to-moderate income part of the city. The project also included an exhibition of the photographs in the book. It remains a benchmark project because no other ethnic group has duplicated that effort.

P.H.: Is there a relationship, personal, ethereal or metaphysical with you and your subject matter? How do you communicate emotion and spirit in your subject matter?

V.B.: I am a storyteller: my perception of "power" in a story is highly intuitive. I know it when I see it. I recognize it when I hear it. I was a columnist for *Gannett Suburban Newspapers* in the early Nineties. I write proposals for a living. (I'm also a photographer.) I know how to move people with a story because I understand human nature. At the heart of all of my work is the portrayal of the Spirit in human form. If I had to narrow it down to a science, I would say this: "The human spirit is conveyed through the eyes, mouth, and hands." That's where you'll find "emotion and spirit" in my subject matter.

P.H.: Have you heard of "Sankofa" — in the native Akan language it means, "Go Back and Go Get It." Do you think that African precept has any significance or meaning to your work?

V.B.: Of course! "Se wo were fi no wosan kofa a yenkiw" (the Akan translation of that quote) is incised on the pedestal of the-first-of-five life-sized bronze sculptures being created for an urban-heritage sculpture garden to honor the enslaved Africans who lived at Philipse Manor Hall in Yonkers — six of whom were among the first to be manumitted/freed by law, sixty-six years before the Emancipation Proclamation. The impetus for the Enslaved Africans' Rain Garden initiative is another example where I looked around a community that I know well, discovered a rich history, and used my aesthetic to map the sense of place for Black history before "revitalization" and gentrification erases that history.

The permanent installation for the Enslaved Africans' Rain Garden will not take place until 2019. Meanwhile, the five sculptures will be temporarily installated and unveiled as each is completed. The unveiling of the first sculpture, "I'Satta," will take place at the end of March 2017 at Sarah Lawrence College. The second unveiling of "Themba the Boatman" will take place in November 2017. Please visit www.enslavedafricansraingarden.org to learn more.

P.H.: Finally "Nyame Nnwu Na Mawu" means "God never dies and cannot die." That particular Akan symbol has meaning around God's omnipresence and the perpetual existence of God's spirit. Would you say any of this meaning or symbolism plays into your work?

V.B.: I am a believer. Being an artist makes me a believer: I am extremely aware of the voice of God— others call it "intuition." I think of my work as a kind of documentation of conversations with God. My work is more about the triumph of the human spirit than it is about the color of skin. I believe this is why my artwork resonates in galleries, public places and on social media worldwide. Inside, we are all the same. People see that in my work.

2/13/17

#(UN)DEFINE VISIBLE/INVISIBLE BLACK WOMEN

ARTIST JENITA LANDRUM AND STUDIO J

Studio J, located in Phoenix, Arizona, is operated by artist and curator Jenita Landrum, who has been at this game for nearly four decades now. Jenita has been a professional artist, entrepreneur and manifestor for thirty-eight years, crafting her own beautiful space with a constructive critique of what it means to be a Black woman within the paradigm of the American experience. Her mediums of choice have been watercolor, acrylic and mixed media, but she has harnessed the forces of hope, self-love and unadulterated realness to powerful effect. She has created a community of artists through her entrepreneurism, setting up a shop that is in reality a liberation space for women. Studio J is a temple of power in contemporary America.

Here is what Jenita, a Black woman in possession of her own power in every way, had to say about some of her incredible work upon the planet:

Patrick A. Howell: Jenita, can you talk a little about Studio J and how that space represents your artistic visions and goals?

Jenita Landrum: Studio J was my first art studio in Phoenix, Arizona. I just graduated with a BFA in painting. At that point I just wanted to keep creating, it was a space just for me. I outgrew that space and opened another space in Downtown Phoenix on 5th Avenue. I named it North 5th Avenue Studios and Gallery. That was larger; it was large enough to have a gallery and had enough space to host five residential artists. That space challenged me to be a curator, artist and business owner. It was in the North 5th Ave space that I became conscious about my artistic vision, the need for exhibition opportunities and how important it is to not wait for an opportunity to define what my mission and goals were going to be in this creative life. In order to fulfill my vision, mission and goals I needed a graduate degree because no one was taking me seriously. After receiving my MFA, my work took off. This was at the same time as I opened The Art Loft Studios and Gallery, fifteen years ago in downtown Columbus, Ohio. The Art Loft allowed me an entrance in to the art community. It took off with the help of national and international artists such as Sam Gilliam, Maurice Evans, Annette Lawrence and a host of others. It was important at that time to launch myself and many other artists by providing exhibition opportunities, community collaboratives, art workshops and mentorships. The launching of my career in Columbus took me to Africa and Germany, and meant I was the recipient of individual fellowships, commission and residencies.

Upon my return to Phoenix I needed a space to create new bodies of work, so I opened Studio J I, a studio/event space, and Studio J II in Scottsdale, which served as gallery and event space. Studio J is a creative space for artists to work. I showed my work in the spaces but also it created opportunities for beginning, emerging and local artists to show in a gallery. I see my experience as an artist/gallery owner as a warmup to what I see myself doing in the near future, which is purchasing a large multi-functional building/warehouse that can encompass all the arts. The space will provide residency for artists in any medium. It will have a performance space, classrooms for workshop/ camps for children, an art gallery and a gift shop, kitchen and sound/computer classrooms.

P.H.: Much of your work deals with the themes of "invisibleness" and cultural norms, appropriating resources — watercolors and pop icons, studios and exhibits — to reflect how societal norms render images that make Black women into caricatures of themselves. How have you seen society change in the forty years since you began your work? Have you achieved the aims or goals you set out with your work?

J.L.: As a Black Women that entered college in the 1980s, when doing research it was hard to find positive images that looked like me and didn't objectify our bodies — they were somewhat invisible or not easily accessible. Part of my drive is to leave a body of work that celebrates and focuses on what makes Black women resilient, powerful in their beauty and to lift Black artists to a higher prominence. I was blessed to attain three degrees from public universities. In formal education you were told that you were not good enough, that your creative images were not viewed as creative because they were Black. In critiques you had to be ten times better than other students; you were graded unfairly if you showed Black aesthetics. You had to defend your Black reasoning based on the norms of art historical praise. If you wanted to graduate, you didn't dare open dialog, embrace concepts or use images that define what was art to you. It happens, often on calls for entries or for curator choice for exhibitions; if your work represents African American Art images your images may be seen as less then.

Today there are some changes in how Black women are viewed, but the Black genre is still low on the totem pole and is mostly viewed in Black venues. The Black aesthetic has lots of opportunities during the months of January and February. I do think Black female artists are breaking molds and creating the best art ever today. We have learned to create with two faces, one face is your personal connection to self and the other face visual acceptance. The art world is slowly embracing Black artists but not enough Black women are sought after or accepted in major exhibitions. My goal is to connect with Black women that are working within their Blackness and are pushing their consciousness to continue making Black art that is provocative, educational, art that pushes out of the box, art that uses skills to bring more importance to Black female artists and in general. I have not achieved my personal goal as an artist, but as an artist, I'm always reaching to define what is art to me.

P.H.: What is art to you? Is it a personal expression? It is politics? Is it a social platform? Is it a way of life? What does "art" mean to Jenita Landrum?

J.L.: Interesting question. I'm asked all the time, "What is art to me?" or "Where does my work come from?" I will take you back to my undergraduate experience at art school in Detroit, Michigan — it was there that I realized that my art was perceived as wrong. Creating art from a Black perspective and from my own experience was not accepted. It was confusing and hurtful but it felt so right to me. I completed studies at a public university in Tempe, Arizona where I felt further rejection because I wanted to paint and draw Black faces and explore the Black consciousness. But I kept working on my personal aesthetic using the tools that I learned. Once in graduate school in Columbus I was determined to do the work that I wanted to. I wanted to create work that had meaning, that was beautiful to look at; it would be work that would grab hold of you long after a show, it would lay on your consciousness, it would be lasting. It is work that has a voice and gives a voice to the viewers.

My art is very layered, I work in series. The concept in every series begins with me, my thoughts, what I see or a feeling from social norms and systems that may be unbalanced, or can withhold inequalities and that may reflect on self — identity and genderism. My work is only completed after it speaks to me. It has to say something to me then it takes on a political, social or feminist platform that comes through a Black voice and Black perspective. Art is also a way of life for me. I embrace my Blackness, I celebrate my womaness and marvel at my creative spirit. It was not my intention to be called to lead. I was told by the great painter Samella Lewis and Jacob Lawrence that it wasn't enough to just do art, but you must embrace art, do all that you can do to further African American Art. I have followed the lead of many great artists that came before me. I honor them by doing what they did, to uplift, encourage, mentor and create opportunity for the Black artist voice. Through my work, it has led me to have a voice and be the voice. Art to me means living a true creative life that is never knowing. But it also searching for what feels right in my creation, and to define what is beautiful to look at.

1/17/18

THE SUBTLETIES OF PASTELS BY STRENGTH OF SPIRIT

NATIQ JALIL, ARTIST AND PAINTER

Natiq's work typically starts out with a little scribble doodle action — something that came from a dream.

That's when he says he likes to do his work — right at the moment when the world is waking up and the dream world loses its footing in reality, just before all the noise is about to start — that's when Natiq Jalil's powers are at their height. Those *might* be Natiq's powers — translating dreams into reality. That's how a Natiq Jalil piece comes into being, a process of synthesizing magic and beauty into material for human voyeurism. I'll say this too — he's at home within himself. The soft pastels that come across in his work are an homage to beauty and the world that is in the midst of all the violence and ugly realities that can, at times, seem so overwhelming. They come from a space that Natiq Jalil shares openly and willingly with the world. That is strength, courage and honor so, there is a code there too.

His work is mixed media, with a strong focus on watercolor and ink, and typically features women and their essence. He is highly attuned to shapes, colors, and moods. But, let's talk with Natiq and find out about his work directly from the creative.

Patrick A. Howell: Natiq Jalil, what does your name mean?

Natiq Jalil: The name Natiq means "one endowed with speech," and the rest of my name means "servant of the most exalted."

P.H.: Why do you paint in watercolor? Does it relate to the subject matter of your work, women? Upon visual evaluation, you seem a strong brother, very masculine, powerful. Why are women the subject of so much of your work? What about the feminine spirit inspires Natiq? Is there a marriage of opposites with you and your work?

N.J.: I've used most media in my journey as an artist, however, I've found the most freedom in watercolor. In my early work, I struggled with feeling confined by the "rules" of the medium I was using. With oil, it was the fat over lean rule, plus the long drying times and difficult cleanup. With acrylics, it was the super short drying times, which made it hard to blend, and the damage they did to my brushes. I disliked the way charcoals and pastels stuck to my fingers and smudged easily. With watercolor, I've been able to quickly capture my subject matter, pack up, and move on. Plus, I love the spontaneous aspect of them. I'm able to let them run, let the colors blend into each other, splatter, etc. There's no limit to what can be done with them. They are definitely the love of my life, right now.

In the beginning, I only painted men, Black men in particular. My earliest experiments were self-portraits. Black men were always spoken about in negative and aggressive ways, but never with adjectives such as beautiful, inspiring, captivating, or human. I sought to capture those things.

Eventually, I found myself putting more and more of my emotions in my work. I started using organic and floral shapes in my work (due to my mom's influence. She does flower arrangements and would often tell me the meanings and attributes of the plants she used). When people would see the work, they invariably started to feminize my work. They'd focus on the flowers in the man's beard and totally miss the message of growth, happiness, sadness, or pain. I attribute this to homophobia, to be honest. Needless to say, I didn't sell much work.

This made me think of the "boys don't cry" philosophy. When a man expresses anything more than a small set of "acceptable, masculine" emotions, such as excitement, anger, and aloofness, he is told to "man up," grow a pair, get out of your feelings, stop acting like a bitch. This is what I saw in the eyes of people who viewed my work.

Eventually, the thought occurred to me to put a feminine face on my work. My thinking was, since you are going to feminize my work and dismiss it, how about I help you out. See? I feminized my work for you, now listen. I didn't know whether I'd get the work I desired, but it ended up working. People looked at my work and immediately connected the pieces to pain, struggle, triumph, and every other thing I felt. The unexpected side effect of this is that, until someone meets me, they often assume I'm a woman. Go fig. It's wild.

My message now is that men are human beings, too, with a full set of emotions and the ability to fully experience them and convey them. In telling people the story of my individual works, they are often moved and wonder how I'm able to, as a man, capture such a wide range of deep sentiments. I tell them that it's in all of us. We just aren't taught that we are allowed to show them.

So, in a way, my work is a true marriage of opposites. To the point where people are perplexed by the artist, himself.

All of the emotions are mine. I've just found that women are the mirror to my own experiences. I've found that I've been able to speak more freely with women, connect to their hidden thoughts, be vulnerable with them, and more tangibly relate to their everyday lives. The models I've worked with have often felt comfortable to share with me feelings, thoughts, and experiences that they'd never even considered mentioning to another person. Their stories always end up being incorporated into the work. Their emotions and mine. It's an amazing connection.

P.H.: What is it about the period between being asleep and awake that informs your work? Do you believe ancestors speak to you then? Do you believe the world is quieter then and easier to focus upon? Do you channel spirits in your work?

N.J.: The period between being awake and asleep is almost magical. You have the last little threads of a dream in your head. You open your eyes and you can touch, taste, smell, and hear your dreams. Everything is tangible in the most ethereal and surreal way. In those moments, I am left with questions without answers, wondering about what some obscure image in my mind could mean.

It becomes a race to quickly transfer these fleeting images to the canvas or paper before they disappear. I often never truly figure out how the strange symbolism of my dreams is related to my life, but I do feel them. Maybe these elements are just a part of me that is so familiar that I've never noticed. I don't know. What I do know is that capturing these retreating dream fragments is quite the adventure. The ultimate high.

I believe that the ancestors absolutely could speak to us in our dreams. They could be telling us stories of their lives. They might even want us to share their stories to the world. There are so many possible ways to look at it.

In the moments shortly after waking up, and I'm mixing colors, scribbling out loose shapes, and dripping colored puddles on paper, it's like Zen. Everything is quiet. Everything is serene. Hours go by and I don't even notice. It's just color and lines and poetry. It's surreal. Getting into the zone is like a spiritual experience. I don't know whether I channel spirits into my work, but I do know that I imprint a piece of myself into every piece.

P.H.: On July 9, you will have your work at Cell Therapy: The Past and Future Diary at the Carnegie Public Library in Braddock. Also, I noticed upcoming events with "Train of Thought." There is a very ethereal approach to your work. Why is that? I noticed also the spiritual quality of your work, as well as the word "spirit" throughout your bio and website. What do you see that most of us miss that allows you to operate at higher frequencies?

N.J.: Reading your questions made me realize that I seriously need to update my website. My Cell Therapy show was last July. It was amazing. It was some of my most honest work. I excluded any pieces that I felt weren't done completely in the moment. If it wasn't a piece that I completely lost myself in, it didn't make it into the show. That show also featured a live performance by Crystal Noel, an amazing poet here in Pittsburgh, PA. She and I went out to dinner after that show and now she is my fiancée. So, needless to say, that show has a lot of meaning to me.

Train of Thought is my ongoing labor of love. I initially started this collection of work when I was living in NYC. I'd literally paint and draw pieces on the trains as I traveled back and forth between Manhattan and the Bronx, where I lived. The trains were almost like a spiritual place to me. New Yorkers never look at each other on the trains. They stare at some fixed point between themselves and nowhere, completely oblivious to their surroundings. I was often the only person looking around. I'd look at them all until I found my subject matter. Then I'd capture them as quickly as I could before they exited. In my mind, I make up a story about where they'd been that day, who they'd spoken to, what they'd eaten.

Over at the Carnegie Library in Braddock, there hangs a piece from this collection. I'll send you a picture of it. It is of a young woman who got on the train with some of her friends. They were loud and very animated. But what drew me to her were her eyes. Even though she was laughing, she looked like she would break out into tears at any moment. I tried to capture her as quickly as possible. I started with her eyes. Then her nose. Then her mouth. It was around then that she and her friends got off the train. I finished the piece based entirely on the emotions she left me with. There was definitely loneliness. Heartbreak. Weariness. Maybe even hopelessness. It was all there. That was what the Train of Thought project was about.

There were other times on the train where I'd just freestyle it on paper. I'd take an element from this person or that one, some pattern on the floor, a billboard I'd glimpse as the doors of the train closed. Those pieces are very satisfying. They were literally the story of my train ride home.

Now that I'm in Pittsburgh, the project has changed a little. I've turned it inwards. It is now about the beauty of people of color, police brutality, protest, love, accomplishment, Black Lives Matter, fearlessness, miracles, and rebirth. It's about whatever is occupying my mind at the moment. Sometimes I am in transit, like I was in NYC. Sometimes, I am sitting there with my fiancée and my daughter. Other times, I'm at a poetry event. It is spontaneous and in the moment. One day, I hope to display the full collection in its entirety.

As far as upcoming events, I am putting together work for a three-man show called *Natural Flow*, with Marcel Lamont Walker and Gregory Garay. It is an exhibit of sequential fine art. The other two artists are comic book artists, and our work will literally tell a story. I'm also working on pieces surrounding social justice issues and the vast, dark emotions of people of color living in a Trump presidency. I'm hoping to put together an exhibit of these works, also.

As far as what I see that most people miss? When I look out into the world, I immediately see lines, circles, colors, and textures. I see how to draw the world before I even see the world itself. I see people in the same way. It is as I speak to someone that their image resolves itself into a flesh and blood human. I know that probably sounds weird. I used to believe that everyone saw the world in this way. It wasn't until someone informed me of my weirdness that I saw myself as anything "other." That was probably the moment that I realized that there was a true difference between "regular people" and artists.

I think that I see the abstract when others see the concrete. When I'm painting, I tend to closely study my subject matter, and then close my eyes. Whatever colors I see on the inside of my eyelids are the colors I use. That's how I show you exactly how I see the world.

2/11/17

AFRIKA GALAKTIKA

RAJNI PERERA ILLUSTRATES A FUTURE POWER PEOPLE

What happens when we are no longer "here," amongst the living? Where does our knowing, being and consciousness go? How do we get back to where we come from? How do the future and the past intersect with one another? How do our future selves intersect with our aboriginal selves to create our present being? What is the difference between the constructs of feminine and male energy?

These are some of the questions inspired by Rajni Perera's work. These questions are evidence as to how the work of artists as Rajni Perera are catalysts to our globe and a brilliant struggle to move into the new power paradigm. The artwork of Rajni, particularly the gallery showing inspired by her 2013-2015 meditation and heroine Afrika Galaktika, is aligned with the future expressed by so many artists and writers of the Afrofuturism movement.

The Toronto-based artist was kind enough to lend insights into her process, inspirations and the impact of her work on individual perspectives and how we see ourselves.

Patrick A. Howell: Which one — *Star Wars*, Frank Herbert's *Dune*, *Lord of the Rings* or *Star Trek* – which is the greatest science fiction/fantasy franchise? Or do you believe that title belongs more to Marvel's *X-Men* or *Avengers*? Or, perhaps, it is an altogether different franchise not as well known?

Rajni Perera: I really like *Star Wars* and *Star Trek* — the science fiction world I create out of lies closer to that of Jean Giraud's, Frank Frazetta's and H.R. Geiger's work from the earlier *Heavy Metal* magazines, the anime series *Robotech* and similar ones like *Voltron*. Manga stories like *Lum*, anything by Osamu Tezuka, the huge crazy epics by Hayao Miyazaki... not much from the West in terms of inspiring the look of my work, although I did some *Top Cow* comics (*Witchblade*, *Gen 13*) growing up. So I'd have to side with "not well known" on this one, I guess.

P.H.: The X-Men's Storm, Halle Berry's Catwoman, Pam Grier's Foxy Brown, Sheba Baby and Jackie Brown, Zoe

Saldana's Superhero Gamora from *Guardians of the Galaxy* are all Black heroines who have had an impact on world popular culture or the "global imagination" if you will. Which is your favorite all time heroine? Why?

R.P.: I really liked Foxy Brown. The special thing about blaxploitation for me was that it wasn't the same as a Hollywood-style heteronormative ideal. The issues of Black America were not covered by mainstream media, so a subculture had to be created out of necessity. Culture is, among other things, a mirror. When a mirror is too small for everyone to be able to see themselves, other mirrors have to be made. Again it is from subcultures that I'm really inspired, from which I gain the most insight. My first heroines were She-Ra and Captain Dana Sterling from *Robotech*, but I didn't see myself or my friends in those worlds. I wanted to make one for us.

P.H.: Are there any artists — performance, literary, painting — that represent your aesthetic or are you and your work a once-in-a-lifetime experience? The issues of ethnicity, cultural heritage, gods, monsters, the taboo, reverence, are all explored within your work without limitation on imagination, subject or what is believed to be the popular normative.

R.P.: Of course there are. This is 2016 we're talking about here...I'm pretty sure Nep Sidhu comes from the same planet as me, Wangechi Mutu, Andrew Thomas Huang. So does Motohiro Hayakawa, Inka Essenhigh... who else? Lots. Their work also inspires me quite a bit though I don't know if we're contemporaries per se. Flying Lotus, Thundercat, Hiatus Kaiyote, Shabazz Palaces, Björk... they're all musical artists but I see a matching aesthetic there, their work drives me and inspires me.

P.H.: Afrika Galaktika is a triumph of thematic, visionary, stylistic work. It is quite literally out of this world. What was the process for creating this gallery showing? What were the inspirations you pulled from to create the work? I noted the influence of comics, fantasy, Afrofuturism and aboriginal cultures. I noted very strong thematic constructs against mainstream perceptions of women, global "Black" culture, and "white power."

R.P.: I think I was always waiting to make this series, due to an underrepresentation of diasporic people and attitudes in the genres I loved so well. Right out of school I did a series called "The New Ethnography" highlighting the ongoing colonization of the colored body in popular Western culture, and Afrika Galaktika is very much an extension of that aesthetically speaking, although it is much more about our bodies' absence in a particular subculture.

P.H.: You hail from Toronto but your work has been exhibited all over the world — places as diverse as Houston, Sri Lanka and Germany. Is there a common emotion associated with reception to your work? Do different cultures respond differently to your work? If so, how?

R.P.: Yes they do. In some places there is a strange empowering effect of the work; the same as if you were to sculpt an idol and place in a made-up house of worship. I think this comes from the specific amalgamation of references and influences which reflect deeply in the (mostly millennial) audience, such as a strong belief in a non-white-male-focused future, a shout out to Japanese animation and manga aesthetics, a love of one's roots and their hand in concepts of adornment, ritual and powermaking, a love of space travel and our belief in it as some sort of salvation, science fiction in general. These are some things that I feel contribute to the reception of the work in most places, or themes that I notice. In other places it is met with criticism — sometimes because I'm not Black, others because I don't have a specific type of education. And that's alright, I'm creating from a very specific here and now and I think there is value in that.

P.H.: How do men and women of color respond to your work?

R.P.: I have a good response to the series overall. A lot of WOC, especially science fiction lovers and comic book nerds feel the same way in regards to wanting to see ourselves in fantastic futures, which offer a very different feeling of possibility than say, only seeing ourselves in stable, egalitarian worlds, which is something we still have to fight for. I want something more than that. And so do most WOC.

P.H.: What do your children think of your work?

R.P.: My daughter loves everything I paint unconditionally, but she is biased after all.

2/12/17

L'AFRIQUE!

INGRID BAARS FUSES FANTASY AND FUTURISM TO CREATE AN AFRICAN FORM HERETOFORE UNSEEN

I first saw Ingrid's work as a post on social media and immediately fell in love with it. I invited her to be a participant in an exhibit I'd planned on the Black female form. I chose her work to be on

the invitation. I was so taken by it in person that I purchased the piece at the close of the show and it's hung in my home since then. The sheer majesty and beauty of the photo enhanced by her subtle surrealist abstracting of the form is unique and quite inviting. Ingrid is a masterful artist.

— Danny Simmons, African American Abstract Expressionist

It's no secret — some of the most creatively and powerfully endowed spirits on the planet come infused with melanin in the skin. Imagine, a multi-trillion-dollar industry focused on getting it all wrong! That's why it can be so frustrating to have the mainstream Hollywood machine portray African souls. Yes, 2016 seemed like an exception, with an August Wilson adaptation with Denzel at the helm and Viola in the wings, *Moonlight*, and a "dark horse" candidate featuring mathematicians that helped astronauts get to the stars, *Hidden Figures*. The body of work celebrated by Hollywood has been, well... wanting. I have dealt with these simple-minded caricatures that Hollywood would make of us all in previous pieces featured in the *Quarterly Black Book Review*, Denene Millner's *MyBrownBaby* and *equities.com*. Actually, I've done more than that.

This agenda of the nay-saying cabal of Hollywood sycophants has nothing to do with the depth and breadth of expression and creativity expressed by international sculptors, screenwriters, poets, authors, bloggers, photographers and painters, such as Ingrid Baars. The first time I saw her work I was spellbound. I was literally dumbstruck by the eerie beauty, futuristic illustrations and phantasmagorical art expressed in her work. Ingrid has termed the ongoing project "l'Afrique!" stating on her site that she is "inspired by the richness of the African

Culture heritage in all its diversity, incorporating as it does both the human and non-human form."

The images represented below hypnotized me into such a tailspin that I spent three days in 2015 transfixed on a story that came into my spirit from merely looking at the images. The story conveyed the melancholy through the fantastic narrative of a man mourning the passing of his young wife and young daughter. Caught up in the ongoing trends of health and fitness, I called the story "Kombucha... on Tap!" and it was later published in the *Foliate Oak Literary Magazine*. As the work expressed itself to me, I attempted to show emotion, spirit and complexities of the human and spirit worlds, with little regard for racial identity. I was concerned with the humanity we all share in our most real moments — which can oftentimes be quite surreal. Then I started posting her work on Facebook and Instagram, recognizing that it was also hanging on the walls of art patrons and community leaders like Carmelo Anthony and Barbara Streisand.

Ingrid Baars is from Dordrecht, the Netherlands and lives and works in Antwerp, Belgium. Her work or the body of "l'Afrique" are a communication of Black identity in a white culture, aboriginal or primal aesthetics intertwined with Afrofuturism. Her work, as the work of so many of our artists, is not stilted. It is glorious, an expression of humanity, or at the very least, a vision unharnessed. There is a stunning cross-pollination at once jarring, fascinating, haunting and intoxicating in her work. European Victorian dress is juxtaposed with licorice Black skin; haunting beauty outlined with macabre sensibilities; outer-space astronauts clothed in Victorian and Bohemian tapestries.

Ingrid is not of African descent — she is European with a soul bronzed mahogany. And this might go to my earlier point of racism and discrimination being a much more complex than simply assignments of white and Black people. It is a global complexity of systemic and political agendas. When I asked Ingrid about her reception from people of African descent, she said: "It never really occurred to me that anyone with dark or white skin tones would respond so profoundly to the content of my series 'African Women'.

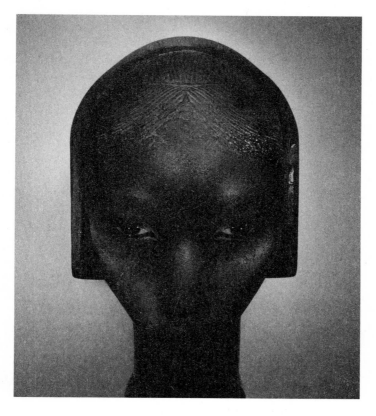

"I wasn't prepared for the effect it has on many African and African American women and men who respond to me with deeply touching messages where they thank me for showing 'Black Beauty'. I'm very grateful to be able to contribute to the awareness of African beauty. There is also a small group of people of African American descent that cannot accept that a white woman creates 'Black art.' This is not something I chose to battle with. I'm an artist, I respect African culture and the beauty in it inspires my work."

Baars's unique style of working is a one-person endeavor with a preliminary photo shoot, then the manipulation of the photography and the integration of the photos with high-end fashion and traditional African sculpture. The works manifested are timeless and without boundaries.

There is a higher frequency to which Ingrid subscribes in creating work that is as much about the past as it is the future, inhabiting such a strong space in the here and now. Furthermore, her work goes outside the simple constructs of Hollywood typecasts of Black or white and combines humanity with vision, fusing cultures in a manner that is surreal. Ethereal is a term aptly applied to her work, where a vision outside institutional constructs invites imagination, fascination and vision of a present and future.

Conversely, she noted of European reception to her work: "Also mostly positive but different. Europeans hardly ever mention the color of the women in my images. They respond to the aesthetics and the emotions in my art. The complexity of reception, if there is complexity it is about the emotions felt by viewers. For some people it's too much, they mostly see 'sadness' or 'pain' or they experience my art to be disturbing. Everyone has had their own opinions about my work. The quality and mystique always garners the most conversation."

Ingrid Baars's works are made entirely by her, with creative participation by many beautiful souls — models, lighting experts, make up, technicians. Her vision is fine-tuned to higher frequencies. She is not limited by a current harness that is blinding us to our collective humanity. Skin fair, and well-minded, she is part of a humanity with one foot in the present and another in the future. Incredibly powerful in presence yet unwaveringly beautiful, Baars's artwork offers a state-of-the-art appreciation of modern surrealism. It shatters all restrictions concurring to the symbolic nature of the female body. Her oeuvre is unique, both for its wonderful idiosyncrasies and its fervent poetry.

2/25/17

THE MANIFESTORS

I AM

BY MARVIN L. MILLS

It's True spirit in people, rising
From the ashes
And to the limits of the universe
One where dark (skinned) matters
And intelligence is wielded
In creative fashion
With the heart on its sleeve
Either wrestling with pain
Abundant with joy
Or somewhere in between
Speaking Its language
And approaching Its resting
Place

MASTERING FORM OVER FUNCTION

RICH FRESH, BEVERLY HILLS' TAILOR

"I respect people in a range of industries who are going against the odds and making things happen that impact culture. I admire anyone who is turning a dream into a reality. In fashion, I admire anyone who takes risks, calculated risks."
— Rich Fresh, clothier to the stars

There are only a few things you need to know about Rich Fresh. If you feel as if you know his work but can't quite put your finger on where from, it's OK. He's everywhere with clients walking the red carpet from the Grammys to the Oscars. He's on the run to private residences, to weddings, to awards shows. He's in the boardrooms of bankers and attorneys alike. He impacts the culture in one of the global epicenters of trend (Los Angeles) with a touch that is at once distinct, curious and peerless. When it comes to clothing and dressing men, he is the best at doing what he does. He's been doing it a while and he makes it look easy. But, it is best to let him tell you — his expression, like his clothing, is one of a kind. Check it.

Patrick A. Howell: What does spring fashion portend for the gentleman — what are the trend forecasts?

Rich Fresh: Honestly, pretty much the same as usual but a little bit more fun. Men's fashion doesn't change that much. Guys are getting away from getting buttoned up and overly conservative — stepping away from neckties and socks and shoe strings. I think they are simplifying their look and the steps it takes to get properly dressed. They are starting to care a little bit about their overall image and brands are beginning to change their overall silhouettes. Menswear is just a little bit more interesting than in the past.

P.H.: What are your business goals this year — in business terms? What are some of your personal goals?

R.F.: Business goals are more of the same. I still do bespoke. Growing the brand, growing distribution, growing the services I offer. Bringing more of my production into Los Angeles from overseas so I can oversee every aspect of production.

I am also developing a small capsule collection of men's trousers. That is a very overlooked market and it is a huge problem for a lot of men, regardless of age, race or income. The way pants fit or what they say. There is a monotony of pants, you know what I'm saying. There is an opportunity to solve a problem there. I am developing a capsule to solve that problem for the spring. We'll see where that goes.

I'll also have a few TV spots that I will be popping up in over the next couple of months starting in March on TruTV. So, lots of interesting developments in the fashion world as well as the entertainment world.

But you can keep up to date by following me on social media like Instagram. Por Favor!

P.H.: It has been said you are a marketing and branding genius. But you are also, by my experience, an exceptional sales and business development mind. For someone looking to get into the business, what kind of skills do they need?

R.F.: You can't look to get into the business. This isn't that type of business. You don't wake up one day and say I just want to do that. You don't wake up and want to be Beyoncé. You don't wake up and want to be Kanye. You either are or are not.

If you're just looking to get into the fashion business in general — there are schools, there are a multitude of resources. You gotta put in the work. You gotta put up money. You gotta lose money. We only make this look easy. It takes decades to master.

P.H.: For the uninitiated, how is what you do different from Men's Warehouse and Brooks Brothers? Who are some of your more prominent clientele?

R.F.: That's like asking how is Nobu different from McDonald's. That's how. It's the same way. There is no comparison whatsoever. There is no comparison. They both serve food but you can't compare the two.

I've worked with a lot of heavy hitters in the entertainment industry. I try not to drop names. Anyone who needs help in the industry who needs perfections and needs someone on it until it is done. I'm the one that they call. When it's your moment, I'm the one that you call. Film A-listers. Finance A-listers. Music A-listers. Anyone who wants it done right and doesn't mind paying for it.

P.H.: What is the bespoke suit all about? You use "bespoke" like a verb. e.g. "If you want to get bespoke, you best set an appointment with Richie Rich, a.k.a. the Rich Freshman."

R.F.: I use bespoke like a noun, like an all-inclusive noun. It's really an adjective. Bespoke is the process of clothing. "You should do bespoke." The term just means nothing exists. Everything is determined and then it is created. There is no pattern to work with and then it is modified. There is nothing waiting and then we are going to change it up. It starts with a thought, then finding the fabric, then drawing the pattern, then building the pattern, then drawing the pattern, then cutting the pattern, then cutting the fabric, then sewing the fabric. Then completing all of the various assemblies of putting this garment together. Then trying it on the client and finishing the garment and ensuring the perfect fit. That's bespoke. That's that big boy treatment. When you're really doing it — that's bespoke.

P.H.: You're into trousers this season? I mean, what goes into making trousers part and parcel of sartorial splendor?

R.F.: It's a process. It's architecture. I don't build houses. Someone who designs cars, homes, kitchens — It's a very similar mind, a very similar process. It's like *The Matrix*. We really just look at numbers and lines all day — that's it. And we just have to build from our imagination and actualize a concept. Making trousers that matter, making trousers that I would be proud to wear. Making trousers that people are going to see and say, "wow." It takes a ton of designing. It takes a lot of forethought. It takes a lot of trial and error. And then just producing them. And knowing that they are going to be dope. And that's all that matters.

P.H.: Is it harder to dress a woman or a man?

R.F.: It's harder to dress a man in terms of range. It's easier in terms of steps: shirt, jacket, pants, shoes, square, tie, done — easy. You only have a certain amount of range but you can't really flex. But I think for a super creative sometimes you just really want to go crazy. But I think it's really fun to dress women. I'm picking up a number of really cool women this season. We'll see a lot of really cool patterns. But we'll see that same with men as well. I'm going to play with menswear as much as I can without crossing the line but I'm going to tap dance all over it! Lol.

But I think with women you can just have an idea and just go. But with menswear I can have an idea and then I have to scale it back and I have to have all these derivatives of my original idea. The creative process is easier with women, but menswear is more simplified and streamlined which makes it easier to do. But with womenswear, I think it's easier to be free.

P.H.: Who are your role models and inspirations?

R.F.: Me, me and me.

Anyone defying the odds. I'm not a respecter of a person per se. And I don't care about industry. I respect people in a range of industries who are going against the odds and making things happen that impact culture. I admire anyone who is turning a dream into a reality. In fashion I admire anyone who takes risks, calculated risks. They don't care what will be said and does what is real to them. Those are the people I admire. People like Kanye.

P.H.: What is your personal style influence or preference for the spring?

R.F.: Sexy. I want men to be cool with being viewed as being sexy. Not just handsome or hot. Or whatever the term we are using these days. Genuinely sexy. There is an overwhelming amount of confidence that is exuding from that human's pores. That's sexy. So everything I do is going to be sexy. It's going to be Italian but just sexy. Like heartthrob, like Sixties Italian sexy hearthrob. Sexy-crazy. LA is the perfect backdrop for that type of persona.

P.H.: As a designer, what trends do you personally want to see this season? What trends are you setting with your clients?

R.F.: I've always been an advocate of no belt. I am a no belt proponent since 2000. Before people even thought it was smart. People told me it was stupid and no one would buy pants with no belt loops. That trend of button fly trousers has remained consistent and it will remain. But I do want to see things get simpler. Less lining, softer shoulder, fewer buttonholes, less frill and more oomph! More attention to fabric quality as opposed to thread color. I want to see men play more with pocket choices. You look around and everyone is wearing one of four options and that is unacceptable. These are trends I would love to see emerge over the coming season. But they are trends that will be emerging from my camp.

2/20/17

PHENOMENAL WOMAN

HANNA WAGARI, MARKETING MAVEN AND BRAND DEVELOPER

Having been wonderfully involved with this marketing maven for nearly twelve years, I would say the brand Mombasa is the spiritual practice of manifestation — creating something from the spirit. Mombasa is what happens when a soul takes its time in the realization of the vision of one's life. Brand Mombasa is how a woman — Hanna Wagari — with a career in branding with multinational cosmetic brands, nutritional, retail and biotechnology brands draws the line from the spiritual world to one of material affects. Mombasa's tribal and kindred spirit unfolds and renews herself within the spirit of her adopted daughters.

There is no age better than another. The commitment to give of yourself and the knowledge that the time is right are what's important.
— Iman, Fashion Icon

Business these days, in its current regime, is the business of barbarism. It is about the "kill or be killed" ethos to command the almighty dollar. *Anything for the almighty dollar in the United States of Capitalism, right?* At least pay attention to the wrong sources and they will report this self-fulfilling narrative again and again and again. *The right to demean and take life in the pursuit of empty riches is widely celebrated as a virtue in American culture.*

The Mombasa brand, by conscious deliberation and intention, is different. It is about free souls, the good word and good works. Mombasa is about channeling positive energy and *giving*. It is about the elegance of simplicity. Its founders Hanna Wagari and Regbe Surafel come from Ethiopia, a land of free spirits and birthplace of Christianity.

Patrick A. Howell: What is the story behind the Mombasa brand?

Hanna Wagari: It was dreamed into life by two longtime friends — myself and Regbe Surafel. My background is branding and she is an artist so it was a perfect partnership to start a splendid adventure of unique jewelry collection and accessories.

P.H.: What was the inspiration?

H.W.: The inspiration has always been our heritage with both of us being Ethiopians. The rich culture and history of the motherland is always an inspiration. We wanted to make a difference in the lives of women in Ethiopia through our business. We launched the business with our "Signature Collection" featuring these mystical Lalibela crosses which are handmade in Ethiopia. We also partnered with a fair trade manufacturer to make our "Made in Ethiopia" leather goods collection.

P.H.: What is your mission?

H.W.: Our mission is to help women through our business. We partnered with I Pour Life, a non-profit which does incredible work with the leprosy community in Korah, Ethiopia. Their 10x10 WEEP is a women-led family empowerment program that seeks to end the cycle of extreme poverty and social isolation for these women living with leprosy. They teach women skills-based training, financial education and a start-up capital for a business. These businesses are funded by donations to I Pour Life. I worked with the founder Julie Higgins in my past life and as soon as we launched Mombasa, I wanted to be a part of her mission because I believe in her vision.

P.H.: Who is the Mombasa woman?

H.W.: A woman who wears Mombasa is well traveled, passionate about the world around her and effortlessly signals her impeccable taste and a cultivated sense of style.

P.H.: Who is your style icon?

H.W.: I don't really have one. I have always had my own style. When I was younger, I wanted to be a fashion designer. However, my parents, like any other immigrant parents, wanted their children to be doctors or engineers. So my initial major in college was electrical engineering but I quickly changed it to business with a minor in marketing.

P.H.: Where are you sold?

H.W.: We are an online business that sells through our website, shopmombasa.com. We do trunk shows seasonally to introduce new products to our customers locally in the LA area. This gives us a chance to meet our customers which is always fun. We are a startup so we rely on social media marketing and we are pretty active on Instagram and Facebook. It is a great medium and gives you instant feedback from your followers. We also have an email list of opt-in customers and prospects that we market to with promotions and new product launches.

P.H.: Is there an art form to the selfie? You've had some very well received ones on Instagram.

H.W.: I don't really like taking pictures but I started taking selfies to show the jewelry. It seems to work.

P.H.: You've been a professional marketing and branding executive for over twenty-five years now. How is traditional marketing and branding complemented by social media marketing?

H.W.: As a start-up we don't have a large budget to do traditional media buys and the jewelry space is very competitive for paid search so social media has been a great platform for us. Instagram and Facebook draw the most traffic to our online store. Additionally, we are focused on growing our opt-in mailing list for email marketing.

P.H.: Has your brand been in fashion shows?

H.W.: Mombasa recently participated in the OC Fashion Week. The Mombasa brand's friend, fashion model Sara Ishag, invited us to place our jewelry on the models for Belorussian designer Tatiana Shabelnik, who brought her globally inspired collection "Contrast" to the runway. The show took place at Soka University's Founders Hall and the show wowed the audience. We were honored to work with Tatiana and grateful for the opportunity to collaborate with her. We will be collaborated again at the American Heart Association Charity Event on April 1st in Beverly Hills.

Now you understand
Just why my head's not bowed.
I don't shout or jump about
Or have to talk real loud.
When you see me passing,
It ought to make you proud.
I say,
It's in the click of my heels,
The bend of my hair,
the palm of my hand,
The need for my care.
'Cause I'm a woman
Phenomenally.
Phenomenal woman,
That's me.
— Maya Angelou, "Phenomenal Woman"

Now, for the macro portion of the story.

Mombasa is the chic manifestation of a story that reaches back from the bible with stories in the books of Genesis, Kings, Esther and Job of a country of "peoples with burnt faces" (for example Genesis 2:13 or Psalms 68:31). Ethiopia or the land of Cush *(Kush)* is spoken of in prophecy (Psalms 68:31 and Habakkuk 3:7). Mombasa is how a sacred spirit of the universe works through its people to fulfill those prophecies of a New Age and the new time. Mombasa is about the work of phenomenal women *for* phenomenal women.

4/27/17

BLACK PANTHER WRITER IS CREATING THE FUTURE

NNEDI OKORAFOR, AUTHOR AND AFROFUTURIST

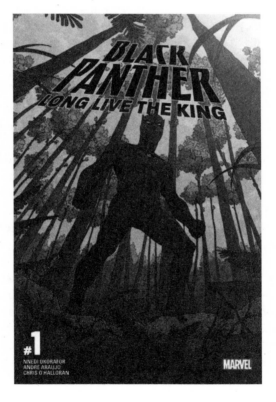

Sometimes, the mysterious galaxy will express her wishes in precise terms. Neon signs. Words in books. Unseemly coincidences. Images jumping from books onto the silver screen. Distinct shifts in the universe. Nigerian-American authors at magical places on Balboa Avenue in San Diego...

Did you know the Igbo griots of West Africa are the most talented of all the African tribes at the art of storytelling? They are the repository of oral traditions; they create reality by speaking it, and have been doing so for millennia. Storytelling is the most basic and fundamental technology of world culture. Just as the modern self-driving car was made possible by the invention of the wheel, storytelling has made possible civilization. As Hollywood/Bollywood director Shekhar Kapur has noted, "we are the stories we tell ourselves." Our stories influence politics, science, innovation, culture — they influence the future.

What if the likes of George R.R. Martin (*A Song of Ice and Fire*), George Lucas (*Star Wars*), and Stan Lee (*Marvel Comic Universe*), seers of contemporary American culture of resistance, dreams, and fantasy — purveyors of what has been long ago and what will be yet — all agreed upon who the next great one is?

Well, they have, and her name is Nnedi Okorafor. George R.R. Martin will work with Okorafor on her 2010 novel *Who Fears Death* for a HBO series; Okorafor penned an original official *Star Wars* short story about the giant creature (aka Dianoga) at the bottom of the trash compactor in *A New Hope* for Lucasfilm; and now Okorafor is chronicling the adventures of the Marvel hero king Black Panther in the comic book series *Black Panther: Long Live the King*. Proudly Nigerian-American, with roots in the Yoruba and aforementioned Igbo tribes, Okorafor is a shining star of Afrofuturism.

I caught up with Okorafor at Mysterious Galaxy Books in San Diego where she was reading from her award-winning *Akata Warrior*, and made note of some answers she gave to questions from audience members:

Q.: What are your inspirations? What did you draw from when you wrote *Akata Warrior*?

Nnedi Okorafor: I actually have an obsession with things that are forbidden. A lot of that story comes from things that are forbidden. It started with the masquerades. Most African cultures have a masquerading tradition, especially West Africans. They tend to be manifestations of the ancestors and the spirits and the ancestors. So, it's very theatrical to have people who dress up in these really elaborate costumes and when they put these things on they become that — they become that spirit or that ancestor. In Nigeria, the people who get to put on the masquerading costumes tend to be men and they are part of a secret society. Growing up I had a lot of interactions with masquerades and was always curious about them. They could look monstrous, they could look bizarre, they could look comical. The masquerade happens during Christmas, Easter, weddings, funerals, all of that. And because my sisters and I were American-born, they would harass us the most. When I was asked about them I was told I was not allowed to know anything about them because I am female. That's when the curiosity began.

With African language it's the same thing. I learned about a magical writing script that is the only African script to not be influenced by the Roman or Greek alphabet or hieroglyphics. It is completely indigenous and so I was fascinated in that way. When I asked my great-grand-uncle about it, he said, "Why are you asking about that?" He said I needed to be saved and he proceeded to try to save me because it was evil, and that made me curious.

Those things that were forbidden, especially within Nigerian culture, were the basis of Sunny's world.

Q.: Could you tell me about "chi?"

N.O.: In Igbo culture, one's chi is one's personal god. Everyone has a personal god. When something positive happens to you, it's because you have a good chi. If lots of negative things keep happening to you, usually the explanation is your chi is problematic or there is something wrong with it. Interestingly most Igbos happen to be of Christian leaning, and that doesn't matter. It's like when people say there is a difference between religion and one's culture — that's how you can have two forms of spirituality co-existing. Even though you may be Christian, your culture is Igbo, so therefore you have these other spiritual aspects that co-exist with the Christianity, even though you would think they completely contradict one another.

Chi is very different from this idea of your personal energy. I think they have nothing to do with each other. It's also different from a guardian angel. And it's not an ancestor. Your chi is you — the spiritual part of you.

Q.: As mentioned, *Akata Witch* and *Akata Warrior* were published six years apart. How much does it change your approach to writing a novel when you feel as if you have to remind people what happened in the previous novel?

N.O.: That's an interesting question because that was the exact problem raised by my Nigerian publisher. My Nigerian publisher hates the beginning. She said the prologue is not going to be in the Nigerian edition. For me the way I approach it is probably the same way I approach the Binti books. Some parts needed a bit of a rehash, sometimes referring to the previous book, maybe a sentence here or there, but other than that, I just kept going. With the *Akata* books I wanted to continue the story where it left off and that is how I wrote it. It's just one big story and this is just the next big chunk of it. I think with the prologue, I knew that especially with American readers, it adds to the marketability, so I knew it needed that beginning of 'this is what happened in the previous book.' But I remember feeling so bored writing it.

Q.: Despite being futuristic science fiction, your work contains many emotive qualities, and its settings are human and fleshy. Is that intentional?

N.O.: That's a good observation. I never really thought of it but it makes sense. I grew up not reading a lot of science fiction. If it was telling a good story, I tended to read it. So I like reading everything but I didn't read a lot of science fiction. I didn't feel as if I existed in those worlds. They were very white and very male. Not that I needed all of them to have an image of me in them. I just needed one, and I didn't have one. But they also felt cold and sterile. I would think about spaceships on which people have lived for months and I couldn't understand how it could be so clean. One of the things I am always obsessed with is a sense of smell — just think about it: the spaceship would be very lived in, very warm. Some of the more recent science fiction films are addressing that — they don't look as sterile and as clean. Things look beaten up. Things look used. That's the way it should be. That's important to me. Also, when I am writing any sort of story, I am very close to the character. I am very close to the place where the story is set. So textures and smells and temperatures—all those things are really important. That's why you won't see me writing about a place that is cold because I don't like the cold at all. When I am writing something I have to be there and I don't want to be in snow.

I like to get really close to the character and when I am close to the character, I experience the sense of those characters. If I am going to write about Binti — if I am going to write about a character who leaves Earth on a ship — the reader is going to get a sense of everything about that ship. It's not going to have that coldness that many stories have.

The emotional aspect is important to me even if I am writing hard science fiction. I've written science fiction in which there are no mystical elements at all and the science is a big part of it. But those stories are also very visceral. I like it to be real. No matter what I write about I believe what I am writing. That's very important. If I don't believe it, I will not continue with it. I think that's where that comes from.

I think that gives a much more hopeful vision of what the future could be. I am an irrational optimist. Even when I am writing about dystopia or things going wrong, there is always going to be hope. There always is. That's because I believe there is always hope, even in the worst of times. *Who Fears Death* gets very dark but there is always hope in there. That's important to me. But it is also my own personal philosophy as well.

Q.: Can you tell me more about your HBO project and what that has been like for you?

N.O: *Who Fears Death* has been optioned by HBO with George R.R. Martin as an executive producer and Michael Lombardo, who used to be the president of HBO and recently stepped down to pursue more projects, as an executive producer. So it's really cool to have both of them involved.

It has been interesting. I'm the type of writer that likes to experience different types of writing. I'm obsessed with that. Not just writing novels but short stories, comics, TV, film, screenwriting — I obsess over storytelling. For me this is my chance to get to see how a TV show is made; how a novel can go from being in that form to TV. And one thing I love about TV that's different from film is film

consolidates and makes things smaller. But TV expands —
stories expand. And you have all these writers involved that
are not you and you see how that shifts the story. And HBO
is a perfect place for *Who Fears Death*.

At this point in time, it has been optioned and now we
are working together. We had a meeting a few months ago
and chose a screenplay writer for the pilot. And just to be
clear — we had five writers and I was in the room too. I was
involved; Michael Lombardo and other executive producers
were there, while George R.R. Martin was on the phone
because he was unable to make it. We interviewed five
potential writers. All were Black. Four of them were female.
The writer we chose happened to be the one male writer.
HBO knows what we are doing here.

Q.: What is your creative process? How does a book come
to you?

N.O.: For a long time, I always knew there was going to be a
part two to *Akata*. The ending of *Akata Witch* was different.
It wasn't necessarily a cliffhanger but I knew there would
be more. This was the type of book where I had to wait for
it. So, I took that time, absorbed it, and then wrote. It was
a lot of work — I wrote *Akata Warrior* while teaching four
classes: Composition I, Composition II, Creative Writing,
and Journalism. And I still banged that thing out in the
middle of that because for me when a story comes, it comes.
No matter what I have going on around me, I will write that
thing. So I wrote it and then came the editing; you add all
that together and that's why it took six years. I had to wait
for it. I couldn't force it. I had to let it organically grow.

5/1/18

CHRONICLES IN THE CITY OF ANGELS

PUBLISHER AND AWARD-WINNING AUTHOR DR. TOM LUTZ

Tom Lutz is a good fellow, an interesting interview, and a good read. Accomplished and world-traveled, Lutz is a University of California, Riverside, distinguished chair with writing in his DNA and coursing through his bloodstream. He is responsible for quietly manifesting the infrastructure of Southern California's literary landscape.

Having won one of America's most distinguished awards in 2008 — the American Book Award for *Doing Nothing: A History of Loafers, Loungers, Slackers, and Bums in America* — he launched the *Los Angeles Review of Books* in 2011, currently attracting approximately six million page views and with four print issues per year. He is in the midst of a prolific writing career and the journal is off to a magnificent start to the new millennium.

The *LARB* also boasts one of SoCal's most innovative and dynamic young teams of editors, correspondents, artists, and graphic designers. *The New Yorker* said its West Coast counterpoint is "one of the instant jewels of the internet." *Forbes* magazine added to the chorus, calling *LARB* "a perfect example of disruptive innovation." Walter Mosley named it "a counterpoint and counterbalance," and Margaret Atwood said: "The *Los Angeles Review of Books* is one of the bright spots, a phoenix rising from the ashes."

Of his own work, Lutz stated: "The older I get the more I realize that the only real pleasure is in doing the work, in the process, in the writing, in the making."

The above rhymes with the four touchstones of this burgeoning kingdom in a city of angels at the beginning of the twenty-first:

- *Los Angeles Review of Books* (which includes *LARB* Radio; *LARB* Quarterly Journal; website; *Guernica Magazine*; the publishing house workshop in conjunction with the University of Southern California and its coming publishing imprint)
- Tom Lutz's teaching at UC Riverside (exceptional pedigree with post-undergraduate bonafides from Stanford and an east coast upbringing out of an Allen Ginsberg poem or Jack Kerouac novel)
- His widely anthologized life via books (six, with seventh & eighth forthcoming travel journals)
- His ongoing global travels, bringing it all together and just getting the danged deals done

Yes, Tom Lutz is erudite but has not lost his common touch. His life's work seems to lift the convention of literary traditions and place them under a glowing light where the best and the brightest are attracted to its shine. A sly twinkle glittering from his eye, he knows his way around a deal and the vagaries of US publishing. His eyes brim with passion as there is no shortage of ambition, just as his prose is minimalist. I joked with Tom after a chance meeting at the recent Red Hen Press 24th Annual Benefit Luncheon (MC'd by founders Kate Gale and Mark E. Cull). Something about a fabled wolf who is at home with sheep—none of his ambition, productivity, or curiosity are dulled. He is piqued with consciousness, positivity, and a goodwill that is infectious. A higher consciousness, balance, and goodness characterize his style and works, a sharp transcendentalism that is warm, undulating, and uncommon amongst accomplished men.

Patrick A. Howell: You received the 2008 American Book Award for your book *Doing Nothing: A History of Loafers, Loungers, Slackers, and Bums in America*. 2008 was a really interesting time, a little bit different from where we are now — the economy was on the brink of collapse and Barack Obama had just become president. How did that book award change your life and literary life, if at all?

Tom Lutz: The American Book Award is the greatest honor I've experienced — Ishmael Reed and the other people who founded the Before Columbus Foundation originally started the awards in response to the lack of diversity in the National Book Awards, as a way to promote multicultural literatures. Because I was very interested, in that book, in talking about the way race and ethnicity play into ideas of work and work ethics in American culture, I am especially pleased that it was recognized by the group of extraordinary writers in that organization.

I'm not sure it changed my life much... it certainly made me feel better about everything for a while, and it does so again when I happen to think about it. But recognition doesn't really mean much, does it? I was recently named Distinguished Professor at UC Riverside, and it doesn't make me feel more distinguished, really. Publishing books or articles feels good momentarily, but the older I get the more I realize that the only real pleasure is in doing the work, in the process, in the writing, in the making. I love that—the recognition is very minor, comparatively.

The timing for the book wasn't great. We love slacker characters — like *The Big Lebowski* — in times of plenty; in recessions or depressions, when work is hard to come by, they don't seem so funny.

P.H.: You have carved out a little niche for yourself in life — writing, publishing, and standing out for your nonfiction, including the aforenoted *Doing Nothing*, but also with work appearing in *The New York Times*, *Chicago Tribune*, and *Los Angeles Times*. Two of your books — *Crying: The Natural and Cultural History of Tears* and *American Nervousness, 1903: An Anecdotal History* — were 1999 and 1991 *New York Times* Notable Books. What's the secret to writing great creative nonfiction, Tom?

T.L.: I wish I knew! I think those three books — *Crying*, *Doing Nothing*, and *1903* — are more research nonfiction, a slightly different category. The travel books, and some of my shorter pieces, are clearly creative nonfiction — in that they are meant to be enjoyed as pieces of writing, meant to give narrative pleasure — whereas, research nonfiction should have some news to impart. I mean, we hope the research stuff is pleasurable, and the creative work has something valuable to say, but they are different genres and have different requirements. For instance, I know more about crying and more about the year 1903 than just about anyone alive, but I cannot say that for any of the sixty or seventy countries I visit in the travel narratives.

P.H.: You were in Ethiopia recently at a really interesting time in that country's history (potentially Africa's and the world's) with the election of Prime Minister Dr Abiy Ahmed. Sweeping reforms are taking place in the country and Dr Abiy is infinitely more popular than the previous Ethiopian People's Revolutionary Democratic Front (EPRDF) party. As someone who has traveled the world — well chronicled in *And the Monkey Learned Nothing: Dispatches from a Life in Transit* — what were some of your observations? You did not get the opportunity to include those observations in your 2016 opus.

T.L.: No, a few moments from the Ethiopian trip will be in the third volume, which I'm trying to finish this coming year. When Dr Ahmed was elected, Ethiopia experienced a moment a bit like the election of Barack Obama — there was a sense, even more widespread than it was in America, of hope and change, of a new world being born. I was there for the Ethiopian New Year, which was on September 11, and Prime Minister Ahmed had encouraged the diaspora to come home for the celebration. A friend of mine from Los Angeles, Elias Wondimu, founder of Tsehai Press and Harriet Tubman Press, went home for the first time in twenty-four years, having been exiled by the previous regime. As I stood with him in his cousin's house, we watched Prime Minister Ahmed meet the dictator of Eritrea on the Eritrean border, and they hugged each other; soldiers from the two armies, who had been fighting each other for twenty-plus years, laid down their weapons and hugged each other, and then citizens from both countries ran into the former battlefield and embraced. Elias and his family were in tears — we never, never thought we would see this day, his cousin said to me, and it happened because Ahmed unilaterally declared the war over, acceded to the Eritrean desires for where the border should run, and just said, enough. There have been, for decades, pronounced ethnic conflicts, and Ahmed, who is half Oromo and half Amharic, represents in his person, like Obama, a bridge across the divide. It was a thrilling time to be there, and everyone, from the monks in the hills to the children in the street to the academics and taxi drivers, felt the momentousness of the change.

P.H.: Tom, you seem to have an interesting take on the Millennials, again with *Doing Nothing* being inspired in great part about your son, Cody, eighteen at the time. Or, as Oscar Wilde noted, "To do nothing is the most difficult thing in the world." How are Millennials different from others — such as the Baby Boomers or Greatest Generation?

T.L.: One thing studying history has taught me is that these descriptors — this generation is like *x*, that generation is like *y* — are not very precise. In terms of sexual mores, some people in their twenties today are more like people who were in their twenties in the 1950s than they are like our generalizations about Millennials. In 1903, you can find people saying things that sound like it's 1875, and people who sound like it's 1925. And one person's greatest generation — honest, hardworking, patriotic — is another person's horror — patriarchal, racist, close-minded twits. Boomers Bernie Sanders, Donald Trump, Samuel Jackson, Bill and Hillary Clinton, Oprah Winfrey, Rush Limbaugh, Mick Jagger, Arianna Huffington, Dolly Parton, they are all born within ten years of each other. How can you think of them as a single generation? And the same is true for Millennials: they are megachurch conservatives, they are sexually fluid urbanites, they are immigrant strivers, they are lazy, overprivileged suburbanites. Some have great work ethics, some don't. People driven by a work ethic have been around since the Industrial Revolution, and people who are or want to be slackers have been around exactly as long — the two need each other — and that is true in every generation.

P.H.: No offense here, Tom, but you are the definition of an erudite reformed yuppie; at least according to the unofficial Jack Kerouac-Allen Ginsberg-Charles Bukowski diagnostic manual (*JU-NM-PR Diagnostic Manual*). You were born in New Jersey, schooled in Massachusetts, did your postgraduate at Stanford, and, this is where the reform comes in, traveled the world with a very specific set of impressions and the highest form of education. As a so-called "Black" man speaking with a so-called "white" man (we are all people), where do you see the future of race relations for our America and your son Cody in the coming millennium, particularly within the hyper-partisan ethos that currently characterizes the culture and politics?

T.L.: Whether we use the *JU-NM-PR Diagnostic Manual* or some other measure, or the *Jack Kerouac-Allan Ginsberg-Charles Bukowski Diagnostic Manual*, I am definitely a white guy, not just so-called, but evidently. But, still, I tell my own story a little differently. If you just look at my CV and don't check the dates, it can look like a straight line. But I started my adult life in the working class, not as a yuppie (I despised yuppies), but as a marginally employed construction worker, cook, and bar musician (much of the time playing in Black and Latino bands), and I had my first kid when I was twenty-one, and then a second and third all before I had a college degree, much less anything like a professional job. And the first professional job I got was as a teaching assistant, and then as a low-paid assistant professor in the Midwest — this was a step up the prestige ladder, but it wasn't otherwise very upwardly mobile. I made a better hourly rate as a carpenter than I did as a teacher for the first fifteen years. And I spent my early time in academia continuing to play in bar bands on the weekends and take some remodeling jobs to make ends meet for the aforementioned children. On paper it might look yuppie, but the reality was much funkier. Now, I have a very good job at UCR, and nice house and car, and have all the trappings of a yuppie, even though no longer young and probably not upwardly mobile anymore. I'm pretty much at the top of the academic ladder. That makes me a yuppie, I guess ...

The future of race relations is a more interesting question. I see the future at my day job at UCR, where the undergraduates are 17% white, the rest Cambodian, Vietnamese, Chinese, Armenian, Filipino, different kinds of Latinx and Black, and many others, mixed and unmixed. As a historian, I can trace a centuries-long tradition of American inclusion and mutuality, and, side-by-side with it, a centuries-long tradition of exclusion and oppression. My Mexican American son-in-law, when someone suggests that the arc of history bends toward justice, will often say, "That has not been my experience." A hundred years ago, 70% of Americans would have agreed with Trump's racial ideas, and 20% would have disapproved. And so, while it is depressing that 40% of the American people now say they approve of Trump, 55% do not, and 5% are out to lunch. It's not good, but it represents progress. It shows the arc of history bending toward justice. When we as a nation, in a very few years, become majority minority, the arc will bend a bit farther.

But then there is Ben Carson, and the conservative Cubans, and even the workers outside the Home Depot from Honduras and Guatemala who approve of Trump and want the wall, and the millions of white racists will continue to reproduce themselves — the Promised Land is a long way off, and we, each and every one of us, need to commit and recommit to justice in order to even approximate it. I've written a bit about the 1910s and 1920s, when what we came to call multiculturalism was being invented, the Harlem Renaissance was happening, the NAACP founded — and that time of great progress was also the rise of the modern Klan, race riots in Atlanta and Tulsa, the epidemic of lynching. Progress often looks like two steps forward and one back, and often causes a virulent response. Trump is a big, virulent step back, but that doesn't mean we aren't also taking two steps forward.

1/11/19

ONE FOOT IN FRONT OF THE OTHER AND REPEAT THE PROCESS, TAMARA SKIPS ACROSS THE GLOBE

DR TAMARA PIZZOLI, CHILDREN'S AUTHOR

Do not shrink from moving confidently out into the choppy seas. Wade in the water, because God is troubling the water.
— "Wade in the Water," Old African American Spiritual

I asked Dr Pizzoli about a photo (in an Italian passage way with her feet in a puddle pool and the Roman Colosseum in the background) and she said it was shot in Rome during the summer of 2015, shooting content for the *In Nero: Portraits and Narratives* short documentary. When I saw the photo, it reminded me of the old spiritual, "Wade in the Water," which was used by the great Harriet Tubman to communicate with our ancestors who had escaped the bondage of American Slavery. The secret meaning of the song signaled that it was time for our ancestors to get off the trail and go into the water to make sure dogs couldn't sniff out their trail. Clearly Dr Pizzoli has elevated her game and that of current generations and those to follow to a higher frequency, signaling that it is time for generations to explore the world. At least, that's what I take away from it.

I first met Dr Tamara Pizzoli at the Harlem Book Fair in 2014, just around the corner from the Schomburg Center for Research in Black Culture. Her pavilion at the outdoor festival was a ray of light, absolutely beaming, where many a passerby more often than not formed a line to purchase her book and talk to the vibrant author. New soul energy radiated from the stand — *the new new*. As I noted in my first article for Denene Millner's *MyBrownBaby*, "She bears a striking resemblance to the characters in her books. In fact, she transforms the immediate radius around her into the very same color-filled goodness splashing her pages."

Indeed, this is the vibe for the former kindergarten schoolteacher's children's books. The books are slowly growing into a library of modern classics that I am confident will sit alongside the masterpieces of Ezra Jack Keats and Dr Seuss. The Dr Pizzoli classics include *The Ghanaian Goldilocks*; its follow up *F is for Fufu: An Alphabet Book Based on The Ghanaian Goldilocks*; *Tallulah the Tooth Fairy CEO* and a series of illustrated West African fairy tales.

I had the opportunity to catch up with Dr Pizzoli on her current projects and am grateful for the time and energy she took to answer questions. As always, thank you Dr Tamara Pizzoli.

In watching my own three-year-old son, it got me to thinking two things: 1.) When is the last time you saw a Black boy as the main character of a fairy tale? And 2.) That's a story that needs to be retold, from that perspective in particular, because fairy tales teach our children so much, but, probably the first thing they teach them is how to think critically.
— Dr Tamara Pizzoli interviewed for Denene Millner's *MyBrownBaby*, December 17 2014

Patrick A. Howell: OK, let's just cut to the point Dr Tamara Pizzoli. How do you come up with this amazing material? I see stories with the creativity, flare and color of the rainbow impacting children from Egypt to Brooklyn to Dallas.

Tamara Pizzoli: All of my stories are somehow based on experiences I've had or ideas about or from my sons. Both *The Ghanaian Goldilocks* and *Tallulah the Tooth Fairy CEO* were inspired by my eldest son, Noah. *M is for Marrakech* is a book of cities around the world, and includes places I've been to or would like to visit soon. I was on an ABC kick for a while so I published *M is for Mohawk* as well. I think the way the alphabet is presented in both books is visually stimulating and fresh. It's a clear break from the *A is for Apple* we're used to seeing. *Auntie Nappy* is written as a letter of sorts to my sons explaining the untimely death of my sister, Nefeterius, and trying to make sense of such a difficult transition for our family. So yes, everything I've published so far is rooted in experience, but I have a series of upcoming fairy tales that are set in places in West Africa that I've never seen or visited, but I'd love to one day soon.

As far as being a mom to bi-racial children, it's interesting. I'm not concerned for their physical safety or about them being bullied. With the recent events going on in the states that have prompted the #BlackLivesMatter movement, I'm grateful right now to live in a society where ignorance abounds but guns do not. Stupid is one thing. Armed and stupid is another. My biggest concern right now, especially since my boys are so small, is that they'll have the misunderstanding that being bi-racial is a novelty. Italians really do love children, and even though Rome is a major city in the world, it's not as diverse as one would think. I read today that only 8% of the Italian population is made up of immigrants. My children are often stopped and told how beautiful they are, how adorable they are, pinched on the cheeks, kissed, have their hair tussled.
— Dr Tamara Pizzoli interviewed in *Brown Girls Fly* by Chelle Roberts, January 29 2015

P.H.: You have three sons now. Your work and lifestyle speak volumes of the limits you have placed on yourself and your life style — zero. Unless, of course, you want to consider zip or nada. What are your visions for your children? What gifts do they possess? How do you envision their future in the lifetime that comes after ours?

T.P.: Yes, I have three sons and my visions for them include the desire for them to be safe, well loved, loving, happy, blessed, creative, well educated, comfortable, kind, healthy and on the right life path. I respect them as individuals so I'm just so grateful to be able to guide them as a mother through their unique journeys. They're seven, four, and three months old... so the gifts that are visible vary, of course. Noah is sensitive and has a great sense of humor. He's a natural storyteller and great with language. He's caring and gentle and in touch with all things spiritual. Milo is hilarious and bold. He's fearless in many ways and has a vocabulary out of this world. His ability to deliver a joke is unparalleled. Zen, my third son, is so calm and pure. He has this ability to bring people together (I think all babies do, really) and can already use sign language to ask for milk. They're all treasures and wonders and they teach me just as much about life and love as I hope I teach them.

With constant traumatic imagery of Black bodies being sprawled across the media recently, it is our belief that Dr Pizzoli's books, including Tallulah the Tooth Fairy, offer much needed, timely, and relevant image activism to counter the negativity that is all too often seen in the media.
— Dr Pizzoli's team interviewed by *AfroPunk*, September 29 2016

P.H.: *Tallulah, Ghanaian Goldilocks* and *Marrakech* are delightful books that seem to increase in accolades and distribution as time goes on. Would you ever consider taking the properties and working with them as animation or CGI?

T.P: Thank you! Yes, I have active plans to expand the existing content I have, particularly *Tallulah the Tooth Fairy CEO* and *The Ghanaian Goldilocks*, into animated platforms.

To me, being an AKA (Alpha Kappa Alpha Sorority) means continual lessons in and demonstrations of the characteristics that would describe the type of woman I would hope to always be — committed to service, grace, poise, class, dignity, high achievement, and promise. It means carrying the baton that's been passed to me along with so many other young Sorors and adding unique and relevant patchwork to this incredible, interwoven quilt of excellence that began over a century ago through contribution, character and a common goal — progress.
— Dr Tamara Pizzoli interviewed in *Rolling Out* by Cecilia Walker, July 7 2016

P.H.: You have several business brands you are working with, like English School House and Pizzoli Media. What's next business wise and creatively?

T.P.: I have so many creative projects going on. One of my main focuses right now and in the upcoming new year is The Nef Gallery. It's a site where I curate high art that is available for purchase. I'm also working with the graphic designer who illustrated my first six books and expanding into curriculum development using my stories as a literary base. I'm also launching an eight-episode web series called *In Nero: Black Girls in Rome* that's loosely based on my life here. So many things to do and try! I'm really excited about it all.

Reading from diverse literature is such a gift for children and adults alike. The cultural nuances and lessons presented with each story are true gifts. I think every single occurrence in life is a

story, so it makes sense that we are introduced to and explore new concepts through stories.
— Dr Tamara Pizzoli interviewed by *BC Books and Authors*

P.H.: Name five sources of creativity that you can always rely upon to get your juices flowing.

T.P.: My children, a conversation with my mentor, Tom, a conversation with my partner, Charles, a glass of red wine, a conversation with a stranger or a new friend

Now, what's interesting is that a couple of days ago I wrote a story that I still haven't named. It, as in the story, woke me up and would not let me sleep. It demanded to be written. I just listened to the urge and what emerged some six hours later is really something phenomenal. Truly. I can't wait to share it.
— Dr Tamara Pizzoli interviewed by *The Mahogany Way,* May 23 2015

P.H.: When is the best time for creation? The best conditions? Environment? Treats?

T.P.: The best time for creation is any time an idea is asking for your attention. I prefer to be alone but if that's not possible I will take the time, even if it's two minutes, to jot down something at least so that I can revisit it when I have the space and attention to be able to devote to it. I think the best treat of all is seeing something that was once just an idea exist in reality.

1/13/17

Dr. Tamara Pizzoli has since had another child and is now partnered with Big 5 publishing firms in NYC.

WORLD BEE BUZZING, MAKING SWEET, SWEET HONEY MAGIC IN SENEGAL

JOSHUA BEE ALAFIA, INDEPENDENT FILMMAKER

Joshua is a creative force. I've worked with him on a few projects, including my upcoming web series In Nero: Black Girls in Rome. *The energy that he brings to filming is the same that he brings to friendship — it's a calm, can-do vibe. Once he flew from NYC to Rome to shoot for my web series with a layover somewhere and once he hit Rome we left for Morocco immediately, and he was all smiles and good vibes the whole way. As an indie-creator, working with that type of positive energy plus quick execution is beyond an asset — it's a gift.*
— Dr Tamara Pizzoli, CEO, Pizzoli Media

It's interesting. I realized after the interview that joshua and I have been travelling in the same circles for a while now. We were both in Oakland around 1995. I was working in San Francisco at Wells Fargo Bank, just beginning my career in finance as an executive assistant. I lived by Lake Merritt. Joshua was interning at the Bay Area Video Coalition and working for a bootleg FedEx delivery service called Express It. In 1999, when I was working by Wall Street at 75 Park Place but living on 17th Street and 7th Avenue in Park Slope, he was living in Flatbush. Now, I look at our Facebook friends and realize that we have Dr Tamara Pizzoli in common, another sweet, magical soul filled with rainbows and delight. She and I met at the Harlem Book Fair in 2014. So I guess joshua and I have been making our way to this conversation for a few years. Given his practice of meditation and his lifelong focus on unification and healing; given his laid back manner, there is a part of me that doubts if there is anything happenstance about our meeting. But then again...

***

joshua bee alafia, a seasoned filmmaker, redefines the art of independent filmmaking. If international independent filmmaking means "making a film outside the major filmmaking process," he has mastered that process. In fact, he is currently writing a book about no-budget filmmaking called *Chasing The Sun: No-Budget Filmmaking in Cuba, Brasil, Ethiopia and Brooklyn.* He is now looking to add Ghana to that eclectic list with his new project, *The Healers*, an adaption of the 1979 novel of the same name by Ayi Kwei Armah.

Indeed joshua bee alafia (small caps intentional) has made a career of making movies outside the mainstream which marry an African ethos, narrative and knowing with an auteur's avant-garde style. He has been fearless. He has been tireless. He has been faithful to his craft and his knowing. His website www.rootsflix.net states it is dedicated to:

The Art in the Spirit of Liberation. We believe in sharing art that liberates internal and external oppression, delusion, dysfunction and negativity. We are committed to bringing films that celebrate earth, life, love and that creation rebel spirit that makes a film, "roots."

Roots, huh?

Rootsflix features films as *Cubamor*, a story about a Nuyorican, Lazaro, who goes back to Havana to study music after proposing to his longtime girlfriend. Or, there is

Zar-O, made in Ethiopia about a "homeless youth in Addis Ababa [who] becomes the prophet of the New Millennium bringing forward an ancient Axumite prophecy." It also has an early film starring David Oyetokunbo Oyelowo — the British Nigerian actor who starred in Ava DuVernay's instant classic *Selma* — called *Shoot the Messenger*, as well as *Blackout*, with a young Zoe Saldana, Jeffrey Wright and the legendary Melvin Van Peebles. Then there is *The Last Dragon*. Everybody knows that one with Vanity and Taimak, a.k.a. Sho-nuff — *Who is the master!?*

Anyhow, I got the chance to talk with independent filmmaking master, joshua bee alafia, about his craft and magic.

Patrick A. Howell: What was it about the opportunity to make Ayi Kwei Armah's 1979 novel *The Healers* into a film that captured your attention?

joshua bee alafia: I consider *The Healers* to be a liberation narrative that disrupts our conditioning and causes powerful chain reactions of internal illuminations. African Americans have such a deep wound from our ancestors being enslaved and it has affected our relationship with Africa. We haven't really had a writer break down the anatomy of the betrayal, how the corruption happened and how the chiefs were persuaded and seduced materially. It's a story of a young man choosing between selling his cousins, becoming a king or becoming a healer. It's a love story. A murder mystery. It's about the fall of the Ashanti Empire and how it happened and it's just a very healing story. The effect of reading it in tandem with *Two Thousand Seasons* is truly healing and liberating. *Two Thousand Seasons* is another one of Armah's masterpieces which is told in a pluralized communal voice — something which is very hard to achieve. I became a huge fan and would just push his books to everyone I knew. Took me ten years to manifest it but I finally got to Senegal.

***

I asked joshua bee alafia about his special journey to Senegal to meet a mentor and inspiration. Below is his story:

Those who have had disappointing meetings with folks they've admired have said, "never meet your heroes," for ages. There's some truth to the saying, you can have your idealization of the person shattered. And I've had my share of disappointing experiences meeting folks whose art, writing, films, and music I admire and enjoy. I've just chalked it off as we have different tastes, ways of being, etc. I've grown to not take those little disappointments personally. When I finally read Ayi Kwei Armah's The Healers in 2007, after picking it up and putting it back on the shelf at Afro-centric book stores from coast to coast because it was an import and $25, I not only felt I'd found an amazing story to make into a film, but a great teacher in this master storyteller, who, on his website, had information on an ongoing writers' workshop he conducted in Popenguine, Senegal. I wrote my friend Salim Rollins exclaiming that Popenguine may be our Mecca, as we both had dreams of repatriating to Africa some day and creating an intentional artist community. Ten years later, I got my chance to meet my hero.

Several months ago, I wrote Armah's USA distributor and told her of my intentions to option The Healers and adapt the book for the screen. My email was forwarded to Armah and he responded, and we began a dialogue. Armah wasn't interested in talking unless I had the financial backing to do the film justice, and the fact that I have been making films outside the mainstream film outlets on micro-budgets didn't engender his faith that I could begin this conversation with any real ability to realize the film. I enlisted the help of a producer to help edit my responses to some discouraging emails as I was beginning to respond emotionally with passion that wasn't serving the conversation. Eventually, she just purchased tickets for us to meet with Armah face-to-face, as email wasn't the most functional forum for the discussion. Armah agreed to an hour meeting.

There are times in life when we are given affirmation that we are moving in a manifestation current that is carried by momentum of both internal and external forces in our favor. Alignment with destiny, is the feeling we get when things flow with little effort. That's how our trip to Senegal started, smooth flight, super fluid immigration control, folks looking out for us arranging our hour and twenty-minute cab ride to Popenguine from Dakar, good food and nice folks at the hotel and boom, it became time to meet the maestro. Armah had a warm, upbeat, polite and welcoming tone, as well as a bit of joyful apprehension. He introduced us to his former student and current collaborator, Ayesha Attah, who has already used her knowledge to publish two novels, is working on a third, and works with a group regularly to translate hieroglyphic texts. We entered his office space and all sat down.

The room was filled with books and light. I admit I was a little geeked out to look at his work space, specifically where his computer sat. We exchanged a few pleasantries and got to the business of me explaining my intentions with the book. I explained how I didn't see it as a micro-budget film, and that I sought to engage actors who have strong track records in Hollywood productions to facilitate the film's broad distribution. Our exchange was pleasant. He fed us a delicious lunch and we looked at his other books and bought some too. We kept talking and the hour meeting became a seven hour conversation that ended in a feeling of excitement about the possibility of making a beautiful film out of his exquisite story. Epic films like this one are just dreams until the financial resources come to make them into realities.

The day after our meeting, as we ate breakfast, Ayi Kwei surprised us by sharing a chapter of the book he was in the midst of working on. We continued talking about meditation, the social revolution started by Gautama Buddha and his wife Yasodhara, Gautama, The Outlaws of the Marsh *and* The Romance of the Three Kingdoms *(the epic Chinese novels he has his students read), and the liberation and unification of Africa, as we walked around the town and along the beach. We eventually sat beside the ocean, fully engrossed in the moment and conversation. Suddenly springing to his feet after remembering it was one of the days he tutored neighborhood children, Ayi Kwei abruptly excused himself, walking away without looking back. We remained still for a while, in a daze of gratitude, before taking a celebratory swim.*

After a great swim, we met with Moussa Sene Absa, one of Senegal's great filmmakers, as Ayi Kwei had pointed out his beachfront home to us. Moussa was in the middle of a think tank with six young writers he had brought from Dakar with the intention of writing a television series. They were busy talking about plot twists and character arcs and very hospitably paused to let me take their portraits and interview Absa about his work as a mentor, filmmaker and artist in general.

The trip home had some little bumps to remind us we were still on Earth. A customs officer wanted a bribe in Dakar, and again in Morocco, but we were floating. Tanned, laden with excellent books, and empowered with an enhanced vision of the film The Healers. *Sometimes it pays to go ahead and meet your heroes, face the music, know their humanity and keep appreciating their work and how it has affected you. I'd much rather know a hero in reality, than keep them an idealized fantasy to preserve an ideal. Sure, it helps if they turn out to be super down to earth and anti-narcissist, and if they live in Popenguine, Senegal, even better!*

***

P.H.: Thank you joshua for your gift of your story. Many more of us enlightened spirits need to make it back to the Motherland if not for repatriation then for business, vacation and rest. I have a feeling, a deep abiding spiritual sense, that the Motherland wants to connect us to the source. What other projects are you working on currently?

j.b.a.: I'm currently looking for the budget to make my Black Arts Movement/time travel/ghost/love story called *The Saxophone Upstairs*.

It wasn't really forced, that first conversation with joshua. It was Sunday morning, I had just finished watching *Meet the Press*. Like so many of the conversations I've had with so many incredible creatives, the conversation is pregnant, nearly bursting with the sweet, sweet overripe presence of possibility. We are part of a conversation which, really, has no beginning and a conversation which has no ending — it is a conversation of the brotherhood, peace and liberation. It is a conversation about coming back to the source within. It is about coming back home.

I came to the conclusion long before I began my journey in finance, before leaving home as a child for adventures in life, that the only technology we people darker than blue ever lacked was that of unity. It's a concept. It's a principle. It's a practice. During Kwanzaa, the third day, or concept of Ujima is the concept of collective work and responsibility. By itself, this concept is nothing new. But, I am forty-five now and have a premium of knowing by way of experience. Ujima means to build and maintain our community together and make our brother's and sister's problems our problems and to solve them together.

3/2/17

NOMADNESS TRAVEL TRIBE

EVITA TURQUOISE ROBINSON, ENTREPRENEUR AND WORLD TRAVELLER

It is a call for Black people in this country to unite, to recognize their heritage, to build a sense of community. It is a call for Black people to define their own goals, to lead their own organizations.
— Stokely Carmichael

Evita Turquoise Robinson has been around the world. Literally. No joke. *Know what?* Let's do a *partial* list of her excellent globe-trotting ways — Bahrain (a small Arab monarchy in the Persian Gulf), Belize (a country on the eastern coast of Central America), the Netherlands, Germany, Cambodia, Puerto Rico, Thailand, Panama, Jamaica, Japan, France, Tanzania, Puerto Rico, United Arab Emirates, Hong Kong, Samoa, Indonesia (Bali), South Africa, Honduras, Greece... She's not even thirty-something. Just up and picks up her bags, travels, plays, experiences, works... creates assets like blogs, videos and keeps doing it. Over and over and over again. Her favorite quote from Dr Cornel West — "Step out on nothing and land on something."

Evita don't play and that global travel thing is only a prologue — like an *opening* to a great literary work by Ralph Ellison or an interlude on an Outkast album. She went ahead and made a business out of it. Calls it Nomadness Travel Tribe. Just like she does with her global travels, she has thrown herself into the world of entrepreneurship, creating a group of fifteen thousand international members.

On May 22 2015, she launched the travel web "docuseries" *The Nomadness Projects*, co-executive produced by HBO's Issa Rae and hosted on Evita's YouTube channel of over 200,000 subscribers. She is a millennial who graduated from Iona College in 2006 and was the commencement speaker, and now holds a board of director position on their alumni association. *These are all indicators to an uncommonly high concentration to excellence.* We could say "Black excellence" and that would be cool, a nice little reference to the anthem of African allegiance and heritage in the Kanye West and Jay-Z song — but this is much, much more than *just* Black excellence. This is about the emergence of global leadership from a generation. It is about the *boom* boom shakalaka boom! after well... the Baby Boomers.

So, now that you have the dossier on Evita, you will agree with me she is a bad lady who don't play, let's talk with her a little and find out about more about her plans for the Nomadness Travel Tribe and literal world domination.

Patrick A. Howell: Evita, where in the world are you these days? And what are you doing there?

Evita Turquoise Robinson: I am presently in Johannesburg, South Africa. What I am doing here is we are doing our pivot in 2017 away from group trips into international pop up events and to launch that we have our weekend of "Johannesburg Juxtaposition." That includes the VIP dinner with some influencers and partnerships we have built in Johannesburg. We are throwing a party with one of South Africa's most well respected DJs, DJ Kenzhero, to kick off the next phase of what Nomadic is doing.

P.H.: Do you consider yourself more of an entrepreneur, innovator, adventurer or trailblazer? Which and why? You can only chose one! OK, two, but in order of preference.

E.T.R.: *I would definitely say innovator. For me it's* always about innovating and doing what is next. Sometimes even with Nomadness we'll use the hashtag — "#whatsnext." If I feel like too many people are doing what we are which happens a lot, especially when you consider we were really the first to really trailblazer the urban travel movement then that is my cue to step it up, do something different and take it to the next level. I would definitely be an innovator first. Second would be trailblazer. Third would be entrepreneur. And last would be adventurer.

P.H.: At this point in your life Evita, you have traveled or lived in over twenty countries on three continents. Where would be your favorite destination to live and why? Where do you have yet to travel that is on your bucket list and what about that particular destination draws your curiosity?

E.T.R.: The favorite destination is probably the most common and the most difficult of all the questions to answer because I have had so many homes around the world at this point. I would probably say Johannesburg, South Africa. More specifically the Maboneng Precinct Neighborhood where I am now and tend to bring the tribe back to. There's just something here that is home from the relationships I have built with people here. I am just a couple months from getting my first apartment out here. There is just something so real about Johannesburg that I guess reminds me of New York — home, home – but also has its own African flavor. I love being in a place where being Black is something that is revered and not a mark against you.

A place I have yet to travel but is on my bucket list? Buenos Aires, Argentina. I have been emotionally building myself up for a trip to my namesake. I am named after Evita Peron — a very powerful woman — the first lady of Argentina. Her former husband was Juan Peron. She was as much controversial as she was powerful and life changing.

I realized that as I grow and I naturally take on what Nomadness brings my way, I am very much an extension of the woman I was named after. So I would like to pay homage to Evita Peron and go to her grave site, former living space and museum to check her out in Buenos Aires.

P.H.: Millennials are known as a generation that travels as a matter of fact. Per Topdeck Travel, a provider of group travel for 18-30 somethings, 88% of millennials travel overseas between one and three times a year. 94% were between 18-30. Given the stabilization of economies v. 2008 and also the global political shift away from globalization (Brexit and proposed American border walls), do you think these trends will continue? Why or why not?

E.T.R.: Yes, the trends with millennials will continue. We are a particular generation that understands the world has shrunk. We grew up in the internet age which is why I think travel is so prevalent and realistic for us where it may not have been for our parents and grandparents. In addition we have made it a priority in our lives and I believe that thought process is something we will automatically instill in our children. So I think that will become a generational shift.

P.H.: How is the Tribe doing? What are your 2017 goals for Nomadness LLC? 5 year goals?

E.T.R.: To be honest with you I don't really believe in five year goals. I believe in very little over two years because I believe it is way too easy to become complacent or not provide tangible actions to something with that sort of time frame. We tend to schedule our calendar six months to two years max. I like to give myself goals in which there are actionable items I can take today that will affect that time frame.

A goal for Nomadness for 2017 is the release for our Nomadness app, finishing the manuscript for my travel memoir as well as television whether it is linear or digital. Those are goals I feel comfortable sharing.

P.H.: You have said, "Everybody is born with homework and it is our responsibility while we are alive to find out what that assignment is." With some of the wild global political shifts, do you think millennials will continue to be as aware and self-conscious as they have been up until now? Are we in a New Age?

E.T.R.: I believe that millennials will continue to be as aware and self-conscious as they have been because we have no choice. Especially if you are talking about millennials of color. This presidential shift alone has woken a lot of people up. That's probably the only positive that has come from the election. It's so jarring that people are awake who have not been. With that, it is about us taking a stance, running for office. It's about us continuing to see the world and that is something that is not just happening in America. As you said, there are actual global political shifts that are happening. And unfortunately a lot of that is fascist. I've heard about a lot of people running for office, myself included. I've pondered it, using my platform on a more global level.

Are we in a new age? That's relative. Every age and generation is new and unique. That is what the essence of evolution is. So I would say yes but I wouldn't say yes with any real standout over the fact that we are always evolving as humans.

P.H.: What does it mean to be a global woman of African descent in the twenty-first century? As you travel the world as an international citizen, do you ever get the sense that Africans have already been the globe over... many times?

E.T.R.: As far as millennial leadership, we have been given this platform in which the world has shrunk so we are more global minded. We are not about the 9-5 hierarchy. For us, we revere freedom over money. We will take a pay cut over being able to use that time to build a family, travel, see things and explore hobbies that we may have. Millennial leadership strives for more of a work/life balance.

We are also aggressive in ways that previous generations just differed. Not saying that they weren't aggressive. We are a different type of aggression. I think we are kind of hard headed but I think that serves us well in being able to go after our dreams and not let anyone or anything tell us that we can't. Many of us are workaholics if we have taken on the idea of being an entrepreneur which is a contrast to sometimes people saying the millennial generation is like-minded.

2/17/17

GRIOT MASSAI

KALIF W. PRICE, CHILDREN'S AUTHOR AND COMMUNITY LEADER

The Gullah peoples of Georgia and South Carolina have a rich legacy that is an exotic mix of Caribbean and American traditions. They are the descendants of enslaved Africans who lived in the lowland regions of Georgia and South Carolina, including both the coastal plain and the Sea Islands. The Gullah enjoy a big though quiet reputation that has endeared them to artists like Julie Dash, whose classic 1991 film *Daughters of the Dust* featured the timeless tale of three generations of Gullah women on the island of St. Helena. Then, there is George Gershwin's 1935 novel *Porgy and Bess* and Zora Neale Huston's 1937 classic *Their Eyes Were Watching God*.

Kalif Price is classic Gullah.

The first time I met Kalif W. Price, it was Sunday and we were in San Diego enjoying Ethiopian lunch with our families at a local store front and restaurant Awash. Awash could have been magically transported from Addis Ababa with an authenticity and vibe that is one hundred konjo, but there was a powerful West African vibe coming from a corner of the restaurant amongst all of the Ethiopian natives who come to watch Sunday soccer, enjoy the injera, tibs and wat and relax. I noticed the regal and distinct brother, a supernova of positive energy realized, loving time with two adorable daughters and his wife. In my mind, though, the unbridled charisma, bold dreadlocks and massive frame reminded me of a lion having lunch with his pride. His beautiful daughters absolutely adored their father and his wife was content with a man as much protector as giver of life and joy.

At the checkout, I let him know. "Beautiful family bro." He radiated a million gigawatt smile and roared, "You too brother!" Sunshine glowed bright into the parlor and the energy flowed like that. King recognized king. He shared a book on the restaurant store front, told me he was the author and I had to buy it for my son. The book was titled, *Maasai Boy, Heart of a Warrior* and was beautifully illustrated by Vagabundo DeVaughn. He signed the book with the inscription, "Christian (future author) — Give thanks for the King God created you to be — Blessed Love, Kalif 2016" (a cool simple sun symbol drawn in). Like that, I knew we would work together because that is the point of business and life, doing work that blends the good with the great. We hooked it up for several weeks later and here is the results of our exchange.

Patrick A. Howell: You are Gullah, right? Do you speak Geechee? Your stories, like *Massai Boy*, come organically from the tradition of the Griot. You are part of the continuum of a story that has told itself as long as the Ghanaian and Malian empires of the 1300s. How does that tradition inform your work as an author?

Kalif W. Price: Much of my relation to my Georgian culture was cut off and suspended early on when my mother and I migrated to California. It wasn't until years later when I developed a strong desire to reclaim and recover the history, knowledge, and culture of my family in the low country that I made consistent efforts to learn, appreciate, and understand all that I missed. I was a freshman in college and had a job loading vending trucks. I saved up enough money to purchase a plane ticket, rent a car and cover my expenses to spend a few weeks sitting humbly by the feet of my Georgian elders listening to their stories. It was through these stories that I learned about my family lineage and the culture of the region. This part of my discovery was also the moment that my latent potential as a storyteller became activated. The beauty of storytelling is that it connects to a much larger web in the oral African tradition.

P.H.: King Kalif, you are also a musician and performer who works with our children, consistently. Those are further instruments of your work as a member of a class of traveling poets, musicians, and storytellers who maintain a tradition of oral history in parts of West Africa. How do the ancestors, elders of the global cosmic system factor into your day to day? Into the art and discipline of your story telling? Which mode of storytelling best suits your soul as a Griot? Writing and authoring? Performing and stage directing? Singing and composing?

K.W.P.: Spiritual obedience is important to me. What I mean by that is, in order to share stories that resonate with, and have power to affect those in need, you have to prepare yourself as an obedient, disciplined, humble vessel for ancient stories from our ancestors and the Creator to move through you. It is truly a healing process for both the storyteller-author and the listening audience. I believe when you are gifted to reach an audience of people with your gift that it is your inherent responsibility to use that gift for the betterment of humanity. Sometimes improving humanity through stories is done through scrutinizing social commentary, which brings attention to social conditioning that is hard to digest or accept. I believe storytellers like Tupac were brilliant at this. In my case, I enjoy utilizing all platforms of sharing stories, from playwriting, screenwriting, acting, directing, song writing, poetry and children books. Recently I have devoted most of my efforts to children's book authorship. Reason being, children are the most impressionable and malleable. I truly know and believe that children are the future leaders of this world they will soon inherit, and the greatest method of instilling values that can shape a humanbeing to improve the suffering of the world is through children. So in short, I see writing children's books as an investment that yields the biggest return. There is a dire need to offer literature of value to our children. As a teacher and mentor coordinator, I work with a population of inner-city children of color who are searching desperately for identity and purpose. When our children have negative cultural identification through their immediate environment and social media, they soon act and behave accordingly. My goal is to reverse their cultural identification with positive images and stories that carry strong principles and values. It doesn't hurt also, that the author in my case is a 6 foot 3, 285lb Black man with a voice like James Earl Jones. I use this to my benefit in gaining their attention when I do storytelling events around town. I am aware that I don't represent the typical children's author, and I enjoy showing our children that we are not limited, but rather we are a people who have limitless potential.

In March of 2016, I had the pleasure of adapting *Maasai Boy* into a stage play, which I directed and featured in. It was truly remarkable to see a sold out audience of children and families enjoy the visual spectacle of my book come to life. This all took place at the Lyceum Theatre in Downtown, San Diego, less than a mile away from a homeless shelter that my mother and I had lived in. My mother was deep in her crack addiction at that time and we had succumbed to the poverty of the streets, eating from soup lines and scrapping around on the streets. It took a spirit of determination to

stand tall on stage years later before an audience whose
children I inspire to educate themselves and develop
positive self-images and beliefs. But this is the power of
spiritual obedience I am referring too. When we allow God
in anything is possible. I am living testament of that.

P.H.: You recently had the opportunity to send your books
to the Maasai tribe in Africa. First was it Kenya or Tanzania?
How did that happen, what was the story there? The Maasai
are a Nilotic ethnic group inhabiting southern Kenya and
northern Tanzania. They are among the best known local
populations due to their residence near the many game
parks of the African Great Lakes, and their distinctive
customs and dress. How did one with the West African
vibes, vibe so strongly with our East African brothers and
cousins? Where in your soul, do you belief the Kalif Price
soul originates? Maasai? Indigo? Mandinko? What do the
spirits and ancestors communicate?

K.W.P.: A little over a year ago I donated few of my children's
books, *Maasai Boy Heart of a Warrior*, to My Chosen Vessels,
a non-profit organization that champions the cause for
providing relief effort for the Maasai people in Kenya,
Africa. My dream was always to have my book make its way
to the Maasai tribe, but I never imagined that this might
actually happen. A few weeks ago I received notification
from MCV that my book was taken to Maasailand, and has
been circulating through the hands of each Maasai family
and child. MCV is in the process of building the first Maasai
school, of which classes are already in session, and my book
is the only book in their library. This is doubly special for
both the Maasai as well as myself, being that their first
book holds beautiful and positive depictions of themselves.
When I was informed about this and saw the accompanying
pictures, my eyes filled with tears of joy to see my dream

come into fruition. And the beauty of this is that it doesn't stop there. I am working with MCV and the Maasai Chief to have *Maasai Boy* translated into their native tongue, Maa. We are in the process of launching a fundraiser so that all 160 Maasai youth can have their own copy of my book. Illiteracy among the Maasai is running rampant. Sadly, in order to receive education in Kenya, they have been forced to disown their culture — from the cutting of their dreadlocks, which the warriors began growing during the beginning of their rites of passage in manhood, to their traditional talisman and attire. The Maasai school is being built on Maasailand directly besides the Chief Sontika's home, which allows the Maasai to receive education while maintaining their cultural traditions. Chief Sontika along with the MCV are spearheading the plan to educate the Maasai people to protect them from illegal land appropriation and their increasing dependence on the industrialization of Kenyan government. Chief Sontika is quoted as saying, "The Maasai people love our traditional culture very much, but times are changing, and we are struggling to survive because we are uneducated." As the Chief, Sontika understands the importance of cultural preservation and education. Educating Maasai girls is even more of a struggle. Maasai girls are responsible for fetching water from a watering hole that is a three mile journey away, which leaves no time for education. The Maasai school built on their land will offer the convenience and time necessary for girls to be educated. This has also inspired me to write the sequel to *Maasai Boy*, entitled *Maasai Girl*. I am working close with MCV to acquire funding to provide every Maasai child with a copy of my book, which I plan to hand deliver to them and have a day of celebrating the art of storytelling.

11/27/16

SHE RULES THE UNIVERSE

KANDIS DAVIS, CELLIST AND LADY OF SOCIETY

When I think of a lady, I get the image of Lena Horne's "Glinda the Good Witch of the South" in *The Wiz* — an angelic majesty of pure goodness sitting upon her cosmic throne among the constellations, her children, spreading the light to all who seek illumination. She is just so sweet. So, so sweet.

But you know what really blows my mind? There are so many of these ladies doing incredible work in the universe, and if our children, our bright stars, knew one true thing, it is that they can truly do anything they set their minds to.

Anything. Anytime. Anywhere. Anyhow. Period.

They would know with the distinct possibility of America electing its first woman president that there are generations of women who have come before and will come afterwards, most unheralded or unknown. Yes, she rules the universe.

For sure, they would know about the super nova, Ms Kandis Davis, the professional cellist, chic and cosmopolitan, residing in Milan, Italy and playing at Olympic stadiums, at fashion week in Milan and in venues throughout Europe — all since the age of fifteen! The Detroit native studied music at Detroit Country Day, Blue Lake Fine Arts and Interlochen, and also was an All-American track and field athlete. She completed undergraduate and post-graduate studies at the University of Michigan, Canterbury University, the Civic School of Music in Milan, and the Magaloff Academia.

Kandis fondly recalls: "I was fifteen years old at the time and turned sixteen while on tour in these marvelous European countries, from France, to Germany to Switzerland and beyond. We, as an orchestra, were hosted by European families of musicians who studied at the counterpart European music institutions, and some families spoke very little English. So many times, my host families and I would 'speak' through the music we all knew, and after dinner we would sit around and play pieces of music, like Beethoven, Chopin, Haydn, that we all knew and this was how we 'communicated.'"

Kandis, a classic violin-cellist (as they say in Italy) continues: "That's when I discovered that music is a language of its own which has no need for words, as it transcends vocabulary and languages spoken by speaking to the soul of each individual listener. That experience in Europe transformed my life as I'd always been told by my parents that 'the world is my oyster,' but when I saw my music speaking to people to whom I could not, I understood more deeply what they meant."

African Americans have a proud history of innovation, creating nearly every musical tradition in America — rock and roll, jazz, blues, funk, soul and hip-hop. American history is also rich with the accomplishments of classical artists like Kandis: in 2002, Tage Larsen became the first African American musician in the history of the Chicago Symphony Orchestra; Misty Copeland is a soloist at the American Ballet Theater; Jessye Norman continues to travel the world performing world-famous, centuries-old operas; and pianist Thomas "Blind Tom" Wiggins (1849-1908) traveled throughout North America, performing the works of Bach, Beethoven and his own compositions.

Kandis' accomplishments are noteworthy: she is the Principal Cellist for the International Festival of Orvieto, Italy and for the Symphonic Orchestra of Pavia, Italy. She has sat on the board of directors of the Benvenuto Club of Milan and was awarded Soloist of the Year by the Civic School of Music of Milan for her virtuoso cello repertoire.

"My cello's name is Mischia and that's the name every cello I've ever played on has had since I was seven years old. Talk about having 'an imaginary friend!'" she laughs heartily. "Mine was made of wood and actually spoke to me and others when I followed my teacher's instructions!"

Kandis was recently selected as the English vocal coach for chorus at Teatro alla Scala to perform the George Gershwin opera, *Porgy and Bess*. This is the first time this opera is being performed in Italy and Kandis was selected as leadership not only for her sterling credentials but her familiarity with the Gullah language. Gullah is a creole language spoken by the African American population living on the Sea Islands and in the coastal regions of the American States of South Carolina, Georgia and northeast Florida. Our first lady, Michelle Obama's roots have been traced to the Gullah/Geechee peoples of Sierra Leone who helped build the United States of America in the 1700s.

Yes, all kinds of sweet goodness and greatness. Goodness gracious. My, my, my. Instead of celebrating women's suffrage with national elections, we can all begin celebrating our rich history 24/7 *NOW*? The rest of the world already is.

Kandis is humbled by the honor. "This honor is so much bigger than "me" and my cello Mischia. It's also bigger than "us" handful of Blacks chosen to participate. This honor bestowed by Teatro alla Scala offers a unique opportunity to send high frequency waves throughout global communities, to raise the consciousness. By the time we have our opening night at Teatro alla Scala, America will also have a new President. As members of a global village, I know our work will reach out and touch the world."

2/4/17

REPEATER'S INVASION OF AMERICA

TARIQ GODDARD, PUBLISHER AND AWARD-WINNING AUTHOR

Photo by Steph Rennie

The Repeater Books manifesto reads: "Repeater Books is dedicated to the creation of a new reality. The landscape of twenty-first-century arts and letters is faded and inert, driven by fashionable cynicism, egotistical self-reference and a nostalgia for the recent past."

Yes, it *actually says that. It says it at the end of this book.* No, it is not a political treatise. Or manifestation in New Age exercise. Or, is it? It goes on to say: "Repeater intends to add its voice to those movements that wish to enter history and assert control over its currents, gathering together scattered and isolated voices with those who have already called for an escape from Capitalist Realism." Repeater Books has been blogging and publishing since 2015 (Mr Tariq Goddard has been at the "game of publishing" a little longer, as an award-winning novelist and as the founder and publisher of Zer0 Books). So the mission is prescient and the product of an acutely astute mind and team. Repeater saw the trend lines in history and got out ahead of Brexit, Trump and the overall contraction of global democratic values and emergence of strongman geopolitical tantrums or grotesque acerbic capitalist agendas. Indeed, the force is so, so very strong with Repeater Books and its manifestations.

It seems that this sort of mission — one with a clear focus, running antithetical to the political shifts of the times — has as good a chance of making a change or difference as any "disruptive" technology. So, perhaps this is "disruptive publishing," or as it is better known, independent publishing, where the most talented new voices come to say the unsayable with verve and creativity, where these new voices have the opportunity to show new sensibilities and shift the culture. Perhaps with its vision and literary thrust of such titles as *No Less Than Mystic* by John Medhurst, *The Equal Opportunities Revolution* by James Heartfield and the radical novel *Resolution Way* by Carl Neville, the Repeater brand definitely seems to defy the new global political normative. With a mission statement that calls for "an escape from Capitalist Realism," Repeater Books is certainly positioned for leadership in the contemporary social climate.

Repeater Books is headed by one Sir Tariq Goddard. Formally, he and Repeater Books are not part of the Resistance. And they are definitely not American. But, in his own way, he is putting out for the good fight. So, he's kind of like Han Solo. Only Han Solo didn't have an English accent. Tariq Goddard does. Also, Han Solo was a swashbuckling pirate despot. Tariq is not. That's not to say he is pugilistic, but I don't think he runs from a fight. He is a gentleman, but shrewd and not in the least shy of expressing a well thought-out declarative and compound sentence, punched with fact and knowing. In style, he is a throwback to the age of the declarative novelist, like Ernest Hemingway — a man's man. He harkens back to a time when authors like Norman Mailer, John Steinbeck and William Faulkner lived, fought and built, and made things happen in the world... when authors were a defining force of popular culture.

Mr Goddard is an acclaimed novelist who has written six novels since 2002. His sixth, *Nature and Necessity*, will be sold through and distributed by Penguin Random House in the United States. His first novel, *Homage to a Firing Squad*, was shortlisted for the Whitbread Book Award for a first novel. *Sports Magazine* recognized his second novel *Dynamo* as one of the ten best sports novels of all time (stiff competition when you consider such classics as Bernard Malamud's *The Natural* or Nick Hornby's *Fever Pitch*). His third work, *The Morning Rides Behind Us*, was shortlisted for the Commonwealth Writers Prize for Fiction. His fourth novel, *The Picture of Contented New Wealth*, won The Independent Publishers Award for Horror Writing. This book also received a development grant from the Royal Literary Fund.

He co-founded the independent publishing company Zer0 Books in 2007 with the late Mark Fisher. Repeater Books, also founded with Fisher, started in 2015, and now boasts twenty-seven titles in its catalogue. Some of the most successful titles have been *Lean Out* by Dawn Foster, *Filling the Void* by Marcus Gilroy-Ware and *The Weird and the Eerie* by Mark Fisher. Repeater Books continues to acquire, publish and sign prodigious new talents, such as NBC's Lesley-Ann Brown's *Decolonial Daughter*, due out in late 2018. All the while, Mr Goddard maintains a disciplined writing schedule that ought to be the envy of any self-respecting author. He, however, is humble about his successes and talents, confessing with a self-depreciating authenticity, "I have come to find that my successes in Europe mean next to nothing across the Atlantic." He seems to understand that his most important work is in front of him and he is well positioned to make a difference where humanity matters.

I received an advance copy of *Nature and Necessity*, and was fascinated with his previous work *The Picture of Contented New Wealth* and the smatterings of personal information found by Google searches. We conducted the interview over a series of emails and FaceTime conversations at the unnatural hour of 1:30 a.m. This will be the first of two pieces; the second will focus on Mr. Goddard's forthcoming work *Nature and Necessity* (all unusual American spellings like "specialise," "favour" and "practising" are kept in their original English form!)

Patrick A. Howell: Who are your literary influences, idols and/or mentors?

Tariq Goddard: Henry James gave me the confidence to go on at length, even if I didn't know what I was aiming at, Norman Mailer gave me the courage to not care about being laughed at, Graham Greene taught me distance and discretion, and Proust that it was alright to look to your own work for spiritual reassurance, which would also be the mark of whether it was working or not. And I think the playwright and my fellow Londoner, Harold Pinter, demonstrated how to construct a world in a handful of sentences plus a stage direction or two. There were and are plenty of others, but these were the most use to me when I was getting started.

Like many children who didn't do well at school, I learnt to specialise early in life, and that was thanks to my English teacher John Stubbs who told me I should write, which at the time made absolutely no sense to me at all, but happily, has since then. So much to his embarrassment (he's a modest man).

P.H.: There is an inner animating spark in you and it burns bright for publishing. I have also noted a hunger to change the world through words, ideas and the culture of literature. Is Repeater Books accomplishing what it has set out to do?

T.G.: Neither I or my colleagues ever viewed ourselves as publishers, insofar as none of us understood the business or published books to facilitate a career in the publishing industry. Our motivation was the fear that lots of books we wanted to get published, or written, never would be unless we commissioned and published them ourselves, and that there turned out to be enough of these to constitute something of a wave, which in itself became a modest publishing revolution as most of our authors were first-time unknowns, who far from disappearing without trace, competed with authors from the big houses and helped influence the climate in favour of projects like ours. The problem with the publishing industry is the "industry" part, with the emphasis on sales, meta-data, charts denoting market share, sales campaigns and the like, and very little on the actual content of books and on how to motivate and support writers.

As enthusiasts that love books, who can spot and cultivate talent and write ourselves, we were uniquely well placed to take advantage of conventional publishing's deficiencies. Our first venture Zer0 Books was conceived really as a gesture with little hope of success, mainly to get as many writers into print as we could and see what happened. Because of costs, not much attention was paid to any other aspect of the process. Repeater is looking to combine that guerrilla urgency with some of the perks Zer0 lacked and that other publishers could offer to our cost: a thorough editorial process, advances where possible, well-produced books, individual cover designs, and far fewer books, allowing us to really get behind those we do release, rather than sticking them in a bottle and chucking them hopefully out to sea.

P.H.: What do you hope to accomplish with Repeater that you did not with Zero?

T.G.: An entrepreneurial venture that isn't, in the last instance, at the service of what it is looking to put out in the world, has its priorities confused and will succeed only by virtue of novelty, sharp practise and luck. A better world is self-evidently a preferable goal to professional success, but as the only way to achieving a better world is to concentrate on what it lies in your power to do, one is more likely to grow out of the other, than emerge by itself. As a novelist my relationship with myself was fairly all-consuming. Publishing was a way of getting away from that and placing myself in the middle of other people's worlds (that of the authors) and experiencing the business end that I had never concerned myself with before, and to do that meant distancing myself from my natural inclinations which is to absent myself from the day-to-day and just write.

Obviously Repeater would fail as a business if we didn't sell any books, so to that end, success is selling enough to continue, but we would also fail if we weren't reaching, touching and connecting to people, which we wouldn't be doing if we weren't selling, so the two have a mutually complementary relationship, providing the books you are selling are the right titles. Anyone can sell a lot of crap, so that in itself would make us no different from anyone else; our aim is to achieve sales with books that would otherwise be ignored, but actually are more deserving of success than titles people believe they should buy, but are forgotten before they're even read.

P.H.: Are publishing entrepreneurial adventures the same as capitalist pursuits? How does Repeater Books measure success? If you could only do one — change the world for the better or create a brand that would stand the test of time which would you choose (not that they are mutually exclusive!)? What is the end game for Repeater Books? Which has been Repeater's most "successful" release to date? With which did you have the most fun? Do you even care about having fun?

T.G.: Our most successful title is *The Weird and Eerie* by our co-founder, Mark Fisher, who tragically died earlier this year. It wasn't much fun for him to write but I and tens of thousands of others are very glad that he did, and for everything else he did for Zer0 and Repeater.

The most fun we had was trying to think of a cover for our first title, Dawn Foster's *Lean Out*, where the thrill of actually seeing what one of our books would look like in concrete form, along with trying to create a kind of symbol that would sum up our mission statement and what we were trying to do as a publisher on the whole, came together and *Lean Out* became our strongest cover thus far I think.

I don't know whether fun would be the best way of summing this job up, perhaps something more like cheerful masochistic euphoria would do.

P.H.: You seem to have made a career of defying convention. In *The Picture of Contented New Wealth: A Metaphysical Horror*, you brought "literary sensibility to the traditional horror story." *The Message* has the unique premise of "a fictional African state in the grip of a civil war provoked by the emergence of the Mahdi, a pretender to the leadership of the Islamic world" and *The Morning Rides Behind Us* takes the band of brothers war movie, incorporating a irony and "black comic tone." Are you a contrarian? Or do you seek those themes of running against the grain, against the prevalent popular disposition? Or is that just life?

T.G.: I don't need to be a contrarian. I've little enough in common with whatever the prevailing tide happens to be as it is, and to say no on principle would be an affectation given that I actually wish my politics, taste and outlook actually were the mainstream. What I have found, as a novelist and publisher, is that books and writers have to be summed up in a pithy sentence or two if they are to attract sales and reviews and deals. And that can work, say, for a book on the delights of Kendal Mint Cake set in the Lake District written by an elderly schoolteacher, or a mixed race campus love affair written by a mixed race academic with an already existing media profile, but often the most vital stories defy easy categorisation, work between the genres, and are often not easily summed up. The writers also may not be superb advocates for their own talent, lack charisma, photograph badly and so on. Finding some of this to be the case in my life as a novelist, meant that as a publisher I began with a series of my own prejudices that I hoped would enable and assist writers who may otherwise have encountered some of the same difficulties as I did. But as with most things, failure to conform to the path of least resistance is a compulsion and a consequence of how you experience the world and respond to life, rather than a set of tricks or gimmicks employed to give the appearance of superficial difference, which is what I find tolerated contrarianism to often be. Basically attempting to not let yourself down is a great enough challenge in itself, especially if you are looking to make a living from doing so!

5/5/17

THIS MOST EXCELLENT GENERATION, OUR BLACK POWER GENERATION (TIME TO GET CRUNK WITH IT)

MARIE DUTTON BROWN, LITERARY AGENT

I got into the publishing business during the heart of the civil rights era. Harlem's congressman, Adam Clayton Powell, was the chairperson of the House Education Committee, and he held a hearing on diversity in book publishing. Publishers were called to testify about their efforts to produce multicultural books and to promote employment diversity. There were a lot of discussions, and many articles appeared about the fact that very few books that reflected the history of African Americans were being published.
— Marie Dutton Brown in *Jewels: 50 Phenomenal Black Women Over 50* by Michael Cunningham and Connie Briscoe

Marie Dutton Brown is one of "the major African American players" in the publishing industry, according to *Black Enterprise Magazine*. But her recognition by one of America's preeminent magazines of business excellence isn't how we know her. We know her by her six decades of work. *We know Marie Dutton Brown by her Black power.* Like so many of the gifted creatives within our culture and tradition, she does the work tirelessly decade after decade (from the 1960s to present) without the spectacle of enormous celebrity.

I mean, it is inevitable that she will end up in the meaningful dedication in an author's book or with headlines in the *Washington Post*, *LA Times*, AALBC (Troy Johnson's African American Literary Book Club) or on

The History Makers. But the lifetime recognition of a thought leader and lightworker who shifts paradigms from staid, recalcitrant formations into new thoughts and new ideas in intellectual, academic and leadership circles where ideologies form a nation's very being? A mahogany lightworker whose literary volumes do miracle work in correcting the gross distortion of Black lives with one dimensional caricatures that is the mass media a.k.a Hollywood Industrial Complex? Perceptions that impact reality and create self-fulfilling prophecies? The volumes produced are miraculous given the political, institutional and social malaise of institutional racism from which they are mined. And as veteran literary agent Janell Walden Agyeman (one of Marie's prodigies) noted in talking with me about this profile, "it is important for the trailblazers to receive their flowers when they can appreciate them."

We honor our own.

Thanks to Marie Dutton Brown, my agent, who continues to support me, and to push me to keep doing what I love to do.
— Linda Beatrice Brown, *Crossing Over Jordan*

Marie Dutton Brown is followed by a generation of authors, women, publishers and literary enthusiasts empowered to take the business of publishing our stories and our histories into the next epoch, upon the higher frequency.

I imagine her hands are elegant rich ebony instruments that spin diamonds of legacies from words. I imagine stars ingrained within the cosmic matter of these hands that are let loose with fastidious work. They are, in fact, Black cosmic hands that come from an ancient soul and immortal spirit of creators. Marie Dutton Brown, just as the work of Sidney Poitier, Toni Morrison or Maya Angelou, comes from the generation prior to Black Lives Matter. When Black lives matter it is because Black power did the dang thang.

This generation represented by Marie Dutton Brown are the Black Power Generation, the architects of our current libraries of books celebrating Black lives and woven into the popular culture, creating a new future unseen. As publishing industry veteran Malaika Adero reminded me, "the circles are small the higher and further back you go in publishing." Their works are the institutional halls through which we research and read our favorite authors, seeing ourselves celebrated against the backdrop of a system that runs on the ruin of Black spirits. These lightworkers are the positive polarity, working against the negative polarity built into the system. The buildings of metaphysical libraries were erected by Black hands, cosmic hearts and Black minds with Black love as the principal energy. *This is Black power.*

"She is determined and hard-working, someone who every day is pushing a boulder uphill and never stops," said CBS newsman Ed Bradley, a client and friend of about 30 years. "She is bucking a tide."
— *LA Times*, August 22nd, 1995

Marie Brown has been an editorial assistant, bookstore manager, book editor, editor-in-chief of a magazine, book marketing strategist and literary agent. She has worked with clients and authors such as Susan Taylor, Donald Bogle, Linda Beatrice Brown, Faith Ringgold, Tom Feelings, and Carl Weber.

Ed Bradley came to New York City because he followed her to the City. She was hired as a Doubleday editor. Both of them came from Philly. He was a radio broadcaster and she was teaching at an elementary school. They were looking to diversify and spread their wings. It was decided that the publishing world did not truly reflect

the population. And there was a consensus that there needed to be more representation of editors.
— Lesley-Ann Brown, NBC contributor and author of *Decolonial Daughter*

I'll say it again because it warrants repeating: there is a whole generation of men and women who have laid out a new vision and *implemented* that vision with decades of tireless, nearly impossible work. They made sacrifices. Some are well documented, but most are not. A few are celebrated. And that's how the race does what it does. Because folks like Marie Dutton Brown take the mission and don't play. They do the work. And that's what Gil Scott-Heron meant by "it won't be televised." It's about African systems, politics, knowing, self-love and *realities. Call it the Matrix or call it the Evil Empire or just call it Make America Great Again.* This is about going outside the current constructs of so-called reality to implement a vision we all know. It's about patience. It is about a faith. It is about hope. It's about execution. It is about *knowing.* It's about getting the dang thing done.

Now, this business about "crunk." The title of this piece says, "time to get crunk with it." And no doubt I've been working the groove well, creating a rhythm that is on the bass side of the scale and curves the walk with a hook, gets the head bouncing and the soul humming. I do doubt a woman of Marie Dutton Brown's caliber would condone such verbiage (or maybe she would), but the sentiment is apropos. Anyhow, time to get really crunk with it.

Cosmopolitan Girls acknowledges a Very Special Thanks to our agent extraordinaire, Marie Dutton Brown, for your guidance, and helping to shape and breathe life into Cosmopolitan Girls.
— Charlotte Burley and Lyah Beth LeFlore, *Cosmopolitan Girls*

Born in 1940 in Philadelphia, Marie Dutton was the daughter of a civil engineer father and schoolteacher mother. She grew up on the college campuses in Tennessee and Virginia where her father taught. She would go over to the department of drama to hear the great Black actor Moses Gunn rehearse. She earned an undergraduate degree in psychology from Penn State University in 1962, when she was a member of a class of African American students that were less than 1% of the population. Upon graduation, she began teaching elementary school but took an opportunity with Doubleday & Company as an associate editor. Ultimately, she would become a senior editor. She would go on to found her own magazine and would found her literary agency, Marie Brown Associates, in 1984. Since, then she has worked with hundreds of authors, served as a board member for Poets and Writers Inc. and served on the Coordinating Council of Literary Magazines & Presses. She has also served on the boards of the Studio Museum of Harlem and The Frederick Douglass Creative Arts Center.

The best way to understand a person, however, is to talk to those who have worked with her year after year and decade after decade. They know the real deal and can lay it all out. So, blogger and NBC contributor Lesley-Ann Brown and Janell Walden Agyeman, consultant with Next Steps Literary Services and former agent, Marie Brown Associates, give their insights:

Lesley-Ann Brown, NBC contributor and author of *Decolonial Daughter*

Marie really stresses the practice of reciprocity and encourages those around her to do the same. She often cites that this is why we are still here — our having a culture of exchanging talents and gifts as opposed to the individualistic mentality our monetary system encourages.

Marie surrounds herself with beautiful images of Blackness and pictures of all the many people whose paths she has crossed or where she's had a hand at some point in their literary/creative journey. If you're lucky enough to see her office, it is a shrine to all things Black and literary. There are books, first edition gems (I once spied the first printing of Sonia Sanchez's *Homegirls and Handgrenades* and *Homecoming*) which I had the opportunity to look at. I met Ed Bradley, Amiri Baraka, the late poet Safiya Henderson, Essence's Susan Taylor, Chaka Khan and many more, all through her.

Marie played an instrumental part in the careers of many of the writers and Black editors that we know today — whether by procuring contracts or just lending her ear, support and advice. To this list I could mention contemporary writer Tia Williams; poet, writer and social critic Kevin Powell; the poet Willie Perdomo; Palestinian-Brooklyn poet Suheir Hammad; Howard professor and poet Tony Medina; Harper Collins editor Tracy Sherrod; and recent Booker Prize-winner Paul Beatty. There are so many more of us who she was there for at the beginning of our careers. I think one of the first books Marie edited at Doubleday was Vertamae Grosvenor's *Vibration Cooking: Or, the Travel Notes of a Geechee Girl* — which has to be one of the Blackest memoirs ever. It's a classic. When I worked for her on 625 Broadway, her office was a resting spot for Blackness and creativity.

Marie surrounds herself with Black art, books and she is indeed a cultural treasure. Her insight into the Civil Rights movement, growing up during segregation, jazz, James Baldwin, Du Bois and countless other topics is incredible. Her knowledge of publishing and Black culture is deserving of a doctoral degree.

I've had many amazing experiences with Marie — one of the most profound was being fortunate enough to see her shackle. Marie has a shackle, from a slave ship that she bought from some hidden away store for about one hundred bucks. The shackle is heavy and the label reads that it is from a slave ship. I think everyone should be able to touch one of those. It's an experience.

Marie loves Black people. Everything she does is about uplifting us and supporting positive stories of us as she understands on a fundamental level, the importance of positive representation. She keeps a crew of writers close in her life, and we're all blessed enough to be referred to by her as her "children."

Janell Walden Agyeman, consultant with Next Steps Literary Services and former agent, Marie Brown Associates

I first met Marie Dutton Brown in 1974, when a professor introduced me and asked Marie to support my application to the Doubleday Publishing Company's intern program, which she did. In the years since, our relationship has blossomed and I now call her my mentor, colleague and friend. I am not the only one. There are dozens of other African American industry professionals who have sought her out for counsel over the years and have benefited from her deep wisdom and generous encouragement.

Apart from having midwifed shelves of books in her long career, she has had a profound influence among numerous African Americans in the book publishing industry, one whose reach has helped nurture generations of Black editors, agents, independent publishers, marketing and sales professionals and authors. "She's the Great Oz," a client once told me, but possessing a consciousness that consistently champions the value of African American and

African Diaspora culture and history and the significance of our contributions to the literary culture and publishing dynamic. She was a schoolteacher before she got into publishing, and she's never lost the passion to educate others while demonstrating our responsibility to help educate or entertain readers with thoughtfully crafted, high-quality books of lasting value.

This work is how we know the current moment of vitriolic racism will too pass. Because it was so much worse before and look how far we have come. It's how we know this violent reaction to the election of a Black president is really just another tired iteration of Custer's Last Stand. It's how we know that the ideologies of racism and its offspring of discrimination will soon be minorities too (in fact their immature violent tantrums already seem like the petty fare of a minority class emerging). We stand in our current moment upon the strength of Black love. And that power grows more powerful with each successive generation... exponentially. But I just call it... call them, the Black Power Generation. You see? Marie Dutton Brown, holding bags of diamonds in those Black woman hands and sprinkling them generously around for a universe to understand. Love is plenty, love is free. It is unending.

3/17/17

THE TRANSCENDENTAL PROFESSOR

DR IMANI PERRY, PROFESSOR AND ACTIVIST

tran·scen·den·tal̩ tran̩ sen'den(t)l/adjective
1. relating to a spiritual or nonphysical realm. "the transcendental
importance of each person's soul"

Dr Perry is a type of a rare academician, thought leader and
cultural critic whose combination of humility, care and brilliance
allows her work to be both felt and critically impactful. So many
people, myself included, count her as a mentor and interlocutor
who is honest — a scholar who cares deeply about Black people
and the state of our shared world.
— Darnell L. Moore, American writer and activist

Patrick A. Howell: Dr Perry, you and I met briefly in 2014
at the Schomburg Museum during the Harlem Book Fair.
You sat on a panel called "Achieving Our Nation: James
Baldwin and American Morality." Do you believe ancestor
Baldwin would be surprised at the lack of progress in
equality in 2017?

Imani Perry: Baldwin would not be surprised in the least.
He saw the direction the nation was going in the 1980s,
and really we are still living with the legacy of the 1980s,
the turn to neoliberal capitalism, the rejection of any
commitment to the public good, a celebration of excess
and selfishness, and a persistent white supremacist global
order. He saw it, it broke his heart, it enraged him, and he

spent much of the last fifteen years of his life warning us about it.

P.H.: What projects, aside from your children, are you currently working on?

I.P.: I have two forthcoming books: one on the history of Lift Every Voice and Sing, the other is theorizing gender in light of the digital and neoliberal eras. I'm also at work on a book about Lorraine Hansberry. I imagine it as a portrait of the artist, and a coming of age as an artist story: a *künstlerroman*.

Dr Imani Perry is one of the most powerful intellectual voices of our time. No matter the platform, whether on social media or television, or in print, she always elevates the national discourse on race and social policy. While her feast of analysis, which I have followed on the pages of the Chronicle of Higher Education *and elsewhere, reveals the cold truth that Black people continue to suffer disproportionately in myriad ways, she also reminds us that we are still a robust, beautiful, and unbroken people. She loves us — our wounds and all.*
— Dr Stacey Patton, commentator and Morgan State University Professor

P.H.: Who are some of your mentors? Who, if anyone represents the Black power struggle in all of its complexity? Barack Obama? Oprah? Dr Cornel West? Or, will "Black leadership" evermore be decentralized?

I.P.: I had extraordinary educators: Robert Stepto, Hazel Carby, Henry Louis Gates Jr, and Cornel West. And there are many other intellectuals, historic and present, from whom I gain constant insight and inspiration although they educated me on the page rather than in person. Among them are Edward Said, Stuart Hall, and Hortense Spillers. I don't think there's ever been single leaders who effected change. It has always been a collective struggle, based in organization and collaboration.

P.H.: Do you think institutional racism will ever be eradicated from the American system? What do you foresee for our children?

I.P.: I don't know that it is our place to ask or answer that question. I believe that we ought to live lives committed to the eradication of all forms of injustice and domination, racism, patriarchy, heterosexism, classism, neoimperialism, and so forth. The only possibility is in the doing.

P.H.: In 2005, you wrote *Narrative of Sojourner Truth*. In 1828 Sojourner Truth became the first Black woman to win a court case against a white man when she sued to get her son out of slavery. You are a Harvard JD. Do you think she ought to be appointed to the Black America Supreme Court? Who else, aside from Thurgood Marshall and former nominee Lani Guinier, would sit on that nine-seat court?

I.P.: I can't answer that question. But I do think that the following are some of the greatest legal minds in African American History: Frederick Douglass, Charles Hamilton Houston, Pauli Murray, A. Leon Higginbotham, Thurgood Marshall, Derrick Bell, and Lani Guinier.

She personifies the best of the Black intellectual tradition but beyond that she offers work that is accessible in a way that exemplifies her deep commitment to liberation and radical Black love, friendship and community.
— Darnell L. Moore, American writer and activist

P.H.: I saw a recent Facebook post on your page with the question, "What are your top five race books every American should read? Not in order. Just the top five." What was your answer?

I.P.: I answered the question in terms of five books that for me capture Black America's journeys and questions. Which wasn't exactly the intent of my friend Jesse Washington, the *AP* journalist when he asked the question. I think he meant books about race (and for that I would actually suggest people read my book *More Beautiful and More Terrible: The Embrace and Transcendence of Racial Inequality in the United States*). But I answered with the following works: *The Collected Essays of James Baldwin*, W.E.B. DuBois' *The Souls of Black Folk*, Toni Morrison's *Beloved*, and *The Selected Poems of Gwendolyn Brooks and Robert Hayden*. I find those types of lists difficult though. Reading should be a lifelong project. There's no short list to understanding race and racialization.

P.H.: On your Facebook page, you recently noted: "As a child, the only singer whose music I played as much as Nina Simone's was Al Jarreau, specifically his *Glow* album, which will always be one of my favorites. So thankful for years of delighting in his voice. May he rest in peace." Truly, Al Jarreau is an American icon and treasure. What is your favorite song on that album and why?

I.P.: His rendition of "Your Song" is my favorite on that album. The extraordinary improvisation, passion and sincerity, are breathtaking. But there are so many more too.

P.H.: This is Black History Month and early next week will be President's Day. Trump surprised the electorate with a victory no one saw, and more than ever Obama's activist

America seems to be in full activist effect. What form do you foresee "the struggle" taking in the coming years? Dr. Martin Luther King famously said, "I have a dream that one day little Black boys and girls will be holding hands with little white boys and girls." Do you think an America, racially at peace, is possible this century before the year 2100?

I.P.: I wouldn't refer to it as "Obama's activist America." What we've witnessed over the past eight to ten years is a response to pervasive and trenchant inequality of a sort that President Obama didn't ameliorate despite the hopes of many constituents. From Occupy Wall Street under Bush, to Black Lives Matter and the Movement for Black Lives, under Obama, to the current rise in organizing and protest, people in this nation are refusing to accept the status quo, a status quo that is profoundly unjust. I hope that the energy to mobilize is sustained and deepened with more organizing around the many areas of inequality and exclusion, and the many injustices that are done abroad as well as at home, in the name of the United States.

2/18/17

SALT, A NOVEL

DANIELLE BOURSIQUOT, NOVELIST

Freedom to choose your fate is Our Father's greatest gift to man and woman.
— Dimitry Elias Léger, bestselling author of *God Loves Haiti*

There are those who are not as well-known as their fellow literary giants. There is Mimerose Beaubrun with *Nan Dòmi;* Suze Baron, *Yo di / They Say;* Roxanne Gay, American feminist writer and professor, who does, however, have her own column in the *New York Times.* There is also Boadiba and her *Haiti Quake Journal.* All of these writers are Haitian or of Haitian descent.

Haitian contributions to the canons of American and world literature are very unique and widely celebrated by literary enthusiasts. Their work is effusive and beautiful like a garden of rare exotic flowers. Like, say, the Hibiscus, a genus of flowering plants native to warm-tempered regions in the world, like Haiti. These flowers have been genetically formed, in part, by the dictatorial regimes and ever more cataclysmic natural disasters of Haiti. These works are ethereal flowers that burn with fire and are rooted deep within a rich African oral tradition. In addition to the works noted above, there is *Love, Anger, Madness* by Marie Vieux-Chauvet; *Anthologie Secrete* by Ida Faubert, reportedly Haiti's first female author, born in 1882 and published at the turn of the century. Also, there is *Masters of the Dew* by Jacques Roumain.

And now there is Danielle Boursiquot. Danielle joins the long vibrant tradition of Haitian authors who have practiced and perfected their craft for world literary audiences, rooted within the ethos of the Haitian creole patois. The vibrant literature has a tradition going back to 1804 and is rich with the French, English and Creole languages. Its masterpieces claim the works of authors such as Edwidge Danticat, author of numerous award-winning books including *Breath, Eyes, Memory* and *Krik? Krak!*. From book signings, readings and panel discussions, Haitian authors are a distinct breed within the Pan-African canon of storytelling. Haiti is a nation that is made up of families of storytellers whose passions for stories are direct descendants of the ancient oral traditions that go back thousands of years. In fact, the story and song of the Haitian-American is central to the quilt of American identity and culture. Many know new soul R&B crooner Maxwell (though most don't know he is Haitian-American). Or co-founder of the Fugees, Wyclef Jean, proudly Haitian-American. In fact, the founding of America's pre-eminent center of Black political power, Chicago, Illinois, was by a Haitian immigrant, Jean Baptiste Point du Sable.

Within this tradition, Danielle Boursiquot's *Salt* is a spellbinding addition, a budding *fleur de hibiscus*. The story of American immigration and Haitian women forging an identity are in the tradition of American coming-of-age stories. It is at its core a quintessential American story.

In *Salt,* Olive Séraphin is racing against time to explain her life to her unborn child. Her journey is marked with love, friendship, and rescue. It is also marked with murder, drug abuse, and the influence of five women who, in their own way, have traced every step she has taken.

I caught up with Danielle Boursiquot to tell us more about the following scene from chapter one of *Salt*:

As Hélène left girlhood, Margo didn't try to make her more lady-like or press her into any feminine confines. Many neighborhood women already thought that it was strange that she had let her daughter run around in boys' clothes for so long and pitied her having such short hair. The opinion of other women didn't bother Margo. She preferred to teach her daughter by example. She didn't think twice about slaughtering her own chickens and goats, or building a small extension to their house by herself. On the days she waited on the porch for her deliveries to come from the city, she smoked her pipe in the evenings on the porch with a sharpened machete within reach. She leaned it against wood railing as she got up to pay the driver extra for bringing her items to her door when she couldn't go into the city herself. A nod and a handshake that almost pulled him off balance secured his services for the next month, and he tipped his straw hat before driving off.

Danielle Boursiquot: This scene, in the first chapter of *Salt*, sets the tone for the relationship between the women throughout the novel. The lessons passed from mother to daughter, aunt to niece, or even between girlfriends are almost never spelled out. The jewels of guidance are shared mostly by example through successes, failures, and sometimes by total accident. Margo was a peasant from the hills. Her journey as an orphan from the country taught her independence, resilience, and a toughness that may have been seen as masculine for her time. Her doing business toe to toe with men, smoking a pipe, and wielding a machete were her unspoken expressions of who she was and how far she was willing to go for what she saw fit.

As she raised her daughter alone, Margo couldn't imagine that this energy would slip right through her daughter without being absorbed. She never dreamed that her brand of love would miss its intended mark and cause her to take extreme measures to prove itself and save her only child. Love is unselfish and it never fails, and sometimes it rises up with a hurricane of consequences when it is misunderstood.

2/28/2018

LITERARY AGENCY

RICHARD KRAWIEC, AUTHOR AND PUBLISHER

I loved reading and wanted to write something that moved me as much as I was moved by the stories I read. But I wanted to write about the people I didn't find in books. Yet.
— Richard Krawiec, publisher of Jacar Press and American novelist

Richard Krawiec believes in words — their magic, music, majesty, industry and power. He believes in people even more, but he uses these words frequently. I mean we all speak and write every day, but he is dialed into another dimension where words are formed by emotional intentions, visionary projections, a bright light dripping with humanity and metaphysical possibilities. He sees where words have the possibility of elevating the human condition. Words are literal symbols and sonar material, magical bits of the universe that can alchemically form moments of good in this old world. If this were the 1200s, maybe Richard Krawiec would be a speaker of spells, a good wizard with clear-water blue eyes and an electric cap of sheep's wool (strands of hair in constant disarray channeling signals of hope and faith from the universe into a temple for that good distribution).

I hope I have not lost you, but that's just a lotta mumbo jumbo to say Richard Krawiec is very selective in the words he chooses to use. He understands their power, and that is not to say he uses them for power because he does not. There is a difference. Richard Krawiec is an old romantic soul who does real magic. He harnesses good and decent possibilities. Words are his medium. Prose spells in most circumstances but he will conjure poetry and playwright matter just as well.

Richard Krawiec believes that when you have a voice you should use it to help those who do not. He believes not only in the power of words to harness and focus a life, but in the necessity to go further — to take personal or professional risks to speak out against injustice. He is a man who walks the walk, for whom what he says is what he will do, both on paper and in deed. His advocacy and integrity run through the marrow of his bones but it doesn't come without cost."
— Melissa Hassard, partner and managing editor of Sable Books

He has sheared off the long woolly beard of his youth that has come to typify wizards. *But I believe it is an optical illusion, a slight of effect. Look in his cool eyes.* The effect of his words, his magic, are no less clear or revelatory. He writes and speaks (in a Boston-brewed accent) sentences that make sense. They are balanced and resonate with a profound humanity and a startling sense of justice and imagination too. He writes them all the time on his Facebook or speaks them to his students at University of North Carolina at Chapel Hill. He writes them in books of poetry and in certain frequencies is renowned for his prose and fiction. But he lives them too. His words breathe and will easily infect others with their earnest vibrancy. He walks the talk at the podium with frequent poetry readings, volunteers in women's detention homes and brings his keen sense of literary justice and healing to homeless shelters in Boston and North Carolina communities where he teaches the art, form, and craft of writing.

Don't we all want to feel like we have a voice? That what we have to say matters? Aren't all our discussions and posts and celebrations and rantings about politics and refugees and the murders of innocents at the hands of police — aren't we all just basically saying: I was here. This is what I saw or thought or felt. This is my witness of what happens on this planet — to others, or myself, and here are my feelings about that. Isn't it all a matter of putting our voices out into the world? Hoping our notes can join, if not be heard through, the cacophony?
— Richard Krawiec, wordsmith humanitarian

He celebrates in them with his activist publishing press, Jacar Press. He speaks at elementary schools to students and gets them jazzed about the power of words, the possibilities within poetry. Richard Krawiec is an American institution, singular in his magic, unrelenting in the demands he makes of himself to marshal good and host it in this old world.

He's smart. And good. Richard Krawiec is a good man when good men are not the way business get's done. So, I guess it's part of his character (not that being "good" is a style, but with all the reality-television-age self-promotion and social media production these days, it is important to make the distinction). "Goodness" per se is not a quality oozing with sexiness and branding and marketing possibilities. But it is essential to the American character.

Well, imagine getting a clear-eyed wizard with lightning for hair, a wordsmith marvel with a Bostonian accent, to sit and talk with you a few. It's not really all that hard. You just open your heart, speak your mind and keep it real. The wizard will retort in the flow — at least that's what I found with our exchange.

Patrick A. Howell: You've been at the literary game for a while, publishing *Time Sharing* in 1986 and receiving critical attention from the *Los Angeles Times* and *Washington Post*. You've published sports books for children (biographies of Yao Ming and Sarah Hughes), books of poetry (*Breakdown* and *She Hands Me the Razor*). You have worked with women in prison poetry programs, homeless shelters and housing projects. Currently you work with children in elementary schools, infecting them with your passion. Basically, you are a lifelong "literary advocate." What exactly animates you in your passion for literature, poetry and all things related to the word? Where does your passion stem from?

Richard Krawiec: I think my passion for writing, and activism, developed from two diverse sources growing up. My passion for reading as a child, and my awareness that I didn't quite fit in anywhere, and other people didn't either. For the reading, I was drawn to books that both exhibited a dogged persistence — *The Little Engine That Could* — but also work that seemed to speak of injustice. I remember crying my eyes out at *The Pokey Little Puppy*, who was denied dessert because he was curious and wanted to explore the world. The message was supposed to be, obey those in authority, but what I got out of it was that he was punished merely for being curious, and that seemed wrong. I loved that he dug his way out of his fenced-in enclosure and roamed. And hated that the "powers-that-be" punished him for it, tried to break his will to make him compliant.

I grew up on Battle Street, in Brockton, where there was literally a different ethnic family in each house — Russian, Lithuanian, French, Dutch, Italian, Irish-Polish. It was a diverse neighborhood that was oddly coherent in the sense that everyone was struggling — not upwardly mobile so much as struggling not to fall back into poverty, it seemed.

Working two jobs, going to night school. Most of the kids were first- or second-generation Americans, if I remember correctly.

We were separated from the Richmond Street projects by a small wooded area, and I spent a lot of my childhood visiting friends in the projects. The projects were a different world in many ways than my street. It was the first place where I saw two men, two fathers, have a fist fight in the street in broad daylight; where I witnessed one man beaten to a bloody pulp and begging, crying for mercy, while his son ran home in shame. Where I witnessed members of a motorcycle gang pull up to a woman's apartment and the nervous, reluctant way she let them swagger in. Ethnicity didn't matter as much in the projects, but poverty, and race, did. I was less aware of the background nationalities of my friends. More aware the projects seemed to break into two camps. African American and white. The groups seemed to despise each other.

It was a different environment in other ways, too, because it was a world where the nuclear family wasn't the common model. A number of my friends were raised by single mothers. Kids were alone a lot to fend for themselves. We did what kids, being curious, often did. We explored the apartments, checked closets and drawers. One of the most stunning moments of my life was when my best friend, M., found, in his mother's bureau, a large hardcover book of photographs featuring a white woman having explicit sex with an African American man.

First, it was stunning that a mother might be interested in photos of people having sex. In those days, the idea a mother might enjoy sex was unheard of. Second, M. didn't know how to receive the issue of race. Back in the early Sixties, you did not see dating between whites and Blacks. I remember he rushed me out of the apartment to be alone so he could figure it out.

The stories of the people I knew, my stories, I soon realized were not covered in the literature we received at school. In those schoolbooks, all the families were white, middle class, two parents and two kids. No one had an ethnic or racial identity. No one was poor, or struggling to make a living. Our stories were not being told. That's what I set out to do. I loved reading, and wanted to write something that moved me as much as I was moved by the stories I read. But I wanted to write about the people I didn't find in books. Yet.

By Junior High (middle school) I was reading Dickens and I began to see that it was possible to write about those who were left out by society. Those whose voices we denied. Those who went unheard. The poor, the miserable — *The Vulnerables*, to use the title for my forthcoming novel from the Paris publisher Editions Tusitala. I like that. Because ultimately it is about those who are vulnerable.

The lens he lives and writes through is love — agape — love for the world and love for all of us on it. His mind is quick, diamond-sharp, well-honed, and he continuously asks the questions to understand both the present moment and the larger scope. Some people are born to write. We should read them and not only listen but listen deeply. Richard is just such a person."
— Melissa Hassard, partner and managing editor of Sable Books

Oftentimes a "literary agent" is described as a business go-between who brokers a relationship between a writer and a publisher for a percentage of the deal. But a literal survey of the two words conjoined suggests more. It suggests a broader anagogic meaning, without the business connotation though not excluding it. "Literary agent" suggests one that services literary culture without concern for one's own gain. It suggests the pragmatism of love where an individual serves a culture of poets, authors, words, readings, libraries, bookstores and books. "Literary agent" suggests an enthusiast in the higher art of words and their affects.

Richard Krawiec promotes literary happenings with a zeal that is not concerned with what is in trend. He promotes it like it is gangster (or wizard) cool because it is. In a time when the President of the United States forms international and national headlines with 140-character Tweets, Richard Krawiec joneses over perfect sentences (complex, simple or fragmented) good books and the flow of poems in a book of poetry. He gets excited about 8th graders and brown skinned high-schoolers jonesing over the possibility of poetry. He is absolutely elated when he sees the effects of words and their possibility taking root in others — when he sees the voiceless gaining power through their own. Words, that is.

Richard Krawiec likes nature, Buddhism and peace. He speaks with candor and a dull warm light emanates from his being at all times. It is small but bright and powerful, a window into a vast soul, a place of uncommon humanity and decency. He appreciates a full moon, will watch a hawk soar and master time so that he may watch flowers bloom. He wants to see literature win but not for its own sake. If he was into ego he might be considered a literary giant. But there are no airs. There is not an iota, not an ounce of that sort of banality within Richard Krawiec's person. He's clean that way. He is a literary agent, authentic. His work is art agency of the American literary flow.

5/29/17

SHE IS GLOBAL, INTERNATIONAL, AFRICAN...
AN ARTIST, A MOVEMENT

MALAIKA ADERO IS THE "GLOBAL I AAM"

Her name is Malaika Adero... She is a renaissance woman. She is a dancer. She is an artist. She knows how to play in the space of words. She is going to talk to us today about the state of Black publishing.
— Max Rodriguez, Executive Director of the Harlem Book Fair

Matthew 5:5 of our Bible says: "The meek shall inherit the earth." In the case of American world literature (sometimes called "Black literature"), the meek *are* the salt of the earth, if not the earth *itself*. Malaika Adero doesn't call a lot of attention to herself. She does her work methodically and pointedly, beautifully, year after year, decade after decade without a lot of fanfare. *Isn't that how angels operate though?* All you see of Malaika are the volumes of books that she has birthed as well as the regular celebration of our global village griots and ancestors under the expanse of large colorful wings. *This is royalty.* She is part of the thirteenth-century continuum of West African history from those kingdoms of Ghana, Songhai and Mali. She comes to us from the tradition of the griot — a storyteller or praise singer who is a historian and often seen as a community and cultural leader, oftentimes an advisor to persons of royal designation (think Miles Davis, Nelson Mandela, Prince, Toni Morrison, or Spike Lee amongst countless others). Malaika has been and is all that, now.

Charles Harris, executive director of Howard University Press and a twenty-six-year publishing industry veteran once observed that, "One of the reasons for having the publishing institute is to go out and sell publishing as a career opportunity to members of the minority communities." "As it is," he said, "the Black presence in publishing is miniscule."

Malaika has spent nearly forty years in the aforementioned publishing industry. Born in Knoxville, Tennessee, she was an inaugural student for Publishing Institute at Howard University in 1980. Since then, she has worked on dozens of novels, including many *New York Times* bestsellers, with authors such as Common, Blair Underwood, Reyna Grande, T.D. Jakes, George Clinton, Nelson Mandela, James Meredith, Victoria Rowell, and Zane. One of her early and most celebrated projects was *Miles, The Autobiography* with Quincy Troupe, which won the 1990 American Book Award and for whom Quincy Troupe and Miles Davis acknowledged Malaika not only for her co-editing but for bringing the idea to Simon and Schuster for publication. It was published on September 15 1990, almost thirty years ago. Just last week, however, Malaika curated a tribute at the New School for Toni Morrison, winner of the 2016 PEN/Saul Bellow Award for Achievement in American Fiction.

Within the world of literature and Big Five publishers, the name "Malaika Adero" is golden, *like royalty*. "Malaika Adero" — *non-stop, don't stop, can't stop* — it's a legacy thing and she, the 'djeli' as griot is pronounced in french, is a *movement. She moves, it happens. Volumes of knowledge, wisdom and systems just drop.*

I have worked with Malaika at the National Black Writer's Conference for two years. She is not only extremely well informed but very passionate about Black literature. She is very knowledgeable.
— Clarence Reynolds, Director at the Center for Black Literature at Medgar Evers College, CUNY

The first time I met Malaika was in 2014 at the Harlem Book Fair. I sat next to her as Max Rodriguez, the executive director of the *Black Book Review* and Harlem Book Fair, introduced her to the world through C-Span. She didn't know who I was. As a matter of fact, I had to introduce myself to her for this article. But I knew who she was — *Yessir!* I mean, *Yes Maam!*

Max said of Malaika that day:

I have the honor and privilege of introducing a dear friend, a colleague and a professional. Someone who has, through intellect, intuition and sheer will power, worked and made her mark through publishing. Her name is Malaika Adero... She is a renaissance woman. She is a dancer. She is an artist. She knows how to play in the space of words. She is going to talk to us today about the state of Black publishing. They left us a legacy, they left us in charge, they left us a body of work, and the lessons and the instructions are just for us to pay attention to that now and to carry on.

I was surprised and honored to have a global village elder, an accomplished griot, right there, just sitting there next to me. Malaika is an elegant lady whose grace, pragmatism and focus underscore every detail she attends to. But more so, there is a glowing power and immaculate strength, with the volumes of projects she has dropped like libraries over a thirty-plus year career. She keynoted the Harlem Book Fair, which also featured the talents of Sonia Sanchez, Dr Imani Perry and Walter Mosley with panel discussions on American morality, multiculturalism and the African American identity. Malaika said in the 2014 address:

> The Harlem Book Fair is one of my favorite book events. One — because it is in the neighborhood I live in, so it's easy for me to get here. The other, as you heard from Dr Muhammad, as you heard from Max Rodriguez, is this setting here. Dr Muhammad talked about Arturo Schomburg who laid the foundation here as a Black bibliophile for this collection to rise, for this center, this depository, that is so important not just for us in this community, but in the world, to be built. Dr Muhammad's leadership and the family of the Schomburg are carrying the beacon for the legacy that Arturo Schomburg, James Baldwin, our recent literary giants who he named who recently passed on — Maya Angelou, Amiri Baraka, Jayne Cortez... there have been too many that have passed on recently... They left us a legacy, they left us in charge, they left us a body of work, and the lessons and the instructions are just for us to pay attention to that now and to carry on...

I was flattered by Max [Rodriguez's] invitation to make this talk. He calls me up and just says so casually, I'd like for you to talk about the state of Black literature in fifteen minutes... How was I going to talk about this thing we call Black literature, this thing we call publishing? Particularly at this time when it's so complicated, there are so many issues, there are so many breakthroughs, so much extraordinary work, there are so many problems. So what exactly will I be talking about? I will be talking about Black people, meaning people of African descent here writing and publishing primarily in America and that reach the rest of the world.

He and I are on the same page to think in terms of "Global I Am." It is how I think. It's how most of the people that are around me think. It is how we need to be thinking more in a systematic fashion in order to reach more people, touch more people, advance our culture and heal the world really. So I can't think of it as a single state. It's more like the world of storytelling.

When I started African American Literature Book Club in the 1990s, Malaika was already established then. We were both working on the advisory board for the Harlem Book Fair. Malaika recognizes what it takes to manifest our Black voices and she has been doing it for decades now.
— Troy Johnson, Founder of the African American Literature Book Club

Malaika says of the Global I Am: "It is a point of view, more than a movement. It is part of a continuum." The legacy of her work is a testament to not only Black literature but her own ubiquity within American literature. Last week she co-curated and produced a tribute to Toni Morrison. The theme of the night was around work that is dangerous because it speaks truth to power or can change the fabric of reality. The judges' citation for the event which Malaika produced reads:

Toni Morrison not only opened doors to others when she began to publish, she has also stayed grounded in the issues of her time. At every turn, she has commented upon and enlarged the conversation about what it is to be Black, female, human, universal. Her brilliant and bracing fiction continues to address what is crucial, timely and timeless.

The event featured the talents of actress Adepero Oduye reading from *The Bluest Eye*; actor Delroy Lindo reading from *Song of Solomon*; jazz pianist Jason Moran, guitarist Brandon Ross, and mezzo-soprano Alicia Hall Moran performing "Round About the Mountain"; and was MC'd by Master of Ceremonies Kevin Young, director of the Schomburg Center for Research in Black Culture. In thirteenth-century Mali, the West African Empire, griots would perform as court musicians relaying wisdom and proverbs through epic song, poetry and story. This might be the twenty-first century, but not a lot has changed in the nine hundred years since.

Malaika said of the event:

> The whole evening was a most eventful experience in a great way — to celebrate someone who is a world treasure. Literature is her. She has an appreciation for all sorts of artists, works and interpretations of her own work. These are values which are important to me as well. Toni has taught me and continues to teach me personally and professionally I walk in the path she has laid.

I kept a folder called "rejects." I had 108 rejections... "Build the plane while you are flying," that became my strategy. Finally, I had the fortune where an editor Malaika Adero actually opened up the email and she read the query letter and she scrolled down and read the first thirty pages. It was a long process where six months went by, send me the rest of it, then another year. Ironically, Atria, the imprint of Simon and Schuster's mission is to "look into windows of different worlds."
— Morowa Yejidé, author of *Time of the Locust*

I wondered, sitting next to Malaika that day at the Harlem Book Fair, why her praises aren't sung loudly and clearly within the national conversation we are always having about ourselves as Americans? "I want more books from her" is what a voice inside my head said. As recently as this week, I wondered about the vitriolic presidential campaign squared around race (Make America Great Again — Really? 'Cause I don't think it's ever been as great as it is now and is gonna be) and the beacon call for elemental humanity and healing in our #BlackLivesMatter movement. I wondered because of what Malaika had noted in her 2014 keynote: "It [Global I Am] is how we need to be thinking more in a systematic fashion in order to reach more people, touch more people, advance our culture and heal the world really." Do we really want to solve this thing and move forward into a future power era, the one that is already here, struggling to be born? We are the ones whose time it has come to lead, who must rebuild. We are the ones with the choices to be made. We have to choose the future we want, the quiet future already here, with collective peace, dialogue and understanding. "I Aam Global," right? Our global village elders have made clear their wisdom.

If I ruled the world, publishing and the bookselling community would be more ethnically diverse; retailers would not be able to return product so easily; and corporations would profit-share with all their employees.
— Malaika Adero, in an interview with John Temple at Akashic Books in 2013

We have learned the valuable lessons of the legacy of Zora Neale Hurston and the Harlem Renaissance. We will not make that error again during the Global International African Arts Movement (Global I Aam). This is a different generation and a different time. Alice Walker resurrected sister Zora Neale Hurston from obscurity with *The Color Purple*. We do our business now — take payment now and tomorrow. Take note, this is royalty. At this point in her career, Malaika Adero is an institution onto herself — a walking, breathing, institution. Under her wings are libraries of books — cosmic stories better suited to ancient hieroglyphics told in American English and cosmic happenings told plainly, printed on paper and at the higher frequencies of e-books — the stories of our people preserved in perfect editorial form for the future power world that arises from our Now. Malaika Adero's name fits nicely in a long line of other djeli, other cosmic soul sistars loosed from earthly constraints — names like Makeda, Ida B. Wells, Phillis Wheatley, Zora Neale Hurston and June Jordan. This is royalty.

Malaika Adero, is currently working on her own book, is the editor of *Home Slice Magazine* and founder of Adero's Literary Tribe/ALT.

1/17/18

FROM VANGUARD TO THE KINGDOM

I got the term "Vanguard" from D'Angelo's 2014 album *Black Messiah*, which he wrote with his band, the Vanguard. It was their third studio album and released on December 15 2014 by RCA Records, bringing an end to D'Angelo's self-imposed exile after his first two albums, 2000's *Voodoo* and 1995's *Brown Sugar*. *Black Messiah* sold over 117,000 units in its first week, debuting at number five on the US Billboard charts. The tour for the album was called The Second Coming. The album is filled with an undeniable Spirit Force and timeless cues. It was an orchestra or choir, signaling that a new time has begun.

D'Angelo, forty-one at the time of the album's release, met with Black Panther founder Bobby Seale, seventy-eight at the time, in Oakland and Berkeley for an interview recorded by the *New York Times*. In the interview, D'Angelo talked about social activism and the Black Lives Matter movement: "What people call a riot I call a rebellion. In my humble opinion, the word "riot" is used by the media to dismiss or degenerate what's really happening. Everybody knows the looting and burning is the voice of the unheard."

Also, after going through my home library, I found Ralph Wiley's classic, *What Black People Should Do Now — From Near the Vanguard*, originally published in 1993 and featuring a series of contemporary issues accenting the struggle at that particular juncture in our evolution as a people. No doubt, this classic also has had an indelible imprint on my conscious and subconscious psyches.

Seers, manifestors, evangelists and prophets are in their own way carrier of the news — the good news. The news is not MSNBC, BBC, Fox News or CNN. The news is not the *Washington Post* or the *New York Times*. All of these organizations have become virtual tabloids covering the carnival and carnage of the twenty-first century's version of Barnum and Bailey's three-ring circus, Donald Trump. News is stepping outside and feeling the sun burn a message of pure light, pure inspiration, onto your third eye. News is the peace that comes sitting at the feet of the beach to hear the waves crash again and again against the turbulence of a particularly tyrannical day until all that remains is peace. Or how the shade and protection of a great tree will seep all the toxins from your body and replace it with quiet nurturing confidence. News is finding out how your son or daughter's day was. News is looking after your mother and father after they have done so for you and experiencing that balance. News is your dog running, leaping, licking and tackling you to say "I love you!" in a language crisp and clear to the soul. News is a smile that changes everything inside you. Yes, the good news is when the air hits you in such a way that your spirit is renewed. That stuff on cable is produced for ratings which provide revenues for parent companies and perpetuate a systematic disenfranchisement of noble souls. It's garbage. We all buy and feed our way into a collective toxic soul. The Good News is well, the good news. It doesn't need explanation. When an evangelist speaks that truth, when a prophet speaks that future, when a seer shows that future or a manifestor makes that future, *we just know.* Dispatches from the vanguard have been disseminated for centuries now and are moving to the center, exposing vitriolic hatred for what it is so that it may be eliminated and replaced with love.

For three years, Donald J. Trump has tried to shut down the National Endowment of the Arts and National Endowment for the Humanities by submitting budgets that did not allocate funding. His $4.75 trillion budget (the largest in federal history) detailed plans to *eliminate* funding for the NEA and NEH. Budgets for both agencies ($29 million and $38 million) have been described as "sufficient funding for orderly termination of all operations over two years."

America's cultural assets are its greatest export. Whether you travel to Paris, Addis Ababa, Dubai, Tokyo, Port of Spain or Panama City, the images and sounds of Denzel or Beyoncé are permanent. The words, ideas and patriotism of Cornel West, Baldwin, Ali, Morrison and Angelou underwrite those sexier assets with ideas, emotional truths and an uncompromised vision of the future by looking the present and past dead in the eye. In the United States alone there are 2.1 million artists. The global art market was valued at almost $64 billion in 2017, up from almost $57 billion the previous year.

Call it academica; call it literature, poetry, plays or essays; call it text, conversations, posts, likes or hearts; call it music or compositions; call it television or movie production, the goal of the griot is to carry on the stories since antiquity — the story of our kings and queens, our kingdoms, our organizations, our ways and our culture, our universities, our love — and to carry those stories forward into eternity. Prophets turn off their mind from the pollution of social media, Hollywood-Industrial-Complex toxins and so-called news. They open the heart that is directly linked to his or her great spirit and they speak in terms that affect reality. It's like Muhammad Ali, saying "I shook up the world! I shook up world!" in his heyday and the next thing you know, hip-hop, athletes as heroes, power of the people, the end of the permanence of white male supremacy as an active agency is all but assured. *He actually shook up the world.* They channel the voices of spirits, ancestors, the marginalized... the voices of the unheard for all to hear.

Patrick A. Howell can be contacted at:

www.patrickahowell.com

AFTERWORD

BY GLOBAL I AAM CO-FOUNDER MARVIN LEE MILLS

They did what human beings looking for freedom, throughout history, have often done. They left.
— Isabel Wilkerson, *The Warmth of Other Suns*

When I first opened the pages of Isabel Wilkerson's book *The Warmth of Other Suns*, I quickly felt resonance with it, and a well of gratitude sprang up in me. This was mainly due to the confirmation that the genuine fire that I found in myself to unapologetically seek world travel, self-discovery and personal *freedom* all at the same time — especially as someone of African descent born and raised in America — had historical and ancestral common thread, even as I had observed the present-day harmony between myself and those I met while exploring various countries. Back in 2011, when I first left America's shores to start a journey abroad, it was indeed in the spirit of seeking the warmth of other suns, taking all of myself and my South Central Los Angeles cultivation out into the world. I don't remember which country I was in, or what year it was when I first read *The Warmth of Other Suns*, but I do remember how I felt learning from the perspectives documented in the award-winning author's work, as much as I remember making the choice to not take a certain amount of clothing on my journeys so that I could pack the big-body text.

But what is *The Warmth of Other Suns,* exactly? It is "the epic story of America's Great Migration," that is, a floor-to-ceiling window into the movement of Black folk from the South of the United States to both the North and West of the United States. *Literal* movements...

Of Black folk seeking the kinds of opportunities which discriminated *less,* or escaping death by the hands of white overseers, or simply wanting to support the ambitions of a family member to manifest *more* in their lives. All this amidst the context of a Southern United States hellbent on maintaining the infrastructure of oppression against African American peoples. Underpinning the entirety of this Great Migration perhaps was one word — spread out at the base and serving as the concrete on which these precious, melanated steps proceeded with faith and imagination — which links all peoples and many movements throughout history:

Freedom.

And, as someone who's been immensely blessed to explore the planet in heavily-melanated fashion as a traveler, digital nomad, volunteer and more, it's been my humble honor to witness the *literal* movement of African peoples all around the world. Whether Costa Rica or China, whether Bali or Lalibela, there *is* a global, international, and African arts movement.

And it is at the vanguard-of-things. Quite frankly, it has *been* at the vanguard-of-things.

One may check the planet's pyramids, or the faces carved in stones, or even the oldest universities in Europe. *Globaliaam* has *been* at the vanguard. Making this world go round.

And I'm blessed to have the beginnings of an intimate awareness of this. It is important to note that the *arts* in *globaliaam* are not limited to paintings, sculptures, words and sounds.

Isn't there an art to *movement* itself? To *life* itself? A former teacher of mine put it well when we reconnected some years ago and I spoke to her of my travels and Truth seeking. Providing a clarity that, quite frankly, I needed to hear: *Our lives are the greatest sermons we preach.*

There *is* an art to how continental Africans pioneered existing on the planet, learned how to read the stars, established wonderful kingdoms, developed high science, and more... and then some were captured, transported across the Atlantic, enslaved, systematically oppressed, and *somehow, someway* became Black millennials in their twenties and thirties *returning* to the land of their ancestors. Becoming the likes of all those featured in this collection of work you've now digested.

I am amazed, again and again, at how beautifully art travels. At how hip-hop has become a global phenomenon. At the power there is in art to transform reality and transcend borders.

Where, as Lupe Fiasco highlights in "Paris, Tokyo," "they barely understand what I speak, but they nod to my beats." We may not understand every word uttered by others. But what limitations exist to understanding the universal language of love and freedom? Singularly.

Dear reader, I do hope that you consider how well *thine* art travels. Not only what you may paint, write, sing, sculpt or draw... But the way you *live. The way you move.* The global international African arts movement is at the vanguard-of-things, and all are welcome to contribute. And, we would all do well to remember: *Every day, we receive a canvas.*

Let us all endeavor to *create* at the vanguard, *by any means necessary.* In searching for freedom, *truly searching* for freedom... Does it not mean at the very least that *movement* will be involved?

Not necessarily a *literal* movement, but perhaps a *literary movement*... Or at the very least a journey, an escape, a

resistance, a rebellion, a demonstration, a *lituation*...
For anyone is *free* to become aware of *freedom* and its
(manufactured or perceived) bottlenecks.

And then, once aware, each and every one of us can...
Move.

Hoping that we can wake up to the warmth of another
sun.

And even though there be only one Sun...

The newness of how it feels we may attribute to our
movement.

And then, a brand new day.

It is perhaps through the *arts* that we *leave* and bring
back vivid messages from the spirit world to the present.
We dig through the past. Imagine the future. To push the
envelope on how, together, we design today.

Yes, we *Be. At the vanguard.*

APPENDIX

There are not enough pages to document all of the creatives globally within art, academia and letters whose visions, craft and works give flight to free spirits and make the voices of the unheard heard. There are also not enough pages here to profile the 1.225 billion Africans from the homeland. We are *all* body to one immaculately creative Spirit Force. The Spirit Force is *one body* of all those souls that are African souls. Those souls of unlimited creativity are now *all over the globe*. In the United States, 12.2% of the population comes diasporic African tribes (including multi-racial African Americans, this increases to 14%). I do know I would like to interview all of us — to record this work and somehow quantify these creative spirits is to document the creative and intellectual genius of America and the world. Here is a partial list:

Aaliyah Octavia Kee,
figurative painter

Aaqil Ka, visual artist

Aaron Ashby, filmmaker

Abdi Ahmed, entrepreneur
and business leader

Abiy Ahmed, author,
visionary and leader

Abdul Ali, author and poet

Afua Cooper, poet and
historian

Aida Muluneh, photographer
and filmmaker

Aissata Pinto da Costa,
abstract artist and
designer

Akwaeke Emezi, writer and
video artist

Albert Othello Glenn,
producer

Alecia McKenzie,
poet

Alicia Hall Moran, singer and writer

Amina Iro, poet

Aminatta Forna, professor of poetics and writer

Amy DuBois Barnett, journalist and leader

Andrea Chung, mixed-media conceptual artist

Angela Davis, activist and educator

Angela Makholwa, novelist

Angela Rye, journalist and political commentator

Anu Prestonia, creator

April R. Silver, activist and publicist

April Walker, author and fashion pioneer

Arthur Aldwyn (Boscoe) Holder, entrepreneur

Arthur Rickydoc Flowers, author and poet

Ava DuVernay, film director and distributor

Barack Obama, author and leader

Barbara Chase-Riboud, sculptor, novelist, and poet

Barbara Walker, visual artist

Bassey Ikpi, author

Benilde Little, author

Bill Duke, film director and actor

Billene Seyoum Woldeyes, writer and poet

Bisa Butler, fiber artist

Blair Imani, author and activist

Bobby Rogers, photographer

Bridgett M. Davis, writer and filmmaker

Brittney Cooper, author and professor

Carolyn A. Butts, editor and publisher

Caryl Phillips, playwright and novelist

Carrie Mae Weems, photographer and visual artist

Cauleen Smith, multimedia artist and filmmaker

Cecil Bernard, abstract artist

Charles Bibbs, visual artist

Charles Gaines, conceptual artist and philosopher

Charles D. King, producer

Charles M. Blow, journalist

Cheo Hodari Coker, producer and journalist

Chéri Samba, contemporary artist

Cheryl Edwards, fine artist

Chimamanda Ngozi Adichie, author

Christine Ntim, entrepreneur

Christine A. Platt, activist and storyteller

Christopher Cozier, contemporary artist and writer

Clarence V. Reynolds, journalist and editor

Colson Whitehead, author

Cornel West, intellectual and leader

D. Channsin Berry, filmmaker

Damola Adepoju, painter

Danielle Boursiquot, author

Darius J. Quarles, contemporary painter

Darnell Hunt, professor and dean of social sciences

Dave Chappelle, comedian

David Dabydeen, poet, novelist, and critic

David A. Wilson, entrepreneur

Deborah Cowell, editor and writer

Délice Mugabo, professor

Demetria Irwin, writer and editor

Denene Millner, author and publisher

DeWayne Wickham, journalist

Diedrick Brackens, textile artist

Dinaw Mengestu, author and professor

D.L. Hughley, comedian

Dwight Trible, jazz singer

Eddie Ndopu, activist, visionary, and future astronaut

El Anatsui, sculptor and mixed-media artist

Elliott Ashby, photographer and producer

Elias Wondimu, publisher

Elnathan John, author

Emily Raboteau, author and professor

Eric Salisbury, visual artist

Erika Edwards, author and historian

Eve Ewing, author and sociologist

Faatimah Heaven Muhammad, model and actress

Glory Edim, author and literary leader

Gopal Dagnogo, contemporary artist

Gillian Royes, author

Haki Madhubuti, publisher and author

Helina Metaferia, interdisciplinary artist

Helon Habila, author and poet

Henry Taylor, mixed-media painter and sculptor

Ida Woldemichael, graphic designer and activist

Idalin Bobé, social justice technologist

Ilyasah Al-Shabazz, social activist and leader

Ishion Hutchinson, poet and author

Jaha Zainabu, poet and spoken word artist

James Gayles, painter, graphic designer and illustrator

Jamea Richmond-Edwards, contemporary artist

Janell Walden Agyeman, literary agent

Janeya Griffin, entrepreneur and innovation strategist

Jason Reynolds, children's author

Javier E. David, finance editor and journalist

Jennifer Nansubuga Makumbi, novelist and short story writer

Jervey Tervalon, author and professor

Jiba Molei Anderson, illustrator and writer

Jimi Evins, painter

Joel 'Kachi Benson, filmmaker

Joel Zito Araújo, filmmaker

John David Washington, actor

Jon McGregor, novelist and literary activist

Joy Reid, author and national correspondent

Julie Dash, filmmaker

Kalamu ya Salaam, poet and author

Kalisha Buckhanon, author and speaker

Kara Walker, visual artist and silhouettist

Katia D. Ulysse, writer, poet, and teacher

Kehinde Wiley, portrait painter and visual artist

Khary O. Polk, professor and author

Kia Dyson, visual artist and painter

Kim McMillon, activist and educator

Korey Matthews, multimedia journalist

Kute Blackson, author and motivator

Kwame Alexander, poet, children's author, and educator

Laini Brown, senior publicist

Latoya C. Smith, literary agent

Laura Bullock, poet and children's author

Laura Pegram, author, educator, and jazz vocalist

Lauren Maillian, entrepreneur and author

Leigh Patel, educator, sociologist, and writer

Leo McGriff, artist

Leslie K. Brown, filmmaker

Lulseged Retta, contemporary painter

Lilly Workneh, senior editor and blogger

Lima Barreto, novelist

Lisa Cortes, producer

Lisa Lucas, literary activist

Lisa Teasley, writer and artist

Lorelei Williams, writer and entrepreneur

Loretta Green-Williams, publisher

Lorna Simpson, photographer and multimedia artist

Luvvie Ajayi, author and pop culture critic

Lynette Eastmond, attorney and filmmaking activist

Maaza Mengiste, novelist and essayist

Marcia Wilson, photographer

Margaret Porter Troupe, editor and philanthropist

Margo Jefferson, author, cultural critic, and professor

Mark Bradford, contemporary artist

Mark Reed, philanthropist

Marlon James, author and professor

Mesai Haileleul, art curator

Marvin X Jackmon, poet and playwright

Melissa Fleury, author

Michael Eric Dyson, thought leader, academic and author

Michelle Bernard, lawyer, author, and journalist

Michael Datcher, educator and author

Michelle Obama, author and leader

Mickalene Thomas, painter and visual artist

Miko Simmons, visual artist

Mitchell S. Jackson, author and speaker

Mulaundo Jones, literary advocate

Namwali Serpell, novelist and professor

Nana-Ama Danquah, author and editor

Nate Parker, filmmaker

Nefertite Nguvu, filmmaker

Nell Painter, historian and professor

Nelson George, author, filmmaker, and taste maker

Nick Cave, fabric sculptor and performance artist

Nolan Anderson, fine artist

Novuyo Rosa Tshuma, author

Nyugen Smith, interdisciplinary artist

Ondjaki, novelist

Oyinkan Braithwaite, novelist

Orlando Bishop, comedian

P. Frank Williams, filmmaker and journalist

Pak Wo Shum, entrepreneur and business leader

Pastor Mark Whitlock, leader

Patrick L. Riley, entertainment journalist

Paul Beatty, author and professor

Pearl Cleage, author, playwright, and activist

Pedro Noguera, professor, scholar, and activist

Peter Kimani, author and journalist

Queen Socks, poet and spoken word artist

Quinn McGowan, cartoonist and storyteller

Rakia Clark, editor

Rania Mamoun, novelist and journalist

Rashid Johnson, visual artist

Reginald Hudlin, filmmaker

Renee Cox, artist and political activist

Retha Powers, author and editor

Richard Ali, poet, lawyer, and literary advocate

Rob Fields, cultural curator and marketer

Ron Kavanaugh, publisher and literary activist

Ryan Coogler, film director

Sabrina Lamb, author and leader

Sakina Saïdi, illustrator

Salongo Lee, photographer and visual artist

Sam Gilliam, abstractionist artist

Sam Hopkins, visual artist and wsculptor

Sarah Lewis, educator and author

Sarah M. Broom, author and journalist

Saul Williams, poet and spoken word artist

SekouWrites, author and journalist

Shadaya Feyijinmi, filmmaker

Shawn Martinbrough, cartoonist and storyteller

Sheila Na'imah Nortley, filmmaker

Sheila Stowell, poet and artist

Shujah Reiph, activist and literary advocate

Spike Lee, film director

Stacey Patton, author and journalist

Steve Barnes, writer and speaker

Sylvia Ofili, writer and teacher

Taiye Selasi, author and photographer

Tarsila do Amaral, modernist painter

Tatyana Fazlalizadeh, visual artist and activist

Teju Cole, novelist and photographer

Tekabe Tadiwos, filmmaker

Teru Mitsuhara, comedian and professor

Theaster Gates, community activist and artist

Thomas Parham, educator, author and psychologist

Tim Reid, filmmaker and actor

Tomi Adeyemi, author and speaker

Tony Medina, poet and author

Tonya Lewis Lee, producer and writer

Touré, author, journalist, and professional gadfly

Tracy Sherrod, literary editorial director

Trevon Facey, filmmaker and photographer

Trevor Noah, comedian and correspondent

Troy Johnson, literary activist

Ugochukwu-Smooth C. Nzewi, artist and curator

Uli Beutter Cohen, leader and writer

Victoria Sanders, literary agent

Viviane Ferreira, activist and filmmaker

Walter Mosley, author and screenwriter

Wangechi Mutu, visual artist

Yared Zeleke, filmmaker

Yona Deshommes, publicist

Yoshi MsBlasian Butler, healer

Yvonne Adhiambo Owuor, author

Zózimo Bulbul, filmmaker and activist

and,

Brook Stephenson, literary activist.
February 12 1974 — August 8 2015. RIP.

ACKNOWLEDGEMENTS

To Mommy, Luisa Jacinta Howell, professor of Spanish, the Panamanian souled mahogany — you introduced me to the arts — literature, music, movies, plays. You are the first love that gave me all my other loves.

To the next generation of brilliant spirits populating the future — including my son SharkHeart (Christian W. Howell, aka the Chairman) and nephews and nieces — Skylar Reid, Megyn Lamb, Emil Rodriguez, Harlem Datcher, Sarah Kellel, Mebruk, Leul; Cecil Yuesei, Amado Soma, Amina — you are humanity's best highest frequency and hope. You are an illuminati, an inspiration, so bright and powerful I cannot imagine it not shining bright for all of humanity.

To the seven brothers and sisters that are everything our father and mother made — the unfolding of your paths are a delight and strange wonderful flight to behold.

To the Victory & Noble Incorporation — it is our time.

Finally, to my family and race of people — the human race — **ONE** love.

Repeater Books

is dedicated to the creation of a new reality. The landscape of twenty-first-century arts and letters is faded and inert, riven by fashionable cynicism, egotistical self-reference and a nostalgia for the recent past. Repeater intends to add its voice to those movements that wish to enter history and assert control over its currents, gathering together scattered and isolated voices with those who have already called for an escape from Capitalist Realism. Our desire is to publish in every sphere and genre, combining vigorous dissent and a pragmatic willingness to succeed where messianic abstraction and quiescent co-option have stalled: abstention is not an option: we are alive and we don't agree.